EARLY AMERICAN POLICY

SIX COLUMBIA CONTRIBUTORS

EARLY AMERICAN POLICY

SIX COLUMBIA CONTRIBUTORS

by JOSEPH DORFMAN
and R. G. TUGWELL

COLUMBIA UNIVERSITY PRESS
NEW YORK 1960

The authors want to thank the Council for Research in the Social Sciences, and the Economic Research Centers, of Columbia University, for grants which facilitated the preparation of the manuscript.

Published in Great Britain, India, and Pakistan
by the Oxford University Press, London, Bombay, and Karachi

First published in book form 1960

Library of Congress Catalog Card Number: 60-8585
Manufactured in the United States of America

CONTENTS

ILLUSTRATIONS

EARLY AMERICAN POLICY

SIX COLUMBIA CONTRIBUTORS

INTRODUCTION

In the 1930s, the authors, in somewhat adventurous mood, undertook to write for the *Columbia University Quarterly* a series of essays on early American economists and political theorists who had been connected with the university or with its predecessor, King's College, in some intimate way, as students or as teachers. Included were such widely known individuals as Alexander Hamilton and Francis Lieber, to whom we have now added John Jay. We have also discussed others not so generally known, but influential in their own time. Among these were the Reverend John McVickar, Henry Vethake, and William Beach Lawrence. It was somewhat novel to investigate American social thinkers strictly in the context of their own political and economic environments; but all of them had been important members of the early community; they had been teachers, publicists, philosophers, or statesmen; and we felt that an evaluation was in order.

Our study of Hamilton was made when his achievement was given lower appraisal than at any other time since his death. The neglect then was almost as extreme as the eulogies have since become. We were impressed by Hamilton's invaluable contribution to the foundations of a struggling new economy with immense potential. The development of the rich and powerful nation of the twentieth century owed more to him, we thought, than had ever been acknowledged. We made a distinction between Hamilton the statesman and the much less creative private lawyer, businessman, and party politician. His great antagonist, Thomas Jefferson, naturally had to be taken into account. It seemed to us that, although the Jeffersonian view became dominant in the American tradition, Hamilton's "inventions" or institutions were indispensable to that very dominance. Usually it is conservatives who borrow progressive policies. In this case the ultrademocrats had to accept conservative formulas if they were to succeed in administering a republic they had conquered with votes.

John Jay's mind ran in the same channels as that of Alexander Hamilton. His contributions, like those of Hamilton and John Adams, serve to bring out the nature of the "radical conservatism," if the description may be allowed, that accounted for the staying power of the feeble-seeming nation that emerged from the Revolution. He was quite clear about the basic kind of government that the new nation required: it should be tripartite, with a strong executive and a genuinely functioning judiciary. It would have been more in keeping with the revolutionary impulse to have clung to the legislative supremacy won by the French and represented in another way by the British Parliament. Jay held more positions of first rank, possibly, than any other American before or since. His services to the nation ought not to obscure his devotion to New York, city and state. His governorship was a distinguished one, and his representation of the state in national affairs faithful.

That King's—and Columbia—should have had two such representatives as Jay and Hamilton as creative statesmen of the new republic in the period of its emergence must always be a source of pride.

The next four figures fall into a later period and help to illuminate the complexities of the Jacksonian era, which seems to have been largely dominated by paradoxes and unresolved dilemmas rather than by consistent policies. They were deeply concerned in policy and they were often advisers to policy makers, especially on such major economic questions as the public debt, banking reform, the tariff, and internal improvements. Their role lay largely in suggesting and popularizing policies, in giving them an intellectual premise, and in developing the professional character of economics and political science.

The Reverend John McVickar, who taught the whole range of the social sciences, and also philosophy, English literature, and religion, was more than a noted clergyman. He was a leader in the promotion of monetary and banking reform and his views were canvassed by prominent financiers and legislators. A high churchman, he was a follower of Hamilton's political philosophy; yet he expressed sympathy for the Indian and found things to admire in Robert Owen, Samuel Taylor Coleridge, and John Ruskin.

His successor at Columbia in the teaching of the social sciences, Francis Lieber, was one of the few important American contributors to political theory in the nineteenth century. He played a significant role in the development of international law, especially the rules of war, while serving as adviser to Secretary Stanton during the Civil War. His proposals that the federal government engage in continuous comprehensive statistical surveys were among the important influences that laid the groundwork for the rise of such great institutions as the permanent Census and, much later, the President's Council of Economic Advisers.

McVickar's student, W. B. Lawrence, had as a young man the advantage of friendship with such statesmen and social philosophers as Jefferson, Madison, Gallatin, Clay, Jeremy Bentham, and Bentham's disciples, the "philosophical radicals." He made himself a name in international law. He helped to popularize Ricardian economics both in theory and as the guide for sound policy. He was ever the "scholar in politics," although his office holding was limited to service as secretary of legation and chargé d'affaires in London, and as lieutenant governor of Rhode Island.

His friend as well as contemporary, Henry Vethake, was the head of two institutions of higher learning and served in five others; he taught primarily mathematics and physics, in which fields he had had the benefit of study under such world-renowned figures as the Germans, Gauss, Öhm, and Encke, and acquaintanceship with such important French mathematical works as those of A. A. Cournot, but his favorite subject, nevertheless, was economics. He initiated it as a separate, systematic discipline at Princeton, Dickinson, New York, and Pennsylvania. Although in later years he lost his reforming zeal, he was in the 1830s among the outstanding promoters of the first great drive for the creation of real universities in the United States.

In our choices there was perhaps a certain piety. The public concerns and activities of our professors were as significant as their academic interests; they were all vital personalities; they made individual contributions to American thought and policy. They fulfilled in a striking way one of the most important functions of an institution of higher learning, which is to nurture creative public service. Columbia was doing this even before it *was* Columbia; the ivory tower was always awash with worldly concerns.[1] They had ideas about these concerns, and they insisted on being heard.

In some of the essays, as formerly published, our affection for the university had resulted in a certain antiquarianism, and this we thought ought to be eliminated out of consideration for our readers. Also there were unpublished papers

[1] Founded as King's College in 1754, the institution became Columbia College in 1784. In 1896, with the growth of professional schools, it became Columbia University, the name "Columbia College" being retained for the undergraduate men's school. A further change of name occurred in 1912, when the university became Columbia University in the City of New York.

newly available and further researches of scholars to be taken into account. It has turned out that none of our earlier views has been much changed; but we think that now we have come closer to assisting in the understanding of certain figures who originated the academic disciplines of economics and political theory in this country and who played important parts in shaping the policies of their era. They shed light on the higher learning of their time, generally so closely bound to theology. They were breaking out of close confines; they were intellectual pioneers in the society of their times. They were inclined to become the American representatives of European thought. They claimed to be disciples of Adam Smith, J. B. Say, David Ricardo, and Jeremy Bentham; they were disciples, because they could invoke the authority of the great masters for the support of the policies they believed necessary for the country.

There was great suspicion of the "new science" of political economy. Theologians feared that it emphasized materialism and took men's thoughts away from an appreciation of spiritual values. College authorities feared that it would deeply encroach upon and eventually destroy the dominance in the curriculum of the classical languages of Greek and Latin. Political leaders whose policies ran counter to its conclusions were quick to denounce it as the vaporings of mere theorists without experience. That the "new science" lived and grew was doubtless due largely to the fact that it was an organic part of the Era of the Enlightenment that characterized the eighteenth and nineteenth centuries in Western civilization, but the Columbia group was representative of the band of scholars that commenced the struggle for its recognition. As McVickar put it, "Hitherto . . . want of science, rather than of virtue, has stamped the errors of our policy. But ignorance is a reproach that should no longer rest upon us. We have the wealth, the talent, and the institutions that are needful to disperse it. Let them be definitely directed to that object—let professorships of Political Economy be established in our colleges, and open lectureships encouraged in our cities."

The appendixes, which include McVickar's short treatise on foreign exchange, two of Lawrence's letters from Europe to President Buchanan, and specimens of Lieber's examination questions in political economy and political theory, should prove useful documentary material for a more detailed understanding of these men and the periods in which they lived.

ALEXANDER HAMILTON

ALEXANDER HAMILTON: NATION-MAKER

A great deal has been made of the unusual circumstances surrounding Alexander Hamilton's birth and early training —more than is warranted. There seems now something exotic about a West Indian boyhood; but there was nothing exotic about it in Hamilton's time. The West Indies were then simply other British colonies, and rather more important ones than any on the mainland except perhaps Virginia, and relations with them were closer than those which existed among any but the nearest neighbors in what later became the states. They had the same difficulties with Britain, too, except that their disputes had a more sensible outcome than our own. If the Barbadian model had been followed on the continent our history might still have been linked to that of the British Empire, and might, in consequence, have been less filled with controversy over obvious issues. At any rate, Hamilton did not arrive in the mainland colonies unaware of what was going on here; in fact, he came from an environment more mature in constitutional ideas than the one to which he came. Then too, part of his boyhood was spent in the Danish islands, and they, also, contributed something to his political orientation.

He was precocious. At twelve he was managing a considerable mercantile establishment in Christianstadt and had a start on a formal education which was pursued with ease and rapidity, after he came to New York in 1772, at a New Jersey boarding school and at King's College. But he was not only precocious; he was also clever and attractive, qualities which gained him alliances with the great families of the colony, furnished scope for his talents, and perhaps led indirectly to his tragic death in 1804. A man of genius could hardly have chosen, in all the years of our history, a span of life in which opportunity would be so generous. And Hamilton took advantage of all that was offered. For he had intense ambitions, too.

It might be thought strange that a poor provincial boy should seem to have been born equipped with aristocratic notions, which included not only approval of monarchy and distrust of democracy, but also a thorough conviction, apparent in every measure he sponsored in his life, that wealth was a badge of virtue and that successful traders were the natural protectors of society. But in reality this was a natural outcome of his circumstances. The people with whom he was thrown during his early years were planters and merchants and it was to this class that he belonged. They were, moreover, West Indian planters and merchants. What this means can only be understood against the background of over a hundred years of precariously maintained white prestige in tropical islands where Negro life is lush—as lush as the vegetation which always reburies human clearing in spreading greenery. A rising tide of color was kept back by increasingly savage efforts as the years passed. The gay and shiftless blacks were not wholly immune to provocation either, as several slave revolts prove; and a careless attitude toward life in general can easily extend to an utterly casual extinction of the master class. White West Indians, as a consequence, breathed fear as they breathed the heavy perfume of their flowers and it did something irretrievable to their natures. They were incapable of viewing men as equal; they were incapable of viewing the lower classes as men at all, really. At least, Hamilton had difficulty in doing so; and his utmost concession to a widened franchise had attached to it a heavy property qualification—the distinction between slave and master on the estate.

The famous difference between Hamilton and Thomas Jefferson in these matters, which has been thought to be so important in our history, can, to the extent to which it is true, be explained in these terms. One who went to look at Monticello might not think so, for Jefferson appears to have had, to a fuller degree than Hamilton, all the appurtenances of that planter life, to have lived on the sufferance of his black slaves, and to have been reared in a far more aristocratic fashion. But this similarity was altogether on the surface. Jefferson had the instincts of the small planter and the artisan. He liked to do things with his own hands and in a small way. Furthermore, in his part of Virginia there was more ease of relationship between master and slave than the Deep South or even the Tidewater ever knew. Jefferson looked forward to the elimination not only of slavery but of poverty as a whole. Even at that time freed slaves were not unknown; and to be black was not thought to be beastly.[1] A surge of color was not engulfing everything; it was a white man's country, too. There were farmers as well as planters. Then, too, Jefferson met the world out of a background of more settled gentility than Hamilton could with that question concerning his birth forever intruding. Hamilton came to New York well recommended, a brilliant lad with upper-class manners but with no family and small funds. He had his way to make. He had to prove his right to the aristocratic connections he sought. Jefferson needed no recommendation. He moved naturally in a well-known circle. He could afford the eccentricities of the rich and well-born. He could even afford to be a democrat.

[1] Jefferson held the view that blacks were "inferior." He could hardly have felt otherwise in his time. But he felt that Virginia was changing her cultivation from tobacco (which was by then a losing crop), to foodstuffs, a kind of farming to which whites were held to be better adapted. He thought that after emancipation the Negroes should be exported. In the West Indies no such shift was or could be contemplated.

It would be easy to exaggerate the part King's College had in shaping Hamilton. He went there, in the first place, because the college of New Jersey (now Princeton) would not have him. Why King's should have been willing to put up with his demands for irregularity, we do not know. He wanted to study mostly by himself and to syncopate his course. Perhaps this was easier at King's, which had, besides Myles Cooper, who was president, only two other instructors, Samuel Clossy, who taught mostly in the Medical School, and John Vardill, who was an assistant tutor. This lack of personnel made the instruction primitive at best and such busy overseers may have been glad for a bright lad who needed no driving. It must be remembered that the course was not professional and could only be considered preprofessional for prospective clergymen. Clossy taught the classics and natural philosophy and Vardill was his assistant. Cooper gave lectures in composition, disputation, theology, and moral philosophy. Prevailing instructions, conduct, and ways of thinking were given elaborate justification. Students were expected to regard them as having been formed by the operations of natural law; they therefore exemplified right reason and self-evident truth. Revelation was made some use of in tight places, but slavery, private property, business gain, and royal prerogative were easily justified in a moral philosophy which relied extensively on Old Testament ethics and the natural law teachings of Hugo Grotius and Samuel von Pufendorf.

But Hamilton always went directly into any intellectual enterprise, seizing on its core and throwing aside the nonessential covering, no matter how many layers of it there might be. His was a mind with power and he used it with economy. As a result he got over ground with incredible rapidity. This was true of him at every age. It appears in his student memoranda (some of which could and did serve for others' texts) just as it did in the greatest of his state papers later on. It was a scarcely human force, this devouring mind. And he was able to implement it early with a swinging balanced prose, tuned to the contemporary style, but growing more direct as he grew older, and strangely effective in spite of its formality. He must have given that fine old Tory, Myles Cooper, some bad moments even before the one we have record of in which Hamilton's hatred of masses on the loose triumphed over his detestation of an old gentleman who would hide in an attic from a mob.[2] Cooper thought Hamilton was urging the crowd to pull him out of his retreat and he called out, "don't believe him," before he dodged out at the back.[3] But the young man was telling his inferiors how to behave toward gentlemen; he was not inflaming passions.

At King's College sides were being taken. This could hardly have been avoided even in an institution which dedicated its students to disciplines as remote as possible from contemporary politics—remote, that is, except in the sense of supporting the status quo. These were stirring times in America. The English were bearing down on their colonies; the Navigation Acts were being enforced; smuggling was being more strictly controlled; and Parliament was imposing duties on colonial imports. Everything was heading up to the first constitutional crisis of Hamilton's experience—that in which the colonists separated overseas parliament from overseas king and denied the authority of the one while they affirmed their loyalty to the other. This was the issue so sharply dramatized by the Boston Tea Party when Hamilton had been two years on the mainland. And it was the issue which had its logical constructive protest in the setting up of an American parliament of sorts—the Continental Congress.

[2] Cooper ridiculed the notion that a stripling like Hamilton was the author of some of the sharpest strictures on the utterances of himself and fellow loyalists. John C. Hamilton, *Life of Alexander Hamilton*, 7 vols. (Boston: Houghton, Osgood, 1879), I, 74.

[3] *Ibid.*, p. 100.

The movement was not a popular one—not at this stage. It was men of large property who were framing petitions then, denying the right of the English Parliament to tax "without representation" or to regulate business enterprise without the consent of colonial assemblies who were chosen by and of the propertied folk. These petitions were being addressed to the British king by substantial and loyal subjects. They ventured to inform His Majesty that true liberty meant protecting the fruits of talent and industry and that, as things were, talent and industry were at the mercy of legislative despots. There were other loyalists too, of course, who for years in New York, once fighting got under way, appeared to have chosen the winning side, but who, in this preliminary stage, were on the defensive. They fell back on the theory that the English regulations, however trying, must be put up with or there would be no respect for authority. The argument was hot. Both sides, as is usual, cited learned works in natural law and moral philosophy and appropriated the favor of Deity.

But official King's College never wavered. It stood against rebellion. Vardill had long been writing in defense of Church and Crown. Later, in 1773, he went to England to be ordained, and was appointed Regius Professor of Divinity and Natural Law at King's. Instead of returning, however, he joined what we would now call the intelligence service, using his colonial knowledge in the British interest. Clossy, disgusted with the outbreaks in the colony, returned to England in 1774. In the following year Cooper, after asserting that "open disrespect to government" sprang from unprincipled minds, and rebellion, even if successful, would lead to the country's ruin, was forced to take the unceremonious leave which caused Hamilton to make his first public appearance.[4]

That young man, still a student, took his stand, as his teach-

[4] *A History of Columbia University 1754–1904* (New York: Columbia Univ. Press, 1904), p. 46.

ers did, on the eternal natural laws, "written . . . in the whole volume of human nature, by the hand of the Divinty itself"; but these laws led him to the conclusion that the repugnant parliamentary regulations were null and void.[5] He said that the love of power was natural to men, and if taxation by the representatives of property were denied, then civil society must end. This was so because men by contract form society to protect their property and thus their liberty. Loyalist writers answered that taxes were already laid by representatives of the nation—to be a representative a legislator need not be chosen by all: witness the case of the English masses who had no franchise. Hamilton quickly admitted the principle that a property qualification was essential. He could see that artisans would be dependent on their masters in selecting representatives. In America the propertied class was in the position of the English masses; they had no representatives because they selected none.

So the argument ran. But verbal exchanges at length lost their dramatic value and violence seeped through the brick-lined alleys and washed up to the walls of King's. Instruction came to an end, hurried by a shower of stones. The instructors departed with discretion, conservative to the end and, so far as we know, unabashed by the rough refutation of their doctrine. Hamilton was left undecided as to what he ought to do. He thought of going back to his mother's people where his younger brother was. But he still had the funds which would have seen him through to his degree. He used them, finally, to equip a company of state militia, and so got the customary commission. This was the beginning of several years of action, of life in camp and on the march which ended, as Hamilton's jobs always did, in a thinking task. He became an

[5] "The Farmer Refuted," 1775, in *The Works of Alexander Hamilton* ed., Henry Cabot Lodge, 12 vols. (1885–1886; 2nd. ed., New York: Putnam's, 1904), I, 113. Unless otherwise specified, all references are to this edition of Hamilton's works.

aide to General George Washington through some brilliant maneuvering, partly his own and partly that of some well-placed friends. It became clear, after a bit, however, that Washington's aides were merely that. When the general dared to rebuke him for tardiness one day he drew himself up, stared at the commander-in-chief, and said: "I am not conscious of it, sir; but since you have thought it necessary to tell me so, we part." [6] And they did, too. The twenty-four-year-old lieutenant-colonel demanded a field assignment and got it, ultimately, under Lafayette, with whom he served with distinction until after Yorktown.

Between Yorktown and the peace there were two years. That time was sufficient for the driving youth to become a father (he had married General Philip Schuyler's daughter), a member of the bar, and a delegate to the Continental Congress. All was confusion then in public life; but all was clear in Hamilton's mind. The government had no resources because it had no taxing power; the treasury was empty and the fatal twins of borrowing and begging had been used until "not worth a Continental" had become a permanent and expressive phrase, indicative of the furthest degradation. Crooks operated hand in hand with Congress, playing games with declining dollars, and disgusting honest folk. Hamilton's genius for penetrating analysis never shone so brightly as during this time of trial. The thing to do, he saw, was to temporize, to try for help from France, but above all to establish the principle of federal authority. When he wrote the reply of Congress to the objections Rhode Island made to federal assessment, he went straight to the issue: that position, he said, "would defeat . . . all the purposes of the Union." He went further in a burst of honesty to say, "The truth is that no Federal Constitution can exist without powers that, in their exercise, affect the internal police of the component members." [7]

[6] To Philip Schuyler, February 18, 1781, in *Works*, IX, 233.
[7] "Report on Impost Duty," 1782, in *Works*, II, 183.

These issues developed their critical phases through the fourteen years between Hamilton's leaving the army and his retirement from the Treasury. As far as he himself was concerned they opened with the reading of philosophy and the study of law, proceeding through the great constitutional debates to the establishment of a permanent fiscal policy and ending their creative uniqueness with the *Report on Manufactures* (1791) which established the tariff as an instrument of policy. Through it all—and this is one of the curious characteristics of Hamilton—he wrote as though the responsibilities of statecraft had continuous control of his mind. Most men grow into the recognition of greatness gradually and become conscious of the weight of every word and action only after learning the hard lessons of public office. It was not so with Hamilton. When he was young he approached serious questions with a strange gravity; when he was more mature he met them without compromise and with undiminished vigor. During his years in public office he was not on the side which created difficulties with well-to-do citizens who can be so savage at the betrayal of their class, and so his courage was never tested in that way; but there were occasions when a little withholding of intention, a tenderness of statement, a shift in the directness of action might have helped. These he seldom used; and for Madison, who knew how to use them all, he developed a contemptuous understanding.

The pre-law reading of Rousseau and Hobbes must have set up some lively conflicts in his mind. We have now only the remote residue of the state papers with which to judge the course of his progress in theory.[8] Certainly his profession of "democracy" at this time was sufficiently verbose. He inveighed against the imposition of an "aristocracy of wealth," but close examination indicates that the injustice in this was

[8] Hamilton, "Pay-Book of the State Company of Artillery commanded by Alex'r Hamilton," in John C. Hamilton's edition of *The Works* (New York: Francis, 1850), I, 4.

deplored on behalf of a democracy of property owners. This is, of course, a severe modification of Rousseau. There is a characteristic passage in which he makes clearly the point that a government where a chamber of superior wealth is created to check the assembly chosen by the propertied irrespective of the size of holdings must surely end in convulsions.[9] Somewhat earlier than this he had been much more extreme; indeed the following, written when he was just under eighteen, displays a faith not developed in later writings or acts; it was probably not thoughtfully meant even then: "All men have one common original: they participate in one common nature, and consequently have one common right. No reason can be assigned why one man should exercise any power or preëminence over his fellow creatures more than another." [10]

But this was one of the first of the controversial papers. Hamilton quickly learned the arts of understatement and the amenities of consistency. For a man who wrote and said so much he was remarkably sure-footed. Most importantly, perhaps, he became more and more direct and pragmatic. He was never profound in spite of erudition. Even this *Full Vindication*, early as it was, paid only lip service, so to speak, to so-called theory. When he really got down to business he wanted to know whether what was proposed (opposition to parliamentary taxation of colonial commerce) had also the "sanction of good policy." He put it this way: "To render it agreeable to good policy, three things are requisite. First, that the necessity of the times requires it; secondly, that it be not the probable source of greater evils than those it pretends to remedy; and lastly, that it have a probability of success." And this was the outline of his whole argument after obeisance to "plain and indisputable principles." [11] Hamilton is not the first or last young intellectual to begin by reference to vague prin-

[9] To Gouverneur Morris, May 19, 1777, in *Works*, IX, 71–72.
[10] "A Full Vindication," 1774, in *Works*, I, 6.
[11] *Ibid.*, p. 14.

ciple and to win simplicity only by struggle with himself. But he was certainly fast in finding his métier. His evolution is perfectly illustrated in this first document.

He was not completely free of his entangling alliances. One of his most serious appeared in *The Farmer Refuted* (but only one year later) when he wrote the much-quoted sentences: "The sacred rights of mankind are not to be rummaged for among old parchments or musty records. They are written, as with a sunbeam, in the whole volume of human nature, by the hand of the Divinity itself, and can never be erased or obscured by mortal power." This eloquence might be forgiven any youth of nineteen except Hamilton; and even for him it must be said that he was arguing with a prominent clergyman before an upper-class audience likely to be impressed by respectful references to nature and the Deity. But the body of this thirty-five-thousand-word tract is legalistic argument and precise statement of the economic conditions for a successful American policy. Of these last the most prophetic was the declaration that American independence would come simply through recognition of our resources, geography, extent, and the like factors. This point of view became the real basis of his later statesmanship and has dominated national policy from that day to this.[12]

As the war progressed and Hamilton worked closer and closer to the centers of power his faith even in a democracy of property owners faded. There were dissensions in the Congress and in the state governments themselves; worse yet, there was the disrupting quarrel between them. States' rights were supreme and no general direction was available even for the war. Quotas for revenue assigned to the various colonies were repudiated at will; military appointments were used to placate small-town politicians; militia levies were local and temporary. Gross corruption and inefficiency were every-

[12] To the great trouble of thoroughgoing laissez-faire statesmen of all parties and factions.

where. No orderly mind could contemplate the surrounding chaos except with revulsion. Those who had whatever authority could be wrested from local politicians used their powers in ways which seem peculiar to us now. Hamilton was once so outraged that he publicly denounced members of Congress who used their offices for private profit; and he made a savage attack on Samuel Chase. Here was the case of a prominent and respectable citizen—he was afterward a justice of the Supreme Court of the United States—who thought it not unworthy to get profit for himself at the public expense.[13] This kind of thing, said Hamilton, was ruining the country.

It is difficult to remember sometimes, as such incidents come to light, that there was a certain contemporary justification. Mercantilism was orthodox. It was made to seem quite legitimate to trade with the enemy if by doing so a favorable money balance was secured; and with such doctrines abroad the private side lines of office holders seemed throughly innocent.[14] Hamilton at least shared the mercantilist bias for monetary balances even though his gorge rose against the private adaptation of the mercantilist lack of scruple as to the source of the funds themselves. He believed that the public credit must be secured at all costs; depreciation of the currency could lose the struggle faster than armies could win it. When he was twenty-two he began to show that special talent for finance which enabled him to dominate the fixing of the new nation's fiscal policy. He wrote letters containing novel schemes not only to his military superiors and to acquaintances in the Congress, but also to Robert Morris, the current strong man in this field. This had consequences, for Morris recognized his talent and afterward was influential in furthering his ambitions. The one idea which dominated this early letter writing was the conviction that whatever scheme was adopted for financial regeneration (and he was flexible about that) it must

[13] [Hamilton] "Publius," 1778, in *Works*, I, 199–209.

[14] It is well to say that some laissez-faire believers could also find reasons for such practices.

be a sort which would be profitable to the investing and business classes. It was this profit which would tie them to the government. Every scheme he worked out had this as a feature. He knew his times; he knew human nature as well as Adam Smith knew it; and he did bulwark his government eventually with selfish and respectable support.

It has been noted that all the forces which impinged upon Hamilton tended to reinforce an aristocratic bias already sufficently strong when he left the West Indies. Another of these forces was the study of law into which he plunged after Yorktown, for it was English law. Still another was the conditions he met as a beginning practitioner. He was a penniless man with high connections and family standards hard to meet; he had to make money. Furthermore, he was surrounded by a speculative group who were just then beginning the exploitation of western lands and enterprises. Among these were William Duer, afterward a great entrepreneur, and Aaron Burr, grandson of Jonathan Edwards and son of a Princeton president, who was later to be Hamilton's opponent in a fatal duel. These and others were seeking to found fortunes; Hamilton joined in the game.

The fiscal ideas detailed in the papers written during his army years and immediately thereafter exhibited close reasoning and mature restraint. His ideas shifted somewhat when it came to detailed planning, although he held closely to mutual support between business and government. He saw that the depreciation of the currency which had taken place so far was not caused altogether by its excessiveness; the moneyed people had found depreciation profitable. This led him to the conclusion that these same motives could be used for a reverse effect. He suggested that a bank under government auspices but controlled by private stockholders with limited liability should be chartered, and no other established during its lifetime. The model was the Bank of England; but he went much further than the original in linking public business and private profit.

In his last plan the general government and the states were to deposit with it their specie and the proceeds of foreign loans. It was not only to perform the functions of discount and deposit, but to coin money, issue paper currency, and have allotted to it all the contracts for supplying the fleets and armies. Its notes were to be acceptable in payment of all public duties.

In this scheme the increased issues of paper over specie reserves would make possible loans to the government for which the current rate of interest of 8 percent would be paid. Furthermore this additional paper, by creating business prosperity, would increase the amount of taxes which might be levied and so render the public debt secure. Since people are influenced by such things, the name of the new currency was to be changed. Even if the war should be lost, the British would retain the bank because of its manifest advantages, and the shareholders would not suffer. He warned that the support of the moneyed classes would be forthcoming only if a solid confederation, vigorous administration, and a permanent military force were established.

Similarly, bounties to promoters of domestic enterprise would be beneficial along with tariffs and other favors. Those who demanded that the sovereign should leave trade absolutely alone were running counter to the teachings of experience and common sense. Such views had arisen from the antipathy to wartime price fixing and from the misreading of David Hume's essay *Of the Jealousy of Trade.* But neither Hume, "that ingenious and sensible thinker," nor any other authority denied that government interposition was one of those moral influences often necessary to rectify an unfavorable balance of trade and to restore commerce to the natural, invariable laws of profitable activity.[15]

But the most important function of import duties was to

[15] Hamilton, on this particular point, seems himself to have in part misread Hume, although there were arguments in Hume which might have been used (Hume, *Political Discourses* [Edinburgh: Kincaid and Donald-

supply funds for backing the public debt which might in this way be made fully negotiable; and if it were it could then serve as a circulating medium and as capital. Incidentally this would also allow its holders to incorporate as a bank. The national debt might turn out to be a blessing for a further reason: the masses would be forced to work harder in order to pay the necessary taxes. Thanks to popular maxims, he thought, we labored less than any people of Europe. About the public debt he had strong views always; he suggested seriously the joining of army discontent with that of the public creditors; but Washington felt that such attempts would cause convulsions.[16] Still, Washington was learning to respect and trust the younger man. Robert Morris, also, was impressed and it was through his urging that Hamilton became receiver of Continental taxes for New York State, an officer whose thankless duty it was to collect federal requisitions. The pay was scarcely more than nominal; but it furnished a connection with national finance and with Morris which later developed toward the secretaryship of the Treasury.

One of Hamilton's biographers quite lost his restraint when he came to discuss the events of 1787; he called it "the wonderful year." [17] It was all of that. It was then that Alexander Hamilton had his way with his country. That we have a constitution at all and are a union instead of an association of

---

son, 1752], pp. 82–84). "Of the Jealousy of Trade" was originally issued as a supplement to the 1758 edition of Hume's *Essays and Treatises*. It was included in the 1760 edition.

Hamilton had read Adam Smith and even had prepared a commentary for his own perusal, but it would not have suited his purpose to cite Smith, whose only clear exception to the doctrine of free trade was the Navigation Acts.

[16] To James Duane, September 3, 1780; "The Continentalist," No. 4, August 30, 1781, No. 5, April 18, 1782; "Report on Impost Duty," December 16, 1782; to Robert Morris, 1780, April 30, 1781; to Washington, February 7, 1783, April, 1783; to George Clinton, May 14, 1783; in *Works*, I, 233–37, 261, 267–70; II, 189; III, 319–87; IX, 312–13, 332–37, 341.

[17] Henry Jones Ford, *Alexander Hamilton* (New York: Scribner's, 1920), p. 186.

jealous neighbors, we may well owe as much to him as to any other single person. Of all those who were involved, no other had quite his determination and certainty. In 1786, under Washington's auspices at Mount Vernon, commissioners from Maryland and Virginia met for certain commercial negotiations. The discussion there disclosed a need for more general agreement and the Virginia Legislature appointed commissioners to meet those who might be appointed by other states. The intention was clear enough; several sovereign states were to try for mutual accommodation in interstate trade. But Hamilton took the opportunity at the ensuing meeting to pursue his controlling purpose—the strengthening of union. He could manage the preliminary concurrence of New York because the city's merchants had grievances; he could even become a delegate himself because the meeting seemed to Governor George Clinton relatively unimportant. In fact it was unimportant, except that it opened a narrow door through which Hamilton could go. Only five states were represented; but there were others from which demands for the regulation of trade were beginning to come. Using this as his lever, Hamilton suggested a further meeting. He did it in the vaguest of terms (this on the advice of Edmund Randolph of Virginia), going gently, smoothly forward; nevertheless the recommendations adopted by the meeting for a convention to meet in Philadelphia in 1787 did say that one object was to be the rendering of the "Constitution of the Federal Government adequate to the exigencies of the union." [18] But even this was softened. The delegates were not to have plenary powers. Everything would afterward have to be ratified.

Nevertheless, the West Indian adventurer had really stirred the colonial lethargy. He had caused a questioning of the predilection for local advantage, the resistant dislike of organization and control. The strategy was moving. Yet much had to

[18] "Address of the Annapolis Convention," 1786, in *Works*, I, 335–39.

be given away in compromise. Sometimes it seemed that nothing would be left. He foresaw the long struggle involved in the legislative trading. But he had come to love his country deeply. He did not, it is true, respect her intelligence greatly. He thought her beautiful but not wise. Others, including Jefferson, would think her wise rather than adorable, however, and so rather more than compensate for Hamilton's strange infatuation. The Constitution would turn out to have a queer mixture of democratic conviction and aristocratic noblesse. Hamilton acted rather as though he were appointing and instructing executors to protect and shelter her after his death. He was doubtless inclined to limit unduly the qualifications for her guardians; but there were fundamental principles of power involved. The source of the mandate we cannot now approve; Hamilton preferred to ignore some parts of his nation which seemed to him unbeautiful or unruly; we now take her whole and find her mandate in a majority quite unselected.

The peace of 1783 had given the country no ease. Public creditors were clamant; commercial rivalries had become so intense that the extreme recourse of conciliation had been attempted at Mount Vernon; the states had refused to be assessed except as it suited their selfish plans; there had been armed risings in New England and forcible suspension of the courts to prevent foreclosures. So in forming the Constitution arrangements were consented to, even fought for later, which none of the fathers believed to be wise and which have been a torment ever since. To this even the policy of private profit from public ventures for the sake of establishing a self-interested protector class is not an exception. If it was desired to have business men profit from the establishment of union this was never for the sake of the business men but always in the interest of union. Hamilton has often been said to have been an aristocrat, and he was; he has often been said to have been something less than a genuine democrat, and this is true. But his was a genuinely national, not a class or a local loyalty. He was looking for strength for his nation and he took it where he could find it.

Hamilton had in mind, when he came to the Convention, a modification of the model furnished by the British government of that time. He seems, for instance, to have wanted a heriditary monarchy with so much power that no advantage would ever be found in securing more. In this way corruption would be made impossible—a consideration of great weight to one who had had intimate experiences with the Continental Congress. He thought, also, that the setting up of a House of Lords for the wealthy, well born, and deserving would create a permanent interest in the government from which honors came and would furnish a check on the probable radicalism of a House of Commons. For this last he had, he thought, enough evidence in the paper-money predilections of the state legislatures, their readiness to pass debt-staying laws, and the like. Wealth indicated enlightenment; the propertyless were usually irresponsible. A substantial property interest indicated the practical focus for political power; it was solidly rooted in resource and it commanded active defense. This was the clue to the securing of permanence for the infant nation.

There was more to this argument. In fact, Hamilton was inclined to elaborate it beyond necessity. Liberty could be defined best as freedom to acquire and keep wealth; it followed from this, of course, that equality was nonsense. There must always be the rich and the poor, nobles and commons, creditors and debtors. The advance of industry and commerce would only widen these disparities; wealth would become more concentrated and virtue would be its graceful appendage. All this might be deprecated as a departure from strict democratic principles, but it could not be prevented. It was inherent in a human nature which was self-interested and especially so in pecuniary affairs. If the influence of the wealthy, moreover, should be circumscribed by law, they would secure the same effect by corruption. What is inevitable may as well be called to the support of virtues. Another aspect of the same situation was that too much democracy would, through the rise of demagogues, lead to a despotism which must be less intelligent than that of the wealthy. In pursuing this thought, Hamilton used the authority of Hume's Tory *History of England;* it was shown there that the bribery of Parliament by the Crown was, under the circumstances, a wise way of maintaining an equilibrium. It brought out the dominant traits of self-interest and ambition but it secured their energies for the public benefit.

In effect, the whole lesson of history was that "popular" government could not last long and that while it did last it made misery. What he was getting at was that America would be wisest to set up an Executive and a Senate chosen for life by an electorate restricted to considerable property holders, and to center most of the power in these as against the necessary Chamber of Commons for small property holders—the "turbulent people." But he felt that even this would scarcely be enough; the states would have to be reduced to administrative units of the central government and within each there would need to be placed a representative of the national authority with veto power over its legislative assembly.[19] On the whole, Hamilton's scheme, basing itself on the belief that economic power could never center in the people, in workers and small farmers, would withhold from them a political power which they would certainly use irresponsibly and center it in the wealthy who would use it with decorum.

If all this seems inconsistent with his way of thinking in the early days of the Revolutionary War, it can only be said that with the most reasonable of us there are times when we suc-

[19] "Propositions for a Constitution of Government," and speeches in the Federal Convention, in *Works*, I, 347–429.

cumb to plausible theories which seem to commit us to beliefs we never really have. In 1782, which was not far removed from the time of his youthful obeisances to Rousseau, he had written in one of his reports to Morris that on the matter in question (inducing the New York legislature to meet its federal obligations), he would do what he could but that that would not be much until the whole system of government had been changed. "The inquiry," he said of the legislature, "is constantly what will *please*, not what will *benefit* the people. In such a government there can be nothing but temporary expenditure, fickleness and folly." [20] This was the way his convictions ran and ran consistently. The people could not be trusted even to look after themselves. And when it came to setting up a permanent government for the new nation, his earlier tentatives in the direction of democracy were dropped. This was a serious matter and a practical one. Playing with theories was out of place.

Hamilton was not too well pleased by the final draft of the Constitution. He feared especially the primary position of the states and would have located the reservoir of sovereignty, if he could, in the federal government, a fault which he went some way toward remedying later on when, in one of his remarkable overnight memoranda, he developed full-blown the doctrine of implied powers. But fearful as he was, he knew that great gains had been made and he labored with characteristic energy to secure ratification. It was a bitter and prolonged fight. The arguments he used were those which came out of his now-settled convictions. This Constitution would cause land values to rise; funds would come out of hiding; industry would prosper. The essentials of property protection and security of contracts and persons had been gained. The courts were firmly rooted and wealth need hide no longer. The rich and the well-born had been committed to the country's future. When New York voted, he knew at

[20] To Robert Morris, August 13, 1782, in *Works*, IX, 273.

last that the symbol of his adoration was enshrined; the holy of holies, moreover, was reasonably removed from vulgar disturbance; at thirty-three his life's work was done.

After the adoption of the Constitution Hamilton's ambitions were to retire from public controversy, to retreat from official life, to make a fortune, and to found a family. But the future lay in the past: the consequences of his patriotic passion soon caught up with him; the secretaryship of the new Treasury evolved out of those old letters to Morris, out of talks with Washington, out of the powerful pamphlets which outlined a national fiscal policy. In this phase of his career there developed nothing new; there were merely evidences of the same genius grown mature and of the same capacity for astonishing spells of creative effort. It all tended in the same direction; it was a consolidation of gains made in the past.

The apogee had passed; but it occurs to us to wonder why Hamilton had no thought of becoming President; and why, actually, he never did. The answers to these questions are hidden in the past—perhaps the evidence disappeared in the ash of burned papers. Speculation leads straight to character. The devious political arts always escaped Hamilton; he had, besides, little of that honorable compromising spirit which was part of the steadier Washington's attitude toward life. His fellow countrymen had seen enough of Hamilton by 1795.

His economic program, moreover, had that directness and straight-line quality from which politicians instinctively shy. It had to be smeared and blunted into commonly unrecognizable shapes. It could not be allowed to plow through competing special interests with its shining blades triumphant. It had to be held to more or less. It stemmed from theories of human nature and of government which had been toned down in the writing of the Constitution. That document was a compromise between Hamiltonian aristocracy and the small-proprietor tradition; and the nation's economic policies had to be keyed to that same compromise. Hamilton could not be President; his policies could not remain unmodified. The man and his policies had too high a visibility; they were too clear, too target-like, and therefore too vulnerable.

It was, nevertheless, during these years, and in the midst of a busy administrative life, that the most famous of his economic papers were written.[21] It is not of much use to inquire what help he had with them. The evidence is lost for one thing, and, for another, they were in the line of his thought; so that, unless interest centers in his prose composition, it does not matter much. Duer and Tench Coxe were about; and neither did him much good, probably, either as ghost writers, or as consultants. Duer was essentially a promoter of all sorts of speculative enterprises; Coxe is known to have used Hamilton's money in land purchases.[22] Any official is better off without such help.

One of the earliest developed of his policies was the funding of the public debt; and characteristically he followed the logic of his mind in this, as in other matters, rather than the obvious expedients to which he might have resorted. The result was that his detractors—there are some even yet—declared that no one would fight so hard for a policy out of which so many miscreants made money, if he were not one of them. It did seem strange. Everyone was to be paid in full and almost everyone of the present holders had spent only a fraction of what he would get. The original holders of securities had, in other words, been scared out and speculators were by now the government's largest creditors. Foreigners, rascals, honest patriots —all were to be treated alike. That side of it, said Hamilton, was not important. The government must meet its obligations in full; in no other way could it punish the timid, reward the

[21] The reports included in Hamilton, *Papers on Public Credit, Commerce and Finance*, ed. Samuel McKee, Jr. (New York: Columbia Univ. Press, 1934).

[22] To Robert Troup, July 25, 1795, in *Works*, X, 110.

faithful, and establish its credit forever. Besides there were other arguments, most of which he had used in the days of the Continental Congress. Assumption and funding would secure a future in which the government would be able to get credit at reasonable terms and at any time; even more important, the debt would at once be represented by freely negotiable instruments; and these would be available as capital for the expansion of enterprise; the debt of the government, therefore, would become an instrument of social progress.[23] This tour de force can be called nothing less than magnificent. The government was to pay its obligations; these payments, flowing into promoters' schemes, were to enlarge the nation's private business. That ingenious notion, linked perhaps to the equally old device of deflation, still awaits exploitation by later American Treasury chiefs who believe in government ownership; but nothing was further from Hamilton's mind than this. He was merely determined to draw all enterprisers, large, small, honest, dishonest, into his net.

Related to this, was the scheme for a national bank. Its stockholders were to have a limited liability; it was to be backed by the government's participation in ownership and by

[23] Hamilton evidently regarded capital as something intangible, as anything, in fact, which was convertible into money. Credit and capital sometimes seem to have been synonymous in his mind. This led him to reason that no taxes should be laid on the principal, income, or transfer of public securities, since such a tax would constitute in effect a breach of the contract between the government and its creditors. Hamilton's view of public debt as a mightly instrument for national economic expansion has been well stated by a pioneering investigator of early American corporations: "The operation of a funded public debt as capital was a favorite one with Hamilton. The essence of this view was that such 'stocks' partook of the nature of money and investments—they were at once income bearers and (for certain important transactions) an acceptable circulating medium; thus they served the businessman as admirable security for loans and as economical 'liquid assets,' and their holders were in a far better position to invest in new undertakings than if their investments were in real estate; the typical investment of that day. The idea is often loosely or inaccurately expressed, even by Hamilton, but for his day it was essentially true." (Joseph S. Davis, *Essays in the Earlier History of American Corporations*, 2 vols. [Cambridge: Harvard Univ. Press, 1907], I, 359.)

the acceptance of its notes for public dues; but it was to be privately operated and its profits were to go elsewhere than to the Treasury. By this time Jefferson, James Madison, and Randolph for various reasons, to be classified partly as jealousy, and partly as differences in political theory, had ceased to be friends of the secretary of the Treasury. The proposed bank was a convenient club to beat him with. It was inexpedient, unnecessary and, moreover, unconstitutional, they said, and in substantiation cited the document itself. Where, they asked, were the provisions for such an incorporation as was proposed? This was the opening for the stroke by which Hamilton endangered Jefferson's reputation for sagacity and developed for all the future that doctrine of implied powers without which there would have been needed a new basic law altogether.

There succeeded the *Report on Manufactures*, Hamilton's most famous state paper. Here his pragmatic mind had a notable collision not only with Adam Smith but also with the whole physiocratic school. An unkind critic might say that the attitude illustrated in this document represented merely another instance of that prejudice in favor of "the great, the rich and the good" which has been so often ridiculed; a kinder one would be disposed to see in its bias something prophetic. The city, the factory, the whole, indeed, of our complex industrial civilization, lay imagined within the stately body of this document; and, after all, they came into being; they are here. The encouragement of manufactures was a policy which would increase the national wealth. As for those who were inclined to weigh the farm against the factory, he had a kind of answer: agriculture, he said, would gain an increasing market for its products; and, as a result of this, land values would rise and proprietors would be benefited. As things were, the rural nations were cheated by the drain of their specie into the countries from which they bought higher priced goods. As for the physiocratic idea that manufacturing is incapable of producing any surplus, as rent is produced by land, this was fallacious; even rent was really the profit produced by capital invested in the land, not something produced by the land itself. From this generalization Hamilton went on to his triumphant conclusion that manufacturing was a more desirable activity than agriculture since it yielded higher profits.

It had been argued that a scarcity of labor existed; but that could be remedied not only by introducing machinery but also by using the labor of women, of children, and of immigrants. Adequate capital was available from foreigners and from the establishment of new banks, but most importantly from using the public debt. English business men and sagacious theorists alike were agreed, said Hamilton, that the public debt had been the great animating agent of enterprise; this was proven by the universal inability to explain, otherwise, how England could become the world's fiscal agent and the center of its industry on so small an amount of specie. The linking of the public debt as capital with private enterprise would have certain subsidiary benefits also. The collection of taxes with which to pay the debt services would force the people who paid them to be more industrious; they would therefore produce more and set the country forward in that way. It needed also to be said that if manufactures were not encouraged, public debt repayments would involve exporting specie to foreign creditors; if this were not enough, it could be added that it took good hard money to pay for the importing of useless luxuries which a wholly agricultural class would demand even though it did not make them.

It might be argued that if these enterprises really had a prospect of profit, self-interest would lead to their expansion; but aside from the objection that there would be competition from foreign enterprises, it had to be remembered that man, being a creature of habit, only tardily makes changes which are profitable to himself and to society. Consequently, to secure the confidence of sagacious, cautious capitalists, government should give guarantees against initial losses. Such aid might take the form of duties on imports of manufactures, and, in rare cases, prohibitory ones; but protective duties on raw materials should be generally low at best. These would raise prices only until the domestic enterprise had matured. But better still were bounties and premiums. For the constitutionality of bounties, Hamilton relied on the general welfare clause.[24] This did not mean that the government could manufacture on its own account, with the possible exception of military supplies. It might, however, purchase stock in privately incorporated societies for manufacture. Finally, as a further aid to industry, no taxes on profits or capital should be imposed. Since business men would not reveal the relevant details of their operations, such taxes must be of the arbitrary, imputed kind that were contrary to the genius of liberty and the maxims of industry.[25]

[24] Interpreted by Hamilton to mean that the national legislature can apply money for whatever it determines to be in the general interest of learning, agriculture, manufacture, or commerce.

[25] Some aspects of the *Report* become clearer through an examination of the Society for Establishing Useful Manufactures (S.U.M.). This concern obtained a charter for incorporation from the legislature of New Jersey in 1791 and established a cotton manufacturing plant in Patterson. Its chief promoters were Hamilton, Duer, and Coxe. The prospectus for the proposed company so closely resembles the contemporaneous *Report* that it has been taken to be the work of Hamilton. Two weeks before the *Report* was submitted to Congress, the charter was obtained, in spite of objectors who said that it was dangerous to the landed and artisan interests. Another use was now found by Hamilton for the funded debt. It could be used for the purchase of stock in the S.U.M., and in turn this subscribed public debt could be invested in National Bank stock. This multiple use, said Hamilton, would increase the market value of the public stocks, and so both the venture and the public stood to gain from what the prospectus described as a patriotic enterprise for the promotion of domestic industry. Shares were fully transferable. The stockholders chose the directors who in turn selected the governor and deputy governor. Both the federal and state governments were expected to become stockholders, but such subscribers were limited to a maximum of one hundred votes each. Otherwise voting was solely by shares, although Hamilton in his *Report on a National Bank* (1791) had held that "a vote for each share renders a combination between a few principal stockholders, to monopolize the power and the benefits of the bank too easy."

The reports of Hamilton in 1790 and 1791, taken together, constituted a theoretical plan which only much later was appreciated. The economic organization logically involved was grand and imperial in scope. A fully negotiable funded debt, drained originally from the small-property classes and met by taxes paid by the masses, was to be used by an emerging moneyed class to create profitable speculative enterprises in lands, industry, and finance. This was the intent. However, after the funding and bank bills became law, a vast uproar began. Jefferson privately wrote that a moneyed interest had been created to enslave the "unmoneyed farmers" who "merely" fed the nation. Others, guided by the skillful Jefferson, uttered equally fiery public statements. Holders of the debt in Congress had voted for the measures and some had become directors of the bank. Press and platform rang with denunciations of the "corrupt squadron of stock jobbers" and "paper jobbers." By the funding soldiers were robbed, a hopeless debt and endless taxes were fastened on the country; the real property in the nation, the property of agriculture and industry, was taxed by the bank and the funding, and placed at the disposal of gamblers in the stock market. Vast inequalities had been created over night by jugglery in mere paper by lending shadows and receiving substance. Formerly the members of this new cor-

The company was granted, along with rights of eminent domain, a complete exemption from state and county taxes on its property for ten years. A lottery was licensed to the concern to meet the risks and losses of initial operations. Further profits were expected through the subdivision of real estate. Incorporation made the site in effect a company town. The mass of the labor supply was expected to consist largely of women and children and immigrants "engaged on reasonable terms in countries where labor is cheap" and brought to the United States. To attract sufficient skilled craftsmen that was the provision that "all Artificers or Manufacturers, in the immediate Service of the said Society shall be free and exempt from all Poll and Capitation Taxes, and Taxes on their respective Faculties or Occupations, and from all Taxes in the Nature of general Assessments upon their Persons, Faculties or Occupations"; further, they were exempted from all military duty, except in cases of actual invasion or imminent danger. (*Industrial and Commercial Correspondence of Alexander Hamilton*, ed. A. H. Cole [Chicago: Shaw, 1928]; Davis, *Essays in the Earlier History of American Corporations*, I, 349–503.)

rupt, barren, idle class were in effect paupers; now they constituted a "paper aristocracy" of rich and well-born. This great disparity in wealth could only lead to the destruction of liberty. Had not Hamilton shown by his use of the welfare clause to support bounties that all power and wealth would be usurped eventually by a select class, and the people reduced to poverty and distress, republican institutions overthrown, and despotic monarchy established? [26]

President Washington became disturbed and asked Hamilton for an explanation. He gave his answers with customary facility. The public credit might be misused, but the true ground of safety must be the prevention at all times of attempts to defraud creditors. Governments as well as individuals must maintain their contracts. Unless the arrangements already made were upheld, private property and government would certainly fall, and Washington was warned again that the confidence of the moneyed class must not be alienated. They were the only solid support for government.

Challenged by invective of so bitter a sort, Hamilton is hardly to be blamed for retorting in kind. He did so in answering Washington and in writing for the press. Since the French Revolution was known to have the sympathy of his opponents, he was not adverse to charging them with all the crimes which might be attributed to revolutionists. He was no more troubled by irrelevancy in this peculiarly political controversy than most other politicians have been before and since. Those who opposed his ideas were "empirics" and "speculative thinkers," influenced by pernicious French doctrines. They were, in other words, un-American Reds. Criminally ignorant of human nature, they entertained the dangerous hope of man's

[26] Jefferson to T. M. Randolph, March 16, 1792, and Jefferson to Washington, Sept. 9, 1792, in *The Writings of Thomas Jefferson*, ed. P. L. Ford. 10 vols. (New York: Putnam's, 1892–99), V, 455; VI, 102–9; John Marshall, *The Life of George Washington*, 2 vols. (Philadelphia: Crissey & Markley, 1850), I, 216; Samuel E. Foreman, *The Political Activities of Philip Freneau* (Baltimore: Johns Hopkins Press, 1902), pp. 45–50.

perfectibility when a sound suspicion of his depravity was the only secure basis for public policy. Extending their principles of liberty toward licentiousness, they were at war with religion, morality, government, and property. To "the vain reveries of a false and new-fangled philosophy" preaching change, they sacrificed all that is sacred, revered, enduring, and substantial in society.[27] They worshiped "the idol of popularity" and propagated errors only to be found in the cottages of peasants.

The press battle went on at great length and with the expenditure of vast energy, but Jefferson had the advantage. Hamilton himself wrote for the magazines and newspapers, but Jefferson always got others to write. He used particularly the litterateur Philip Freneau, the cleverest publicist of his day. And this device worked well, illustrating the maxim that officials other than presidents are safest with nothing on the record. Hamilton won many engagements; he was figuratively decorated for gallant conduct; but Jefferson won the war. That is to say, he, not Hamilton, obtained the Presidency. Hamilton had his way about policy; in fact, Hamilton's policies became Jefferson's when he had to assume real responsibility. But by then Hamilton had long since retired in disgust; and Jefferson no longer needed him for a foil.

Hamilton's more discriminating biographers obviously have felt, in contrast with the usual piously patriotic lament over his short career, that their task would have been a more grateful one if they could have ignored the years between his resignation in 1795 and his death in 1804. And certainly there was little in these years to magnify his reputation. He turned inconsistent in his advocacy of public policy; his own mistakes helped to lose for his party the control of the country; and he was gradually drawn toward his own personal extinction by a series of intemperate disputes with Aaron Burr which apparently followed a chosen line of behavior. It can hardly be

[27] To Washington, Aug. 18, 1792, in *Works*, II, 455.

argued that his character went to pieces after 1795, or that his mind lost its former brilliance. He did seem to grow more touchy about his personal integrity [28] and his struggle with Jefferson was reduced to the level of a feud.[29] But mostly the difference is accounted for by his change of scene and activity. He turned now to the law and to money-making. And he did both well. But neither of these enhances a retired statesman's prestige.

One money-making venture had an unhappy outcome. He joined with his financial and political competitor, Aaron Burr, to secure a charter for another bank from the New York Legislature, though he had denounced a previous attempt by others as monstrous because it would result in creating too much paper. Subterfuge was used to secure the charter. It happened that the city of New York was seeking power from the Legislature to create a water works system. Burr and Hamilton convinced the municipal authorities that it would be financially impossible for the city to erect the works on its own account.

[28] He was so anxious to defend his official reputation that in 1797 he published a detailed pamphlet in which he explained that certain impugned relationships of his were not maintained for profit while in office but for the quite different purpose of keeping a mistress. ("Observations on Certain Documents Contained in Nos. 5 and 6 of *The History of the United States for the Year 1796*," *Works*, VII, 369–479.) As a matter of fact the worst that could be said of him was that he had engaged in land speculations involving public grants. (Charles Beard, *An Economic Interpretation of the Constitution* [New York: Macmillan, 1913], pp. 110–11.) But so did Washington. It cannot have seemed so wrong then as it would seem now.

[29] An instance of his littleness at this time is furnished by his change on the Jay pact with Great Britain. He denounced it at first as "an old woman's treaty"; but as soon as the Jeffersonians indicated that it seemed to them a betrayal of American economic and political interests, it became to him one of the fruits of adherence to "reason left to its own light." With one doubtful exception, every article was of benefit to the nation. See, for instance, the advantage of securing a share in the trade with India. Opponents said this was an empty privilege so long as the East India Company retained its strength; but Hamilton, forgetting his hitherto consistent belief in the growing usefulness of the corporate device, insisted that experience proved (outside of "banking and a few analogous employments") the superior strength and enterprise of individual effort. (Henry Cabot Lodge, *Alexander Hamilton* [Boston: Houghton Mifflin, 1899], p. 186; Hamilton, "Defense of Mr. Jay's Treaty," *Works*, VI, 44.)

It would not be able to borrow sufficient funds; the requisite taxes would be too heavy and the work would not be zealously pushed. A private company in which the city would buy shares could easily and quickly accomplish the task. So a bill was passed by the Legislature in 1799 providing for a private corporation, the Manhattan Company, to supply the city "with pure and wholesome water"; but a clause was inserted which stated that it "may be lawful for said company to employ . . . surplus capital in the purchase of public or other stock, or in any other monied transactions or operations." After securing the charter, the incorporators dug a well in the most thickly settled part of the city and, in feeble compliance with their contract, pumped a little impure water. The city obtained no real water supply, but the company entered its real business of banking. In the process, Burr froze out the Hamilton interests, and Hamilton then described the bank as "a perfect monster in its principles but a very convenient instrument of *profit* and *influence*." It was now ostensibly a Jeffersonian "Republican bank" and Republican spokesmen shouted that they now could prevent Federalist banks from coercing borrowers at election times.[30]

Meanwhile, the Federalists were losing control of the government. The foreign-born, particularly, were rabid Jeffersonians and their anti-British and pro-French sympathies made them doubly obnoxious to Hamilton. He felt that the proposed Alien Act giving President John Adams arbitrary power to deport any undesirable foreigners should be administered with an eye to deporting the mass of foreigners—except the

[30] Charles King, *A Memoir of the Construction, Cost and Capacity of the Croton Aqueduct* (New York: privately printed, 1843), pp. 95–96; *Minutes of the Common Council of the City of New York, 1784–1831*, 19 vols. (New York: City of New York, 1917), February 25, 28, 1799, II, 514–15, 517–20; *Act of Incorporation of the Manhattan Company* (New York: Foreman, 1799), p. 11; W. B. Lawrence, "The Croton Aqueduct, *The Merchants' Magazine and Commercial Review*, X (May, 1844), 435; Hamilton to James A. Bayard, Jan. 16, 1801, in *Works*, X, 415; James Cheetham, *Remarks on the "Merchant's Bank"* (New York: privately printed, 1804), p. 33.

merchants among them.[31] They were causing disturbances. Furthermore, the administration should, he said, appoint more judges. This "salutary patronage" would increase the government's influence. The people would grumble at first, but they would eventually become docile. On the other hand, the Federalists should establish a society for giving premiums for new inventions, discoveries, and improvements in agriculture and the arts. Such a society would "speak powerfully to the feelings and interests of those classes of men to whom the benefits derived from the government have been heretofore the least manifest." [32] He began to perceive also that the sources of the higher learning ought to be protected from common contamination. Commenting on the standards which ought to be used in choosing a president for Columbia in 1800 he wrote that the candidate must "be a gentleman . . . as well as a sound and polite scholar; . . . and . . . his politics be of the right sort." He prevented Benjamin Rush from obtaining a post in the medical division.[33]

In the national presidential campaign of 1800 Hamilton was unrestrained in his partisanship. The Republican ticket of Jefferson and Burr must be defeated at all costs. He unsuccessfully begged his political ally, Governor John Jay of New York, to overturn arbitrarily the election procedure in the state. The atheistical Jefferson, he wrote, was too earnest about democracy, and would destroy the substantial interests of society. "From indubitable facts, not from conjectures and inferences," he knew that a revolution was planned with Jefferson as Napoleon.[34] The Republicans won, but Jefferson and Burr having received the same number of votes, the Constitution required the House of Representatives to determine who was President

[31] To Timothy Pickering, June 7, 1798, in *Works*, X, 294.

[32] To Jonathan Dayton, 1799, in *Works*, X, 331–33.

[33] To Bayard, Aug. 6, 1800, in *Works*, X, 385; H. G. Good, *Benjamin Rush and His Service to American Education* (Berne, Ind.: Witness Press, 1918), p. 92.

[34] To Jay, May 7, 1800, in *Works*, X, 372–74.

and who was Vice-President. Federalist representatives, it seemed, might throw their support to Burr. Promptly, Hamilton transferred his invective to Burr, however much it must have hurt to support his old enemy, Jefferson. Burr, he shouted, was a potential dictator—a Godwin! [35]

With Jefferson in the White House, Hamilton found it increasingly necessary to defend the constitutional and fiscal structure he had labored to erect. Jefferson proposed to repay the public debt rapidly. The result would be an excess of money, said Hamilton. This, experience showed, would lower the morality and decrease the industriousness of the nation. In addition, specie payments to foreign holders of bonds and the importation of luxuries would create a defective circulation and less industry. The proposed elimination of the excise duty would be disastrous; it would destroy equality of burden, and if this revenue really could be spared it should be used for the benefit of commerce and navigation. Jefferson's statement in his inaugural address that industry prospers in proportion as it is left to the exertion of individual enterprise was preposterous, for "practical politicians know that [industry] may be beneficially stimulated by prudent aids and encouragements on the part of government."

Nothing was as terrifying however, as the proposed reduction of the number of federal judgeships. This was a violation of the sacred principles of contract and vested interest. It was based on the pernicious doctrine that no legislature can bind its successor—in other words, that no rights can be vested in an individual or collection of individuals, whether of property or any other description, which cannot be canceled at pleasure. This doctrine would prevent the making of any valid pledge of public faith! [36] To fight this "democratic frenzy" he and his friends founded in 1801 the New York *Evening Post*

[35] To Bayard, Jan. 16, 1801, in *Works*, X, 415.
[36] "Examination of Jefferson's Message to Congress of December 7, 1801," in *Works*, VIII, 259–60, 262–64, 282–83, 318–19, 327.

which, according to the prospectus, was "to diffuse among the people correct information on all interesting subjects, to inculcate just principles in religion, morals, and politics, and to cultivate a taste for sound literature." But Hamilton soon found that a newspaper was not the most effective instrument to win the people to his side. He complained in 1802 that the Federalists had not heretofore pursued the wisest tactics. They had always appealed to the ignorant people on the basis of reason. But "men are rather reasoning than reasonable animals, for the most part governed by the impulse of passion." His opponents, he now saw, were aware of this. They praised democracy and equality; they gave lip service to the reason of men; but their appeal was really to the most powerful of passions, that of vanity. This gave them the great advantage of having the vicious on their side. Since mankind was governed more by vices than by virtues, the Federalists must now and then depart from the path of absolute rectitude to win the support of those they despised. The best way to accomplish their ends, he thought, would be to organize a Christian Constitutional Society, devoted to upholding the Christian religion and the Constitution. It should promote charitable societies for the relief of emigrants. Federalist-manned science schools for "the different classes of mechanics" should also be established to check the influence of the Jacobins in the populous cities.[37] This was as low as Hamilton ever fell. Little wonder his biographers have taken no pleasure in the record after 1795 of one who by his shining magnificence up till then had so reduced their resistance to hero worship!

Many statesmen have been praised for the wrong virtues; Hamilton and, for that matter, Jefferson are no exceptions. It has become a habit among superficial historians to oppose the philosophies of these two contemporaries: the great democrat and the determined aristocrat. It is probably because of this

[37] To Bayard, April, 1802, in *Works*, X, 436.

that Hamilton has been a favorite mark of mob-conscious orators and Jefferson has been inflated out of all resemblance to a Virginia politician. It is only fair to remember, however much we may deprecate Hamilton's distrust of the people, that Jefferson had an equal distrust of the majority rule which has become the instrument of all others on which modern democracy most relies. It is also only fair to remember that Jefferson intrigued and maneuvered to become President and so was often less than single-minded in his devotion to his country's good. But even these contrasts can be overemphasized very easily. Neither was the paragon pictured by his partisans. Jefferson's weakness for political preferment was certainly matched by Hamilton's ambition for place and money, and by his degeneration into reaction after retirement from office. But the residue of relevant truth in the contrast furnished by the two philosophies is nevertheless important. The last word is yet to be said on the matters which concerned Hamilton most deeply. Our difficulties in the face of national crises have brought the beginnings of emphasis on the need for some national guidance of the whole economy. State rights are questioned sharply now by political theorists of repute even in those reserved fields which few would have permitted the federal government to invade in 1787. The selection of personnel for enlarged governmental functions has brought home even to demagogues the truth that we are not really all of us equal in capacity. Questions concerning the origin of national policy are as current now as they were when our forefathers dodged the issues they presented. And involved with them now as then is the matter of independence for the executive, the legislative, and the judicial branches. One who believes in majority rule and in popular mandates, whether of a select or a democratic electorate, cannot at the same time believe that these divisions should be allowed to check each other even to the point of governmental futility.

Hamilton regarded his country's future with a realistic understanding of her capacities and judged with remorseless accuracy the sort of constitution she could and should accept. In his method at least, and certainly in some of his conclusions, we can find the guidance we look for in true statesmanship. It was said earlier that no span of years in our history offered such opportunity to a nation-maker as those included in Hamilton's career. We were better prepared for the years through which we later passed because Hamilton lived, and loved his country, when our Constitution was first beginning to be created.

JOHN JAY

JOHN JAY: REVOLUTIONARY CONSERVATIVE

John Jay's first interest in public affairs was manifested in 1774 when he was twenty-nine. He retired to his Bedford estate in 1801 when he was fifty-six. During this relatively short career of twenty-nine years, he held more important offices than any of his contemporaries or, indeed, than any statesman since. There was hardly an issue in the Revolutionary and post-Revolutionary years in which he was not concerned, hardly a large decision in which he did not participate, and hardly an action in which he did not join. He was the confidant of Washington and very nearly his successor. He was an intimate of Hamilton, Gouverneur Morris, Robert R. Livingston, and others of that remarkable generation. The list extends itself almost incredibly: he was the first chief justice and was acting secretary of state before Jefferson took over. Before that he had been for years secretary for foreign affairs of the Continental Congress; and afterward he was governor of New York. He participated in the negotiations for the treaty after the war and negotiated the treaty of 1794 with Britain which has ever since been known as Jay's Treaty.

If to this formidable list of offices there are added his service in the New York Provincial Congress, his membership in the Continental Congress, his chief justiceship in New York (the first), his membership on numerous committees, and his work as ambassador to Spain, a total is reached that exceeds the credits of any American statesman. This cannot be accounted for by saying that it was a time when there was a lack of talent; there were other able men available for every position to which he was elected or appointed. His varied and repeated calls to public service are only to be explained by his possession of an unusual combination of talents and virtues suited to the special needs of his generation.

He had a first-rate intelligence; he was trained in the law; he came of a family whose social position was unquestioned; he was married to a Livingston; he had private means; and he had none of the distractions which so often interfere with men's careers. He was deeply religious; he had a stern sense of duty; he was abstemious in habit; and he was of a strictly moral cast. He could always be expected to do any task he was set to the limit of his considerable abilities; he was faithful to his friends and disinclined to intrigue or even to manoeuvre; he had less ambition by far than would seem possible in a man of such attainments; and he was averse to mere politics and scornful of those who allowed themselves to be swayed by political considerations. These last characteristics were responsible for his absence from the Constitutional Convention—he was elected a delegate by the lower house of the New York Legislature but was rejected by the senate in favor of others who soon left the meeting to return home and organize opposition to ratification. He was, however, repeatedly chosen for the state and national legislatures; and he was easily elected to the governorship.[1]

His elections took place by a pattern that is illustrated by his governorship. At the time of the balloting he was at sea on his way home from a long stay in England; he had been negotiating there in a quiet way and none of those supporting his candidacy knew whether, if elected, he would accept, since he was still chief justice. Similarly he was elected secretary of

[1] But always, it must be remembered, by a very restricted electorate. He was never a popular favorite.

the United States for the department of foreign affairs by the Continental Congress in 1784 after he had been abroad for eight years in Spain and France and must have lost many of his contacts. It was never because he made an electoral plea that he was chosen for office. It was rather because he approached indispensability.

It was not as a mere formality that Charles Thomson, the secretary of the Congress, wrote to him: "I do not know how you will be pleased by the appointment, but this I am sure of —that your country stands in need of your abilities in that office." [2] John Jay's country seemed always to stand in need of his abilities and his integrity. And he never refused an appeal until he felt himself incapable of further service. That time came when he was comparatively young; he lived on in retirement for twenty-eight years; but they were years of ill health and a good deal of sorrow. Before he died the nation was firmly placed among the powers and was stretching out toward the Pacific. The Federalists to whose principles he was so wholly devoted had disappeared; the Democratic-Republicans, of whom he disapproved, were in power; and he had outlived his friends—Washington, Hamilton, Philip Schuyler, Gouverneur Morris, William Cushing, and all the rest. But he must have declined into old age consoled by his unwavering faith in a hereafter to which those whom he had loved had preceded him. And he must always have had satisfaction in having been one of the nation's creators.

How much of what he becomes any person owes to his ancestry, to his parents and his home, to his environment, or to his training, it is always difficult to say. But in the case of Jay it seems evident that he was very much the product of a calculated regime. He was exactly what his father wanted him to

[2] Charles Thomson to Jay, June 18, 1784, in *The Correspondence and Public Papers of John Jay*, 4 vols., ed. H. F. Johnston (New York: Putnam, 1890–92), III, 126. Hereafter referred to as *Correspondence and Public Papers.*

be—a good and useful citizen. This father, Peter, was a merchant and the son of a merchant. It was a Huguenot family, originally from La Rochelle, where it had reached prominence and wealth. In 1685 Auguste, the first of the Jays to come to America, had returned from an African voyage to find the Edict of Nantes in effect and his family in exile. The proscription had left them nothing; and even their religion was forbidden. He went first to South Carolina, then to Philadelphia, and then settled in New York among the numerous refugees already there. By 1746 the family had a modest fortune and John's father Peter was retiring from business and moving to Rye. John was the eighth child; those who had been born earlier had caused concern for one or another reason—one had become "an idle fellow" in spite of his father's attempt to give him an education; two others had become blind because of smallpox; and only one gave promise of being a credit to the family. This last was the eldest of Peter's sons, James, who was to become a physician, be knighted, and remain a loyalist, spending much of his time in England, and being something of a problem for his patriot younger brother.

John was sent, when he was eight, to New Rochelle to school. The establishment was kept by the Reverend Peter Stouppe, pastor of the combined French and Episcopalian churches. The pastor half starved his pupils, neglected his household, had a negligent wife, and, aside from mathematics, which interested him, contributed but little to Jay's education. But New Rochelle was a center of Huguenot culture; most of its people spoke French habitually; and their Calvinism was undimmed by translation across the sea. Jay never forgot his French, and the Calvinism kept a firm hold on him all the rest of his life.

After a few years his father rescued the boy from the disorderly Stouppe household and brought him home to Rye. There he remained under a more competent tutor until, at fifteen, he was judged ready to enter King's College. The man he became can be understood better if the atmosphere of his parents' home is studied. It was there that the shaping of his character took place; what he was by fifteen he always remained. The piousness he absorbed was not so gloomy an attitude as Calvinism sometimes produced; but it served as a rigorous confining framework for all his subsequent actions. It also furnished consolations he could not well have done without in the exigencies of his later career. But most important of all, it gave him that rigid uprightness and uncompromising integrity which were to be his most distinguishing characteristics. His conservatism, his rather narrow interests, his contentment with mild pleasures, and his lack of driving ambition were also confirmed, if not acquired, in the paternal household. Then too a conscientious judgment of right and wrong and a strong belief in liberty became so much a part of his very being that the great choices of his life would be easier for him than for many of his contemporaries who had not had so firm a grounding in tradition, at least in Huguenot tradition. For the sense of wrong remained strong even in this later generation of exiles' descendants; and they never forgot what it was their ancestors had left France to find. It seemed natural to John that he should oppose, without thought of risk, the sort of oppression and unchecked power from which his ancestors had fled. He never really trusted any European nation; it seemed to him that they were all alike in exploiting those they assumed to govern. They dealt with a formidable adversary when they bargained with this remembering Huguenot.

For the earliest shaping of legal institutions in the new nation this narrowness and rigidity perhaps served a good purpose; certainly it is not easy to believe that any of the other lawyers concerned would have understood so well the function of the judiciary in a government of separated powers, or have realized so clearly the limitations judges ought to impose on themselves. We do not at once recall, when we think of them, that Jefferson, Hamilton, James Madison, and James Monroe were lawyers, although all of them took their profession seriously. But Jay was the very model of the professional legalist, happiest when dealing with cases, bringing to them the learning and the humanity which were inseparable from his character, but never forgetting precedent and tradition. He helped to make the constitution even if he was not present at its writing—John Adams would say of him, in speaking of the Federalists of the period, that he had been "of more importance than any of the rest, indeed of almost as much weight as all the rest." [3]

It was not only because Jay and Adams generally agreed on constitutional principles that John Adams had this to say of Jay. It was also because there was no lawyer at the time whose prestige was so high or whose steady devotion to the fundamentals for which the Revolution had been fought was so well known. Through many years of service he had never wavered and never refused a duty. He would refuse one much later, held out to him by Adams himself, then President. This would be a second appointment as chief justice. He would choose retirement then, being not only worn out but also discouraged, and believing that his contribution had been completed; and he may have been right. John Marshall, whom Adams appointed in his place, was, if not more courageous, certainly more aggressive and more suited to the task of preserving the structure erected by the Federalists. For the years to come were to be years of regression. It was perhaps better that Jay should watch them from retirement.

Jay acquired his legal training in the fashion of the time—as an apprentice. But before he passed to the law he spent four years in King's College.

[3] Adams to James Lloyd, Feb. 6, 1815, in *The Works of John Adams*, 10 vols. ed. C. F. Adams (Boston: Little, Brown, 1850–56), X, 115.

The indications are that these undergraduate years were good ones. What can be gathered of them would seem to show that his moralism and his self-discipline were at least occasionally in abeyance, but his youthful spirits were kept within limits. He had a quite normal social life for a young man of family and means, but there was little about it of self-indulgence; the characteristics for which he was later noted were already dominant. He was relatively humorless and serious about himself; and his escapades of record are confined to one in which he may or may not really have taken part. A group of students, in his last year, scuffling in the college hall, broke a table. The president, rushing in, demanded to know the culprit. All refused to tell; in fact all except Jay said that they did not know who was to be blamed. Jay admitted knowledge but refused to name the guilty one. This infuriated the president who, after ranting and shouting, called a faculty meeting to discipline all those present. It is significant that the defense was entrusted to Jay. His argument was that, although each student had sworn upon entering to obey the college rules, there was no rule that required any of them to inform on each other. This did not impress the faculty; and all who had been present were suspended for several weeks as contumacious.

Whether this punishment seemed to Jay an injustice we do not know; but it must at least have been a lesson in the risks of literal interpretation. He was inclined to literalism himself; his punishment may have modified that inclination. The incident, at any rate, did not prevent him from graduating that spring; nor did it interfere with his acceptance as a clerk at the law, which took place immediately after the commencement exercises.

Jay's studies in the college were confined mostly to the classics, to philosophy with a strong religious flavor, and to mathematics. He had had to demonstrate on entrance that he was expert in arithmetic "as far as the rule of reduction." During his course he studied both surveying and navigation and such further mathematics as were required for those arts. In his first year he studied only Latin and Greek, but for cultural orientation as well as for training in the languages. As a sophomore he came to rhetoric and public speaking. Later he read, under direction, extensively in the physical sciences, using John Rowning's *Compendious System of Natural Philosophy* as a guide; and he seems to have been influenced, as were so many students of his time, by Plutarch's *Lives*. Plutarch's heroes were the kind of examples that seemed worth emulating to the revolutionary generations when republics were in the making. Serving as a sort of balance, it seems, was Jay's deep interest in the gossipy Roman historian Suetonius' *Lives of the Twelve Caesars*, translated by John Clark. In the philosophical disciplines he read John Locke's *Essay on the Human Understanding*. As a senior, he would have read the central work of the revered teacher of Adam Smith and friend of David Hume. This was *Moral Philosophy* by Francis Hutcheson, who anticipated Bentham's very phrasing in his criterion of the "greatest happiness of the greatest number." The book itself contained, as was customary with such treatises, an integrated study of philosophy, ethics, politics, and economics.[4]

King's College had only recently been founded; and Jay came first under the authority of Dr. Samuel Johnson. The first president was, however, replaced by Dr. Myles Cooper in 1763; and it was with him that the unruly youths had their difference. Dr. Cooper was not popular with the students, and consequently was involved in a good many disciplinary incidents. Jay must have been fairly exemplary in conduct to have escaped any disfavor until the spring of his last year.

It has to be said that the unexceptionable behavior of his college years was no more than a preview of his whole life's conduct. He never did a dishonorable thing; and like John

[4] "Plan of Education" in Minutes of Meeting, March 1, 1763, Columbia University, *Early Minutes of the Trustees, fascimile edition*, Vol. I, 1755–70 (New York: privately printed, 1932).

Adams he seldom departed from the most severe rule of behavior. This was one reason why he was to be so uniformly trusted. Only John Adams, perhaps, of that early group that brought the nation into being can be compared with Jay in the matter of personal conduct. It was always certain that he would be involved in no questionable activities likely to be disclosed to the embarrassment of associates. He could be expected to give his whole mind to the task before him without worry over possible personal contretemps. It was not a time when many men laid down this kind of rule for themselves. The vast volume of work got through by these two was made possible by single-mindedness and devotion to duty. Neither allowed himself the wearing distractions that were so common among his contemporaries.

That Jay should have been so exemplary as a youth is the more remarkable because for his first two academic years he was unable to live at the college. The building was not yet completed; and there was not room for him until his junior year. In the meantime he lived in the house of Lawrence Roomes, a painter, at what is now the corner of Broadway and Exchange Place. This was ten blocks from the college; and the intervening territory had a good many temptations that another sort of young man might have thought irresistible. In the neighborhood there were many of the licentious establishments that were so notable a feature of early New York. In fact, students approaching the college were forced to pass through streets where soliciting prostitutes were numerous. When in May, 1762, Jay moved into rooms in the college, life must have been simpler and more to his liking. The college was on an eminence at what is now Murray and Barclay Streets, not far from the river. It was a three-story stone building, with accommodations for some twenty-four students. It contained, as well, classrooms, a library, a laboratory, and a dining hall. The regime was an intimate and uncomplicated one under the immediate supervision of the president, who was expected to watch over the religious as well as the intellectual development of the young men.

It was some time before finishing at the college that Jay determined to devote himself to the law. His father easily consented to the decision and furnished the considerable sum (£200) required for his apprentice fee. The graduation of Jay's class was attended with some ceremony, many notables being present, and the President making a lengthy speech in Latin. The ceremony was in St. George's Chapel, Trinity Parish, and of it the New York *Mercury* said that "It would be injurious to the Reputation of the College, not to observe, that ample Amends were made for the Number of Candidates [two], by the Display of their Proficiency in the Elegance of their Performances."[5] This may help to account for Jay's having been one of the orators; at any rate he did make "a spirited and sensible English Dissertation on the Happiness and Advantages arising from a State of Peace." This subject must have offered ample scope for a future eminent jurist, even at the age of nineteen.

It was in the office of Benjamin Kissam that Jay worked until he was granted his license to practice in October, 1768. By that time he was already recognized as a successful pleader who was unusually well versed in the law. It was a reputation he had achieved by his habitual industry and by taking a leading part in the activities of the young lawyers of the city. Even more interesting, he became a member of a social club, joined several dancing assemblies, and generally behaved superficially as a prominent young bachelor might be expected to do. Nevertheless he was already the victim of what is described as "dyspepsia." This result of overwork and tension would follow him

[5] Milton H. Thomas, "King's College Commencement in the Newspapers," *The Columbia University Quarterly*, XXII (June, 1930), 232.

through his life and would be one reason why he felt he must retire at so early an age.

It was five years later, when he was a really prominent lawyer, that he asked Sarah Van Brugh Livingston to marry him. This was after he had unsuccessfully tried to persuade two De Lancey girls to have him. But if Sarah was not his first choice, their marriage was entirely successful. She was to die rather early and leave him alone in his old age; but while she lived she was all that a wife should be. It helped that she was the daughter of William Livingston, one of the eminent men of the city. She is said to have been somewhat dominating and vain; but it is certain that she had the deepest respect for Jay and regarded him as a paragon—which he was. If she was sometimes impatient because he was so judicious under stress, their affection for each other was never impaired.

It must have seemed to Jay that with his marriage and his success at the law his future was marked out in a very predictable pattern. As we know, however, during the very next year the future of all New Yorkers was to be put in jeopardy. All of that colonial city's society, and much of its business and professional life, was to be completely disorganized by British pressure and American resistance.

It is really remarkable how little attention Jay seems to have given to politics and public affairs up to this time. And one of the puzzling problems for his biographers is the rapid change that took place and the direction that his subsequent career followed. The future patriot had been concerned only with his legal career until a challenge to his conscience was offered by the events of 1774 in Boston. Even then, considering his conservatism, it might have been thought that he would be mortally offended by the behavior of the radicals who were taking the lead in opposition to the British.

But it must be recalled that there were very few colonials who in the early years of the disturbances foresaw that independence would be the result of their resistance to oppression. Greater liberty within the empire was what they hoped for; and differences were mostly about how much liberty and for whom. There were very heated patriots whose emotions were excited solely by their own interests. And even the more public-minded of the substantial people were horrified by the riotings and threats of the Sons of Liberty. It was to control a movement that seemed likely to get out of hand that the Committee of Fifty-one was set up. Jay's acceptance of a nomination to this committee was his first service in the Revolution. And it was more to keep the movement from really becoming a Revolution than to promote one that he accepted. He, along with Gouverneur Morris and others, set out to settle the colonial differences with Britain in a dignified way; but they were almost as much concerned that civic order should be maintained.

As usual, Jay was absent when he was elected to the Committee of Fifty-one; he was also absent when the advisability of calling a Continental Congress was discussed. It was when he was elected to this larger body that his career in public affairs became definite. From then on he had less and less time for the practice of law. During the next few years he was much on the road between New York—or wherever the provincial legislature was meeting—and Philadelphia. At first his influence was thrown against the Massachusetts radicals, such as the Boston Tea Party mob. He was against the policy of nonintercourse; and in the First Continental Congress he opposed a declaration offered by Patrick Henry that all government was at an end and that a new beginning must be made. "The measure of arbitrary power," said Jay, "is not full, and I think it must run over, before we undertake to frame a new constitution." [6]

He was usually asked to serve on committees when there

[6] Statement of Jay in John Adams, "Diary of Debates," Sept. 5, 1774, in Adams, *Works*, II, 368.

were messages or resolutions to be drafted. The first of these committees, and an important one, was that appointed to formulate the grievances of the colonists and the means for their redressing. This group, meeting almost continuously, was at least the means of the various delegates' understanding each other. Jay was consistently on the conservative side, arguing for moderation and accommodation, and the Congress accepted this position for the time being; but there were differences remaining which were very deep.

It was Jay who wrote the letter of that year (1774) which, if it had been received with even a minimum of respect in Britain, might have averted the Revolution. It was an appeal to the English sense of justice over the heads of the existing government. It was not lengthy, but it had to a full degree that firm and convincing style that marks so many of the American Revolutionary documents. There was never any excuse for misunderstanding the colonial position; and it was Jay who was often responsible for the composition. That so distinguished and representative a group of citizens should so often have chosen Jay to be their spokesman indicates how readily the New York lawyer had become the useful public servant. He was not unopposed; he was usually on the opposite side from the Sam Adamses and the Patrick Henrys; but he was in the majority among the enfranchised elite. If this reluctant majority became revolutionist during the next two years, it was because a stupid English policy refused the concessions so reasonably demanded.

Jay's *The Address to the People of Great Britain* closed with what, if taken in conjunction with the document of *Association* voted by the Congress within the same week, amounted to an ultimatum. The *Association* was not a revolutionary document. It declared that the colonists now had to maintain a policy of nonintercourse, and it threatened boycott and ostracism for all those who did not conform. But still the *Address* did express the hope that the British sense of justice would prevail, and that a wicked ministry would be replaced by one with whom the other members of the empire could restore friendship and harmony. This, it said, was the ardent wish of every true and honest American.

If this was so, there were a good many Americans who were not true and honest; and they were rapidly getting their own way. They were, in fact, being joined by the reluctant conservatives who got no encouragement at all from the adamant ministers of the crown. But the New Yorkers gave up only after persistent efforts. The Provincial Assembly met early in 1775 and sent still further petitions to the king and to Parliament. But Jay was already a member of a revised Committee of Sixty which had replaced the Committee of Fifty-one and was pledged to carry out the provisions of the *Association*. He had defected from the conservatives. This, however, was more apparent than real. The New York conservatives were in process of dividing between Tories and Patriots. When it came to choosing whether to be British or American—and that choice was rapidly approaching—Jay had no hesitation. But he would have much preferred that such a choice need not be made. He was not a natural revolutionary.

When the news arrived in New York of the battle of Lexington, the crisis was precipitated. The Committee of Sixty recommended that a new committee be elected with wider terms of reference and that a new Provincial Congress be called. This Committee of One Hundred became in effect the government of New York; and Jay was a very active member. He was active, that is, before he left for Philadelphia in May for the 1775 session of the Continental Congress. This congress made still another effort to arouse British sympathy. As its last act in July it sent what would later come to be called the Olive Branch Petition. This was received much as the former ones had been.

The Congress resumed in September. It was fast becoming a national government. Jay at this time was beginning to spend much time on the work of a secret committee formed to correspond with friends in Great Britain and in other parts of the world. A vast volume of this work was got through that winter. At the same time he successfully urged that the New York Legislature substantially encourage certain manufactures with a view to keeping the people "easy and quiet; by being employed they gain bread and when our fellow mortals are busy and well fed, they forget to complain." [7]

In spring he was again elected a member of the New York Provincial Congress; his immediate attendance was requested. He left Philadelphia intending to return shortly. But this exciting year of 1776 was even more exciting in New York than in Philadelphia. The Congress had suggested that the states set up genuine governments; and New York was earnestly complying. Her most experienced statesman was needed; and Jay, by staying at home for this duty, missed being a signer of the Declaration of Independence. It has been suggested that if he had been present he might have cast an adverse vote; [8] but this seems unlikely. As Professor Carl Becker remarked of him, "he had . . . the associating mind . . . which easily shapes its thinking to the exigencies of action." [9] And certainly it was he who wrote the resolutions adopted by the New York Legislature ratifying what the Congress had done.

The next year of Jay's life was wholly given to the task of bringing into being a state; that, however, involved a good many unusual duties, since the British held New York City, and since there were still numbers of citizens whose loyalty to the empire was unshaken. The creation of a new government under these circumstances was a strenuous, even a dangerous, business. Jay himself was much involved in the work of fore-

[7] Jay to Colonel Alexander McDougall, Dec. 23, 1775, in Jay, *Correspondence and Public Papers*, I, 40.

[8] John Adams to Thomas Jefferson, Sept. 17, 1823, in Adams, *Works*, X, 410–11.

[9] Carl L. Becker, "John Jay and Peter Van Schaak," 1919, reprinted in his *Everyman His Own Historian* (New York: Crofts, 1935), p. 289.

stalling Tory activities. He also served on a secret committee for obstructing the Hudson.[10]

The river was never closed; but luckily it never needed to be. Jay was soon relieved of the journeying under the most difficult conditions—sleeping in verminous beds, eating food that made him ill, and being exposed to all kinds of weather—in search of munitions and materials, and was brought back to begin the business of forming the government. The legislature in these years was necessarily a body without a home. It met in various places before settling down at Kingston in February, 1777. Meanwhile it carried on by means of an infinitude of committees, as was the habit in all the colonies in reaction from royal governors. It would be some time before a genuine executive would become acceptable.

Jay was the chief author of the constitution adopted by the legislature in April. He was assisted by both Gouverneur Morris and Robert R. Livingston as well as others; but his influence shows in every clause. It is true that he would have proscribed Catholicism if he had had his way, and would have included some dangerously vague prohibitions against endangering the state and engaging in licentiousness, and that he was defeated in his attempt by Morris; but only he had the skill and knowledge to draw the detailed document. This was not the only occasion on which Jay's Calvinism showed; but the repulse seems to have taught him a lesson about the role of the state in private affairs. In two other matters he was on the liberal side; one of these was the secret ballot; and the other was the abolition of slavery. In the one he had his way; in the other he did not succeed.

[10] The British strategy called for the control of the river; and why sufficient energy was never summoned to effect it remains a mystery. The three-phase plan of attack involved penetration by way of Canada, Carleton and Burgoyne commanding; harassment from the west by stirring up the bordering Indians; and a sweep up the Hudson from New York. The northward march never materialized; and Burgoyne was, of course, defeated. But the possibilities were always evident; and the colonists had good reason for apprehension.

Along with that of Massachusetts, so strongly influenced by John Adams, this New York constitution was a significant accomplishment. It forecast the later federal document in several ways; and it represented the best, even if the most conservative, thought of the period. It provided for a separation of powers, and if not an entirely satisfactory executive, yet one which was surprisingly free to function considering the prejudices of the times. The governor was not given the appointing function; it was entrusted instead to a Council of Appointment.[11] This, as well as the Council of Revision to exercise the veto power, Jay probably knew to be mistaken; but he would usually compromise in matters of this sort; and on the whole the conservatives had reason to be satisfied with the document. The franchise was not notably widened; they liked this. And, curiously enough, the conservatives themselves were afraid of too much strength in the executive. As has often been remarked, this state constitution, serving as it did for forty years, was more successful than the Articles of Confederation, which had to be abandoned altogether by 1787.

Jay was presently elected to the chief justiceship of the state by the convention which had decided itself to select the judges and some other officials. He was mentioned for the governorship too but, seeing how matters stood, withdrew in favor of Philip Schuyler. But the more politically astute George Clinton was chosen, and entered on more than a decade of political dominance in the new state.

But the time had come when Jay had to think more of his country than of his state. For the next two years he served as first a member, and then president, of the Continental Congress, activities which kept him, much to his sorrow, away from his growing family and from the state to which he had contributed so much.

Even in the darkest days of 1779 he remained sanguine in

[11] A compromise very characteristic of the time. It almost made its way into the federal Constitution.

public, looking forward to rapid material expansion and prosperity accompanied by a corresponding growth of population. "Extensive wildernesses, now scarcely known or explored, remain yet to be cultivated, and vast lakes and rivers, whose waters have for ages rolled in silence and obscurity to the ocean, are yet to hear the din of industry, become subservient to commerce and boast delightful villas, gilded spires, and spacious cities rising on their banks." [12]

But from being an active committeeman, assigned to specific duties or to the formulation of acceptable policy papers, he now moved to a considerably higher level. He became one of the select number of men of the Revolution—in the company of Washington, Hamilton, Gouverneur Morris, Franklin, Jefferson, John Adams, Madison, and James Wilson—who determined strategy and policies. As such his clear mind, his hard determination, his ability to stand prolonged work and strain, and his narrow concentration on what was before him—all these qualities served him usefully. And by now he had a clearly developed view of governmental principles as well as a sense of their utility. He had also learned something about acceptability, so that the disorderly, slow, and generally exasperating conduct of affairs in a government that had not yet developed an executive and that dispersed its responsibilities so widely as often to fail in them was not so intolerable as it once would have been. He did not like it; and it taught him new lessons about the structure of effective government; but he did not chafe under it to the point of resigning.

As president, he was regarded as an independent; that, indeed, was part of the reason for his having been chosen. Much of the manoeuvering of this time was centered on an attempt to undermine and oust Washington whose wise and cautious generalship was little to the liking of the New Englanders, and in whose own Virginia there were those who would have liked

[12] Jay, "Circular-Letter from Congress to Their Constituents," 1779, reprinted in *Correspondence and Public Papers*, I, 226

to see him supplanted. This involved also a difference of opinion on asking for French assistance. The conservatives still hoped that friends in Britain would bring about a more conciliatory policy; an alliance with France would make their efforts futile. But as affairs were developing, it seemed more and more likely that French help would be necessary.

There was an acute awareness among the leading Americans that the colonies were counters in a vast game of empire being played out in Europe. The proprietors of the New World colonies had been Spain, Britain, and France. They were contending for supremacy; and the narrow territory along the Atlantic seaboard merely happened to be in a central position for the moment. There was involved the control of all the continent, of the West Indies, and of South America. The writ of the Continental Congress—such as it had—did not run south of Georgia, north of the Great Lakes, or, with any certainty, west of the Appalachian mountains. France claimed Canada and trading rights to the west. So did the British. And the West Indies—the sugar islands—were of importance to both. Spain was nervous about her declining power in Europe and uneasy about her ability to hold Central and South America. To British —and later to American—aggression, these areas as well as all the west beyond the Mississippi, now undisputedly held, would be open if France did not prevail in the power struggle. Spain therefore supported France and opposed Britain, but hesitated to favor the Americans. Besides, she had the added reason that revolution and independence were principles she could ill afford to see established anywhere; her own colonies were already restless.

It is one of the real achievements of the American Revolutionists, among so much else that seems inept, selfish, provincial, and stubborn, that they found the talented representatives who, in the European capitals, especially, but also at home, were able to gauge to a nicety the motives and strengths of the statesmen they dealt with. The Europeans were men of long training and experience; but the Count of Florida-Blanca, the Comte de Vergennes, and successive British foreign ministers were consistently outthought and outbargained by Franklin, Adams, Charles C. Pinckney, Jefferson, Jay, and others of the small Revolutionary band. And independence was established in the end more by diplomatic than by military means—a kind of incident in the imperial struggle for power which the American negotiators always kept before their eyes and shrewdly used for their own purposes.[13]

Jay was soon a member of this distinguished group of diplomats, assigned, however, to Spain, the most difficult of the powers to deal with. He was glad to escape the growing troubles of the Congress over which he presided. There were not only repeated cabals against Washington and irritating shirkings of responsibility, but also positive refusals among the states—as they were now called—to recognize the authority of the Congress or to give its members any independence as representatives. Especially the states would not recognize their financial obligations, and more and more the general expenses of the war were met by simply printing money. The phrase "not worth a continental" was coming into a use that would last as long as the republic that was being fought for. The French, as the American alliance became a recognized fact, were generous with supplies and even with funds; but war is an avid consumer; and there was never enough of anything. What Washington fought with makes his final victory seem an almost miraculous achievement. But the issue was so largely dependent, finally, on the events being disposed in Europe, that Washington could only retreat and thrust, and wait to thrust again; he could not win by force alone. It was political arranging on a grand scale that would determine victory or defeat for the new nation.

[13] On this the study of Samuel Flagg Bemis leaves no doubt. His *Diplomacy of the American Revolution* (New York: Appleton-Century, 1935) is amply convincing.

Jay, in Spain, where he arrived in January 1780, was an envoy designated for a hopeless task. The reactionary Spanish government, set on dead center between its hatred of the British and its detestation of revolution, would do little. Jay was there for two years without even being recognized or officially received. When he left to go to Paris he had, so far as he could see, accomplished nothing. Spain had not granted funds except in trivial amounts, and had certainly not given help of other kinds; and, as an anxious representative of a struggling new government, Jay felt very deeply the inability to make any progress. Things were not going any better at home; his communications were exasperatingly slow and uncertain; and he was tormented by intriguing and contumacious helpers. He did not like Spain or the Spanish; in fact, his puritanical soul was revolted by the constant exhibition of Catholic extravagance. His wife was not well, and neither was he; and it was with relief that he got the news of transfer to Paris in 1782.

He was in Paris until 1784, actively negotiating for the peace to follow the long war. Franklin was already there as the American Minister; John Adams, who was at the Hague, was to come later. The members of this incomparable trio were, among them, to establish the young nation among the old ones. They did not always agree or work together well. Adams never worked well with anyone; and both Jay and Adams disliked and distrusted Franklin. The old philosopher was too worldly, too tolerant, and too much a voluptuary for either of the others to approve. His ripe wisdom seemed to them soft and a little rotten. But the Europeans found him more congenial than his tense colleagues. His was always the soft voice; but often too it was the shrewd one.

The proceedings—mostly at Paris, but partly in London—correspond very poorly with the picture of negotiations that the amateur in such matters would carry in his mind. There were very few occasions when the representatives of all the nations met to exchange views. Some of those who were involved were not really representatives in anything more than a personal sense. There were differences among those on either side who belonged to political factions at odds with each other. The positions of the powers were altered materially at various stages and so their bargaining powers were more or less considerable, depending on their anxiety for progress. And there were times when bargaining was being done with different ends in view by negotiators who concealed from their own colleagues what they were doing. That out of such a disorderly process any conclusion at all should have come was mostly because the great powers at length felt compelled to make an end of conflict. In spite of ineptness and mutual suspicions the Americans did very well. In the end they got all or more than they could have expected.

When Jay, still in Madrid, received his instructions, they were such that they infuriated him. He was told that nothing could be done without French consent; and this meant, if taken literally, that the French were to do the bargaining. This was perhaps a laudable loyalty on the part of Congress to a helpful ally; [14] but Jay could not help feeling that the Gallic faction at home had as usual gone too far; no party at interest could be trusted to keep always in mind the interests of others; and it was apparent that French and American objectives were sep-

[14] Behind the need to conciliate France were strong commercial as well as political factors: notably the attempts to persuade the French government to remove the hindrances to American trade with France and her colonies. Robert R. Livingston constantly pointed out to Jay such lines of argument as that a freer trade would lead to increased imports of French manufactures in return for America's exports of cheap food. In one letter Livingston well expressed the characteristic attitude toward wage labor, an attitude that pervaded the two dominant strains of thought, mercantilism and physiocracy: "It is obvious, that the price of labor is regulated by that of provisions, that manufacturers never earn more than a bare subsistence." In more general terms, "the man who labors gets a bare subsistence, for the moment he does more, the number of laborers of that kind (provided his labor does not require uncommon skill) increases, and his labor is not more profitable than that of the other laborers of the country." (Livingston to Jay, Sept. 12, 1782, in *Correspondence and Public Papers*, II, 338–39.)

arating—for one thing, the French would be bargaining for the Spanish as well as themselves—and that Spanish and American claims would clash in important ways was quite obvious. Jay was disillusioned after his two futile years of humiliation; he shared the gratitude of the Congress to France, but he was a descendant of Huguenots and also he was an American conservative whose feelings had often been rasped by French intrigue in Philadelphia. All this, combined with his positive distaste for association with Franklin, caused him to face his new task with some reluctance. But, having agreed, he set his sharp and suspicious mind to the work of analyzing the motives of his opponents and measuring their every suggestion with the yardstick of hard American necessity.

First and above all, there must be complete independence; second, the nation must have a chance for life and growth. The one was a simple and hortatory demand; the other was much more complex, involving borders, commerce and comunications, the freedom to trade, fisheries, and navigation of the Mississippi river—many matters vital to the economy of the new nation. Furthermore, these were matters about which the powers had been manoeuvering and fighting. They were still not certain what they could successfully ask for and get. It was all very delicate and difficult; and it must not be left to old Franklin who was so enamored with French culture. Adams would be more dependable; but he was not yet present when Jay and Franklin first met in 1782 and opened conversations with the wily Vergennes.

Talking had in fact already begun. Earlier in the year British agents had felt out Franklin to see whether a separate peace might be possible; but Franklin had repulsed them. This was a confused year in Great Britain; presently Lord North's ministry fell and was replaced by one of which the Marquis of Rockingham was the head, but in which Charles James Fox and the Earl of Shelburne were respectively in charge of foreign and colonial affairs. These two were antagonists; and it was far from clear which had the responsibility for American negotiations. There was thus at the first an uncertainty which was a bothersome complication. Fox sent Thomas Grenville, son of the author of the Stamp Act, to deal with Vergennes; Shelburne sent Richard Oswald, a retired merchant with philosophic interests and American connections, to sound out Franklin. Franklin was convinced that Oswald was responsible, and at once sent for Henry Laurens (then a paroled prisoner in London), for Adams, and for Jay. Jay made a quick departure and actually arrived in Paris in June. Adams was more leisurely. He did not arrive for several months; and meanwhile a good deal had gone on.

Jay, after some preliminaries which excited his suspicions more than ever, fell ill, along with all his family, with an influenza that kept him immobile for weeks. And in this period Franklin advanced to Oswald two categories of suggestion for the British to consider; he was obviously optimistic either about good will across the channel or about the political pressures for peace. These were actually very strong, but not yet imperative; after all, Admiral Rodney had just defeated the French fleet of the Comte de Grasse in a decisive naval engagement; and this went some way to offset the British defeat at Yorktown. The war in America was really over; but the terms of the peace were far from being foregone. Franklin thought a venture worth while; and it was a brave one.

Suppose, he said to the British, you think of two categories, one that Americans believe to be necessary, the other that would be of a sort to make Americans your friends and ensure a lasting peace. In the first category were independence, the withdrawal of troops, a settlement of the boundaries, freedom of fishing, and the fixing of Canadian territory at about the existing extent. The other category would include an indemnification for war losses, acknowledgement that the colonies had been oppressed, a grant of trading rights in Britain, and the cession of Canada to the new nation.

This tour de force of Franklin's may have been thought of by the king and some others in Britain as impertinent; on the other hand it may have made much easier such concessions as the Americans did win in the subsequent negotiations. When Jay first saw Oswald he discouraged that unofficial negotiator by lecturing him about the necessity for a prior recognition of independence before exchanges could even begin. This was a stiff-necked position to have taken just when a little conciliation might have helped; but Jay was a stiff-necked individual. He did not propose to lose in negotiation what colonial fighting and hardship had won in the field. Franklin at the time was ill; and Jay, indignant about his instructions, and suspecting that Vergennes was betraying American interests, decided, for once in his life, to act on his own, regardless of terms of reference or of his colleagues. He sent a merchant-economist, Benjamin Vaughan, to Shelburne as a secret agent.

At the moment Shelburne was glad to treat with the Americans alone in the hope of separating the allies. Franklin would have been scandalized; but Jay suggested that the British occupy the Floridas in place of Spain—and perhaps the western territories, too. Jay was probably correct in thinking that Vergennes was prepared to sacrifice American claims in the coming bargain. He had to think of the preposterous Spanish persistence in hedging the new nation about so that it could not possibly threaten the Spanish territories to the west and south. Jay's apprehensions were, he thought, confirmed when he conferred with Vergenne's second, J. M. Gérard de Rayneval, who, he knew, had gone secretly to Britain with French proposals which would have been disastrous to the Americans. Rayneval urged Jay to confer more at length with the Spanish toward whom he was ill disposed, believing his experience with them to have indicated a wholly intransigent attitude.

But Jay also saw in what went on a confirmation of his suspicion that France did not intend to support the American claim to all territory to the Mississippi and to free navigation of the river. Also, it seemed, France preferred that the British should have all of the territory north of the Ohio.

Jay modified his fierce claim to prior recognition of independence so far as to demand merely that Oswald should be accredited to the United States of America; he also saw that Shelburne was apprised of French intentions as he saw them—this was what his agent, Vaughan, was sent to do. Matters were in a fluid state when Adams arrived in Paris to join in the negotiations.

Adams shared Jay's suspicions of the French; and the two seem to have stood against Franklin through the rest of the negotiation. But ultimately all three did meet Oswald and Henry Strachey (appointed by the British to offset Oswald's more sympathetic attitude) and for a month of daily meetings followed the pattern of more formal bargaining. Shelburne made counter proposals through his envoys and found the Americans very stiff. Vergennes and Rayneval, egged on by the Spanish, tried without great success to find out what was going on; but such interference as they furnished seems not to have affected matters much. Jay was the reasoning member of the trio; Adams was more concerned about fishing rights than other things—and was successful; Franklin had as usual an emollient effect. In the end the American border was established at the Mississippi and at the center of the Great Lakes in the north; and there was to be no more than a recommendation to the States that the Tories (Loyalists, the British called them) should have their properties restored. The matter of the debts was settled by providing that there should be "no lawful impediment" to their recovery. All this was arranged by the time Henry Laurens, the fourth commissioner, finally arrived; and he participated only at the very end.

The whole was a result the Americans could feel satisfied with; but there remained two problems. There were still the the French; and there was a certain dissatisfaction at home that the French should have been left out. It fell to Franklin to conciliate Vergennes, and he did it with what grace he could; but Jay had to explain to Congress why it was that the formal instructions to consult had been ignored. It was his argument that Congress could complain only if the purpose for which the envoys had been sent had not been reached. Nevertheless, there was some clamor and a vote of censure was moved. Robert R. Livingston, secretary for foreign affairs, acting on his own, did send a letter of reprimand. The fact was, however, that the terms were so much better than it had been feared they might be that the objectors found few to support them.

This matter was concluded in November. It was not until a year and a half later that all the formalities were completed and Jay could leave Paris. When he arrived in New York in July, 1784, he found that Livingston had resigned and that he had been elected to the secretaryship of the Congress.

It cannot be said that the ensuing tour of duty, lasting until he handed over to Jefferson under the new constitution (this was not until March, 1790) was the most difficult of Jay's career; his several diplomatic assignments were harder—the disappointment in Spain, the necessity for proceeding beyond his terms of reference in Paris, and (yet to come) the negotiations in London in 1794 for the disappointing settlement with the British of outstanding differences that came to be called "Jay's Treaty." But the task he had as the servant of the Continental Congress was never easy and was sometimes bitterly frustrating. In the end it ran on into the period of futility which characterized the latter years of that hopeless body. He had to see the nation fall into disrespect abroad which was a reflection of the disrespect with which it was treated at home among the states. But he was always industrious and faithful, always a strong nationalist, and generally held in the greatest respect by his countrymen—even those who most disliked his political views.

He did not actually take office until December of 1784. The Congress was then in Trenton and he had to satisfy himself that he would be able to appoint his own clerks (two) and arrange a few other matters. He was chairman of a committee to greet the Marquis de Lafayette and served on several others before adjournment. This was the day before Christmas; and on January 11 Congress was to assemble in New York in quarters not yet selected. Jay had this duty. He had also, after his long absence, to find a house of his own. The matter of a residence he settled by building a commodious one on Broadway near what is now Exchange Place, a neighborhood familiar to him from his youth and not far from King's College. The Congress in April of 1785 leased the house at Broad and Pearl Streets that had been Fraunces Tavern, so well known from Washington's visits. For an office Jay had two rooms in this building which he kept until 1788 when he moved to the Philip Livingston house on Broadway near the Battery. As secretary he was paid $4,000 annually, a stipend that was presently reduced as Congress found its resources slimmer and slimmer. Nevertheless, his was a very important post in the new nation and during the next few years he labored to establish its prestige among the others. It was not his fault if he did not succeed.

Very early in his service he saw that he must first create his position. This he did by getting the Congress to accept his view that he alone could conduct correspondence with other nations. In the existing relations between the states and the Congress it also became necessary for him to conduct much of the correspondence with them. Their sense of obligation was strictly limited; they were sovereign; and they hardly more than tolerated the central government. It seemed natural that the secretary for foreign affairs should deal with them—a situation that would in the end necessitate the complete change represented by the work of the Constitutional Convention in 1787.

As secretary, Jay was not a member of the Congress; but he could and did speak and respond to questioning. It was his view that he was not merely a servant of the government but was responsible for shaping its policies; and he held to this attitude very strongly. He could succeed in his aim because he was now a person of great reputation. He was at home in New York, with social connections of the most unexceptionable sort; he had behind him a successful service; and, to tell the truth, he was the most important of the Revolutionary figures still remaining in national service at home. Jefferson was now minister to France; Adams was in London; Washington was in retirement; Gouverneur Morris was practicing law; Patrick Henry was governor of Virginia; John Hancock was governor of Massachusetts; Franklin was living in Philadelphia; Clinton was the boss in New York; Hamilton was engaged in his own affairs. There was no one who could be compared with Jay in eminence.

The ablest men of those years stayed in retirement, serving, if at all, in the state governments. Sometimes those elected to Congress—like Hancock—did not bother to attend. Others seemed to be there with the object of hampering the proceedings; there were in fact several who disbelieved in a central government and would rather see it grow weaker than stronger. There was one fatal weakness, which, more than any other, enfeebled the Congress; this was its inability to lay any taxes. It could only assign quotas to the states; and these were often simply ignored. But also, because there was no control of interstate or foreign commerce, the states could make of themselves small principalities at the expense of their neighbors if they wished, and all too often they did wish. It was almost impossible to borrow. During the war Robert Morris had practically exhausted all potential lenders, issuing bills, printing money, and getting supplies on credit. Except for trivial sums, there was no one and no government willing to finance such a body further.

Yet low as the government stood in the regard of the states and of foreign governments, it had responsibilities. The United States of America was an entity. It had to have a foreign policy. It must settle many issues left over from the Revolution. These had to do with borders, with commerce, and with the relations between the United States and former allies as well as enemies. The British, in particular, chose not to be conciliatory, a policy calculated on a shrewd estimate of American weakness. They proceeded to restrict American commerce everywhere without penalty. The states traded with Britain just as the colonies had.

Then there were the violations of the Treaty of Peace, which, as the years passed, continued on both sides to be notorious. The British did not withdraw their garrisons in the north and west. They continued to arm and encourage the Indians and to harass the territories almost as they had done while the war was going on. On their side the Americans failed to treat the Tories as had been agreed. They neither paid debts owed to them nor restored their properties and rights. Riots followed the effort of exiles to return and there were many instances of violence. Jay wrote to Washington about this in 1786. He said that it was "too true that the Treaty had been violated." And he made this the subject of his report to the Congress in October of that year.[15] For years—until the negotiation of Jay's Treaty—relations with the British gradually worsened. But Spanish relations were no better. The southwestern bound-

[15] Jay to Washington, June 27, 1786, in *Correspondence and Public Papers*, III, 203–4. Jay's report dated October 12, 1786, is in *Secret Journals of the Acts and Proceedings of [the Continental] Congress*, 4 vols. (Boston: Wait, 1821), IV, 185–287.

ary question was perennially in dispute; and so was the navigation of the Mississippi. In 1785 Diego de Gardoqui was sent to treat with the Americans in New York; and Jay, negotiating with him, ran into a serious controversy. This arose largely out of a difference of interests. Southerners were interested in boundaries and navigation; to northerners and New Englanders these seemed less important than commercial rights. Jay thought such rights more important than other matters and he suggested that navigation be sacrificed. This has been more or less explained by Jay's provincialism; and it is true that he had never been further west than New Jersey or further south than Philadelphia although he had been so much abroad. But it is also true that Washington agreed with him. In the end the negotiations simply died for lack of agreement in the United States. But it was long held against Jay that he had been willing to give up the Mississippi to Spain.[16]

On the other hand, French relations gave no great difficulty. This was in spite of a series of unfortunate envoys. There would be trouble later on when the revolution in France began; but for the moment the French were disposed to reduce commercial restrictions and there were no border troubles to be settled as there were with the British and Spanish.

When Jay's new home was finished it became one of the important social centers of the city; and this meant of the country as well, because New York remained the capital. There was at the Jay social affairs a mingling of government officials, professional men of all sorts, especially the leading members of the bar, diplomats, and the most select members of New York society. Mrs. Jay's health was not good and gradually worsened so that she was quite often away at Elizabeth Town where the family had a country place; and Jay was always extremely regular in attending to his duties; they were

[16] This matter is comprehensively discussed in Frank Monaghan's sprightly *John Jay* (New York and Indianapolis: Bobbs-Merrill, 1935), chapter XIII.

therefore often apart. This was a source of grief to both; they had become deeply dependent on each other during the years of their marriage. This was the more notable because it was not habitual in the circle in which they moved.

New York in those years was much given to pleasure; and faithfulness, either to duty or to mates, was not a virtue that was widely cultivated. Taverns were well patronized and immense quantities of alcohol were consumed as matter of course; gambling establishments prospered; cockfighting and similar blood sports were very popular. The new nation's capital was neither austere nor impressed with its responsibility for governing.

Jay moved in this environment familiarly yet apart from many of its activities. He was himself as abstemious and as strait-laced as ever. He dealt with diplomats and legislators who were neither. And many of his closest collaborators—Gouverneur Morris and Hamilton, for instance—were as notable for their lack of these virtues as he was for possessing them. Yet they too were loyal Americans, devoted to their country's welfare, agreeing with him in principle, and in many ways more creative. His narrowness was always characteristic; it seems to have been inherent in his virtue. His health was never robust; the dyspepsia he had begun to have as a student had followed him through his career and would always be a torment. His portrait, done by Gilbert Stuart in his maturity, shows a fine-drawn, lean, and almost ascetic face, and a figure clothed in elegant black, with lace at neck and wrists. He might have been the kind of churchman who had risen by sheer virtue. Actually, of course, he was by now worldly-wise, experienced, and disillusioned. If this did not affect his personal conduct, it at least led him not to expect more than was likely to come from self-interested and locally minded legislators or from diplomats who, however flexible they might seem, had only the interests of their governments in view. He had to be constantly asking for more than he would get from the Congress and just as constantly countering the moves of the diplomats with whom he dealt. And he had to do it all himself. There was little leadership in the public's affairs.

This sort of life for Jay went on until the worsening conditions made the Constitutional Convention necessary, something which he could see was inevitable long before it happened. Things simply could not go on as they were. Either there would be a stronger union or the separate states would succumb to pressures none could resist alone.

Working as he was day by day, in constant touch with all the multifarious affairs of the nation, he knew better than anyone else what its fatal weaknesses were and how these were likely to be taken advantage of by rapacious powers. The Americans had not been forgiven for leaving the British Empire; nor had they been exorcised from the taint of rebellion. Republics were anathema to the dictatorial monarchies of the prerevolutionary years in Europe. And the young nation was surrounded by potential enemies, who every so often looked less potential than actual. Something must be done.

Jay, as well as some others, knew what this must be. The slow-minded Washington, looking at events from Mount Vernon, had sadly concluded that he must leave his fields and slaves for still another public intervention. He could not sit still and see the nation die of inanition. But he was not the only one. Madison, Franklin, and others were quite as apprehensive. All of them were fearful of the divisive forces they must overcome.

There is a letter to Washington, written in June, 1786, and a reply from Washington, which show how apprehensive these two patriots had grown as they had watched the nation decline into feebleness. They were sick at heart. Jay said to Washington:

Our affairs seem to lead to some crisis, some revolution—something that I cannot foresee or conjecture. I am uneasy . . . more so than during the war. Then we had a fixed object, and though the means and time of obtaining it were often problematical yet did I firmly believe we should ultimately succeed, because I was convinced that justice was with us. The case is now altered; we are going and doing wrong, and therefore I look forward to evils and calamities, but without being able to guess at the instrument, nature or measure of them.

. . .

The mass of men are neither wise nor good, and the virtue like the other resources of a country, can only be drawn to a point and exerted by strong circumstances ably managed, or a strong government ably administered. New governments have not the aid of habit and hereditary respect, and being generally the result of preceding tumult and confusion, do not immediately acquire stability or strength. Besides, in times of commotion, some men will gain confidence and importance, who merit neither, and who, like political mountebanks, are less solicitous about the health of the credulous crowd than about making the most of their nostrums and prescriptions.

. . .

What I most fear is, that the better kind of people, by which I mean the people who are orderly and industrious, who are content with their situations and not uneasy in their circumstances, will be led by the insecurity of property, the loss of confidence in their rulers, and the want of public faith and rectitude, to consider the charms of liberty as imaginary and delusive. A state of fluctuation and uncertainty must disgust and alarm such men, and prepare their minds for almost any change that may promise them quiet and security.

And Washington answered:

Your sentiments, that our affairs are drawing rapidly to a crisis, accord with my own. What the event will be is also beyond the reach of my foresight. We have errors to correct. *We have, probably had too good an opinion of human nature in forming our confederation.* Experience has taught us that men will not adopt, and carry into execution, measures the best calculated for their own good, without the intervention of a coercive power. I do not conceive we can exist long as a nation without having lodged somewhere a power which will pervade the whole union, in as energetic a manner as the authority of the different state governments extends over the several states.

. . .

What astonishing changes a few years are capable of producing! I am told that even respectable characters speak of a monarchial form of government without horror. From thinking, proceeds speaking; thence to action is often but a single step. But how irrevocable and tremendous! What a triumph for the advocates of despotism to find that we are incapable of governing ourselves, and that systems founded on the basis of equal liberty are merely ideal and fallacious! Would to God that wise measures may be taken in time to avert the consequences we have but too much reason to apprehend.[17]

Neither Jay nor Washington guessed, as either might well have done, considering their disillusionment at the moment, that no matter of abstract principle, but crass matters of commerce would open the way to the reforms both hoped for so ardently. But it should be obvious that there was ample reason for John Adams's later opinion that, even if Jay was not present at Philadelphia in 1787, he nevertheless had had as much as anyone to do with the result. He was expressing these apprehensions and pointing out generally what must be done to numerous colleagues in the years before the Convention. He wrote to Jefferson later in 1786, saying that the inefficacy of the government became daily more and more apparent. And to John Adams he wrote that affairs were in a very unpleasant situation: "When government, either from defects in its construction or administration, ceases to assert its rights, or is too feeble to afford security, inspire confidence, and overawe the ambitious and licentious, the best citizens naturally grow uneasy and look to other systems.[18]

[17] Jay to Washington, June 27, 1786; Washington to Jay, Aug. 15, 1786, in *Correspondence and Public Papers*, III, 204–5, 208–9.

[18] Jay to John Adams, Nov. 1, 1786, in *Correspondence and Public Papers*, III, 214.

What the main defect was he was quite clear; it was government by legislature alone. There needed also to be an executive and a judicial branch. Writing to Washington in January, 1787, when it appeared that there would actually be a convention, he speculated more at length; this was a continuation of the correspondence begun the previous summer:

The situation of our affairs calls not only for reflection and prudence, but for exertion. What is to be done? is a question not easy to answer.

Would the giving *any* further degree of power to Congress do the business? I am much inclined to think it would not, for among other reasons there will always be members who will find it convenient to make their seats subservient to partial and personal purposes; and they who may be willing and able to concert and promote useful and national measures will seldom be unembarrassed by the ignorance, prejudices, fears or interested views of others.

. . .

The executive business of sovereignty depending on so many wills, and those wills moved by such a variety of contradictory motives and inducements, will in general be but freely done. Such a sovereignty, however theoretically responsible, cannot be effectually so in its departments and officers without adequate judicatories. I therefore promise myself nothing very desirable from any change which does not divide the sovereignty into its proper departments. Let Congress legislate—let others execute—let others judge.

Shall we have a king? Not, in my opinion, while other experiments remain untried. Might we not have a governor-general limited in his prerogatives and duration? Might not Congress be divided into an upper and lower house—the former appointed for life, the latter annually—and let the governor-general (to preserve the balance), with the advice of a council, formed for that only purpose, of the great judicial officers, have a negative on their acts? Our government should in some degree be suited to our manners and circumstances and they, you know, are not strictly democratical. What powers should be granted to the government so constituted is a question which deserves much thought. I think the more the better, the States retaining only so much as may be necessary for domestic purposes, and all their principal officers, civil and military, being commissioned and removable by the national government.

. . .

A convention is in contemplation and I am glad to find your name among those of its intended members.[19]

That Washington was present at the Convention that summer and that Jay was not made Jay's short dissertation all the more important. But these were not ideas that were exclusively his. They were those of all good Federalists. Hamilton, especially, was of a like mind. But Hamilton might have had much more impact on the meeting—which he attended only casually, and at which he made only one major address—if Jay had been there to reinforce him.

As it was, Jay had to use his influence indirectly. This was important in the case of Washington, who wrote him again in March, thoughtfully, and in a melancholy strain, about the issues to be discussed. He was not hopeful that anything would come of the meeting; he was beginning to think that American theory was better than American practice; and he was apprehensive of that jealousy and of those "local views" about which he was to write a famous letter to Hamilton midway of the Convention. All that summer and into the fall Jay wrote and talked about the issues. In July he was differing with Adams about the glorification of Congress in Adams's *A Defense of the Constitutions of the United States of America*, published in that year.[20] He wrote to Jefferson and again to Adams.

[19] Jay to Washington, Jan. 7, 1787, in *Correspondence and Public Papers*, III, 226–28.

[20] Jay to Adams, July 4, 1787, in *Correspondence and Public Papers*, III, 249. Adams had written in *A Defense:* "The people of America, and their delegates in Congress, were of opinion that a single assembly was every way adequate to the management of all their federal concerns and with very good reason, because Congress is not a legislative assembly, not a representative assembly, but only a diplomatic assembly. A single council has been found to answer the purpose of confederacies very well. . . . Dr. [Richard] Price, and the Abbé de Mably are zealous for additional

Like the other nationalists, Jay was not overly pleased with the result of the Convention; but like them, after consideration, he realized that it was better by far than it might have been. And he, Madison, and Hamilton in concert decided on the effort at defense and exposition represented by *The Federalist Papers,* written that autumn. It really did seem doubtful whether nine states could be got to ratify the radically revised government represented by the proposed Constitution.

Jay's contribution to the exposition turned out to be slighter than those of the others, so far as the writing was concerned. Of the eighty-five papers he wrote only five (numbers 2, 3, 4, 5, and 64). But what was to be said was thoroughly worked out in a series of conferences so that they all agreed. It was a powerful effort by three of the best minds of their generation.

The Federalist, ever since the composition of its various pieces, has been regarded as a classic of republican exposition, the foundation argument for the government of delegated and separated powers, the first line of defense of the Constitution that has endured ever since essentially unchanged. There is a tendency to forget that it was written by three contributors who were disappointed in many of its provisions and who regarded it as at best a compromise that would before long have to be modified. The states were too strong, the executive not sufficiently powerful, and the Senate a sop to the small states that would certainly cause endless trouble. Whether or not any of them argued themselves into a more accepting frame of mind, they certainly seemed vigorous enough in defense; and the controversial atmosphere of the next few years, when ratification was taking place with so much dissidence and in such continual uncertainty, tended to make

---

powers to Congress. Full powers in all foreign affairs, and over foreign commerce, and perhaps some authority over the commerce of the states with one another, may be necessary; and it is hard to say, that more authority in other things is not wanted; yet the subject is of such extreme delicacy and difficulty that the people are to be applauded for their caution."

partisans of everyone. There was a polarization of political opinion that tended to obscure any remaining doubts. And then the new government had to be set up, its traditions formed, its personnel selected, and its operations made successful. All *The Federalist* authors were involved in these matters; and all gained stature by their participation. They were already prominent; they were to become more so.

Jay's contribution in the first few issues was limited to a warning against foreign influences on a weak government, a subject he was entitled to treat from long experience. The last of his essays—in the spring of 1788—was a defense of the powers given to the Senate. The reason for the long interval, and for the limiting of his contribution, was a breakdown of his always delicate health. It was thought that he might have tuberculosis this time; and he did not escape from close confinement until the spring. When he did he was involved in a New York riot started by medical students who infuriated some boys by throwing parts of a cadaver out of a window at them. When Jay, with some other prominent citizens, undertook to intervene, he was struck by a stone and severely wounded. He was again invalided for some time. When he began to recover he wrote *An Address to the People of New York* which was very possibly more immediately influential than his contributions to *The Federalist.* That whole document was sufficiently partisan; but it was also legalistic and scholarly. As a modern propaganda effort it would convince very few voters; and it probably had little wider appeal in 1788. But it is true that the electorate was very restricted and possibly an argument addressed only to the elite may have had considerable effect. Jay's *An Address* was shorter, more pointed, and more widely read at the time.

An Address was one of several appeals made by Jay to the people of New York. That he made them in this way, and that they were accepted as they were, is an indication of the honor this particular prophet had in his home community. Other indications of the same respect were the several public recognitions of his services—when he returned from France, for instance, and when, on one occasion, he returned from a tour of duty on circuit. Few public men have been held in such high and steady esteem. It was because he knew this that he felt he could address his fellow citizens as he occasionally did.[21]

The purpose of the tract was to explain in simple terms how it was that good revolutionary impulses had somehow been transmuted into ones which might destroy all that had been achieved. The evils of the Confederation, once regarded as virtues, had compounded. Trade and industry had fallen off, the merchant marine was idle, and the credit of the nation was ruined. It was because there was no way to remedy this sickness except by a drastic reform of the government that the wise and moderate men had met in Convention. They had been of all sorts and opinions; they had arrived at a compromise, not pleasing in its entirety to any of them, but recognizable as one which might work. It ought now to be accepted and tried. He appealed to the self-interest of New Yorkers; they were dependent on commerce and needed to keep their great port free. But mostly he addressed himself to three questions:

1. Whether it is probable that a better plan can be obtained.

2. Whether, if attainable, it is likely to be in season.

3. What would be our situation if, after rejecting this, all our efforts to obtain a better should prove fruitless.

His conclusion was carefully but briefly argued. On all grounds it was desirable to ratify. No better men and no wiser ones could be found than those who had worked out the

[21] It was also why he took so much pains to make public explanations of situations that threatened to embarrass him. One of these was the Littlepage incident, described in some length in Monaghan's *Jay* referred to before. On the whole Jay's integrity was so generally recognized that his few detractors had discouragingly little success.

proposed Constitution. Delay was something the nation could no longer afford. If another convention was held, the forces of dissension would not be less strong. And there were foreign influences that might be brought to bear to hinder agreement. So far as New York was concerned it had better be considered what the situation would be if the necessary number of other states ratified and she did not. The consequences could hardly be pleasant. But his most ardent appeal was stated with moving eloquence, so obviously motivated by his love of his country and fear for her future, that even at this remove in years it possesses a singular power. It was addressed to the highest impulse of men:

> Consider, then, how weighty and how many considerations advise and persuade the people of America to remain in the safe and easy path of union; to continue to move and act, as they hitherto have done, as a band of brothers; and to have confidence in themselves and in one another; and, since all cannot see with the same eyes, at least to give the proposed Constitution a fair trial, and to mend it as time, occasion, and experience may dictate. It would little become us to verify the predictions of those who ventured to prophesy that peace, instead of blessing us with happiness and tranquillity, would serve only as the signal for factions, discord, and civil contentions to rage in our land, and overwhelm it with misery and distress.
>
> . . .
>
> If the people of our nation, instead of consenting to be governed by laws of their own making and rulers of their own choosing, should let licentiousness, disorder, and confusion reign over them, the minds of men everywhere will insensibly become alienated from republican forms, and prepared to prefer and acquiesce in governments which, though less friendly to liberty, afford more peace and security.

This was a call, in the highest tradition, to men's capacities for selflessness and cooperation in the cause of human liberty.

Jay was a member of the ratifying Convention in New York State. He was elected from New York City and had the highest vote of all of the delegates. Hamilton and Robert Livingston were also chosen. Outside the city, Governor George Clinton received a large vote; so also did John Lansing, who had left the Convention in Philadelphia, and Melancthon Smith; but the anti-Federalists were not of the public stature of the Constitution's supporters.[22]

The anti-Federalists may not have ranked with the Federalists in prominence; but they were excellent politicians; and they were able to delay matters in spite of their weak cause. In the end they possessed the strength to wring a reluctant compromise from Hamilton, Jay, and the others. That ratification was achieved at all was largely because it became unnecessary; other states were completing the roll of nine, and New York might be tagged as a reluctant tenth. When consent was given it was with a "recommendation" that another Convention be called to consider amendments. This was not a condition; but it detracted somewhat from the victory represented by the acceptance.

As the controversy over the adoption of the Constitution went on, the old government existed only in a vestigial form. Jay, still its foreign secretary, had in fact no superiors to whom to report, but he kept the government machinery going, especially in the vital area of international relations. He complimented our minister to France, Thomas Jefferson, on the

> late French commercial reforms relative to the United States in the spirit of reciprocity and free trade for they would render the Connection between the two countries more intimate. They bear Marks of Wisdom and Liberality, and cannot fail of being very acceptable. It is to be regretted that the mercantile People in France oppose a System, which certainly is calculated to bind the two Nations together, and from which both would eventually derive commercial as well as political Advantages.

[22] It might perhaps be noted that among the Federalist members from the city—who were all prominent citizens—was that Isaac Roosevelt who was to be the ancestor of famous men in later generations.

Then he presented a vision of liberalization of trade intermixed with the caution of his commercial forbears:

It appears to me that France has not a single Ally in Europe on which she can fully depend, and it doubtless would be wise in her to endeavor so to blend her Interests with ours as if possible to render them indissoluble by giving us all the Privileges of Frenchmen, and accepting in Return all the Privileges of Americans. If they could bring themselves to adopt this Idea, their Schemes of Policy respecting us would be greatly simplified; but the Spirit of Monopoly and Exclusion has prevailed in Europe too long to be done away with at once and however enlightened the present Age may be when compared with former ones, yet whenever ancient Prejudices are touched, we find we have only Light enough to see our Want of more. Toleration in Commerce like Toleration in Religion gains ground it is true; but I am not sanguine in my Expectations that either will soon take place in the due Extent.[23]

Jay was much relieved when the Constitution was adopted to go into effect in March, 1789, and doubly so when, in April, the ballots for President and Vice President were counted and it was known that Washington had been chosen unanimously and Adams, though with less than a majority, still by more votes than any other person. He had thirty-four; of the rest, which were scattering, Jay had the next largest number—nine.

There ensued a period in which Jay's contribution was perhaps as considerable as any in his career as a statesman. He assisted materially in the formation of the new government at a time when his experience and accumulated wisdom were peculiarly useful—when a complete rebeginning was being made and when everyone was willing to listen to the counsel he was able to offer.

Robert Morris, acting as his emissary, invited Washington to use Jay's house until a suitable official residence could be

[23] Jay to Jefferson, April 24, 1788, in *The Papers of Thomas Jefferson*, ed. Julian P. Boyd (Princeton: Princeton Univ. Press), XIII, 106.

provided. Washington, when the letter was presented, was already on his way to his first inauguration. That journey was one of the most remarkable, certainly, in presidential history. At every crossroads there were official receptions; and in the cities on the way there was a display of pageantry never seen before even in Washington's experience. The aging general was fairly inured to this sort of thing after the adulatory celebrations of the peace; but that had been some years earlier and time had weakened his appreciation. But the democracy had to be allowed a hero and the new President braced himself over and over for local celebrations, drinking innumerable toasts at endless dinners, reviewing troops of horse and companies of militia, responding to speeches of welcome, and enduring the accommodations of indifferent taverns. It was part of his conception of his role that he should not accept private hospitality; and it was on this ground that he refused Jay's invitation. But Jay was one of those who turned out to escort him into the city—he came across from Jersey in a barge loaded down with notables—and was among the company of those who surrounded him as he took the oath of office. They were, moreover, much together in the months that succeeded.

There was no one who had more practical advice to offer. Since 1784 he had been identified with the old government—as its most prominent official; and he had developed very definite ideas concerning its weaknesses and how they might now be avoided as a new start was being made. Washington was not familiar with government; he had never been concerned in it except as a military man always asking for funds and always pleading for the support of policies that would strengthen his hand. As a member of the Constitutional Convention, he had been an almost silent member, although his influence had been used to strengthen the union and the executive. Now he had to emerge from an honorable retirement to administer the affairs of a newly constituted federation, with its structure only sketchily delineated and its traditions still unmade. It is no wonder that he relied heavily on the most trusted experienced person available. During all the spring and summer, as the first departments of government were shaped, and the first problems met, the President conferred repeatedly with Jay. It was he who drew up the plan for the State Department; and the two acts establishing it which were passed that summer were largely his work. Meanwhile he was staying on as secretary for an interim period; and he could have been the first secretary under the new organization if he had so desired. Washington, as a matter of fact, gave him a choice of positions, and there was a time when it was generally supposed that he would be the new secretary of the Treasury.[24] Each of these possibilities he discussed at length with the President. But in late August he decided that he might serve best by becoming the first chief justice of the United States as he had earlier of New York State.

The intimacy between Washington and Jay that grew up that summer was useful to both on later occasions. Washington never had reason to doubt Jay's disinterested loyalty; and Jay had the utmost confidence in Washington's leadership.

One of the unfortunate circumstances of Jay's appointment was that there were others who wanted it. Among these aspirants was Robert R. Livingston. After Jay's selection these old friends were separated; and when Jay, in 1792, was a candidate for the governorship of New York, Livingston was his bitterest political critic. But, in spite of this, and of some other envious criticisms, Jay was accepted as the almost inevitable choice; and, until his resignation in June, 1795, was the symbol of the judicial function almost as much as Washington

[24] Jay had shown not only extensive knowledge of monetary and financial doctrines but also a considerable skill in their application in his *Circular-Letter from Congress to Their Constituents* (1779), which dealt with the problem of the great depreciation of the paper money.

was of the executive. They were both gravely conscious that they were establishing traditions and they behaved as their roles demanded. The Presidency still bears indelibly the mark of Washington; but not more noticeably than chief justiceship bears that of Jay. His early service has been somewhat obscured by that of his successor, Marshall; but it was Jay who, for instance, first confined the functions of the court to decision-making and determined that the chief justice should be a judge and not an adviser to the executive or the legislature.

Jay's national service was ended when he was sent abroad in 1794; when he came back he found that he had been elected governor, and this was his last public office. But between 1790 and 1794 he had time enough to habituate the court firmly to its appropriate role among the branches.

Jay's contribution to the separation of powers took the form of a gentle but firm rebuke to both Jefferson and Washington who, forgetting theory, had asked the court whether certain questions might be submitted for decision which were not justiciable but which it would be convenient to have settled as guides to action. Jay's reply (joined in by his colleagues) was brief but significant; it referred directly to:

> the lines of separation drawn by the Constitution between the three Departments of the government. These being in certain respects checks upon each other, and our being judges of a court in the last resort, are considerations which afford strong arguments against the propriety of our extrajudicially deciding the questions alluded to, especially as the power given by the Constitution to the President, of calling on the heads of departments for opinions, seems to have been *purposely* as well as expressly united to the executive departments.[25]

There the matter has stood ever since.

As to the important cases decided during Jay's tenure, there were several which would establish precedent; and there was

[25] Chief Justice Jay and Associate Justices to President Washington, Aug. 8, 1793, in Jay, *Correspondence and Public Papers*, III, 488–89.

one which would be reversed by a constitutional amendment. Of the cases, the first of note was *Chisholm vs Georgia* (1793). Until then the court had met, admitted practitioners, and heard motions, but had not had any cases. This was partly because of a provision of the early Judiciary Act under which the justices served also as circuit court judges.[26] This was a wearing business; and it was partly responsible for Jay's willingness to give up the chief justiceship for the governorship of New York; but it served to keep cases out of the higher court. *Chisholm vs Georgia* upheld the right of a citizen of one state to sue in the federal court against another state. It showed what an important policy role the court could play even if it kept strictly to the cases that came before it. There was nothing in the Constitution that said a state might not be sued; but the framers were not thought to have intended it so; and Jay was guided therefore less by any knowledge of intention than by nationalist views. The decision was regarded at the time as an assault on the integrity of the states; and the anti-Federalists were noisily angry.

Jay's argument in this case was an ingenious one. It rested on popular sovereignty. In America, he said, there was no prince. If there were, he could not be sued; but where every citizen shared in sovereignty, and every citizen could be sued, his sovereignty obviously could not confer immunity. Nor could it confer immunity on any number of citizens collectively.

This was Federalist as well as democratic doctrine; it regarded the states as less important than the Jeffersonians held them to be. And, of course, the Eleventh Amendment (introduced into the Senate in 1794 and ratified in 1798) was a final victory on this matter for the anti-Federalists.

The last term over which Jay presided was that of 1794.

[26] The country was divided into three districts with two Supreme Court judges together with a judge for the district court constituting the circuit court in each district.

In that session *Georgia vs Brailsford* was decided. This again, although it was a more involved matter, infuriated the believers in states' rights and raised again the issue of national supremacy. But the case of *Glass vs Sloop Betsey* had a quite different connotation. The *Betsey* had been captured by a French privateer and brought into Baltimore for seizure by the French consul. The owners brought suit to determine whether the federal district court or the French consul had jurisdiction. Jay, delivering the unanimous opinion, held that the district court did have the power to determine the legality of prizes brought into American ports; he laid down the position that no foreign power could establish a court within the United States, "but such only as may be warranted by, and be in pursuance of treaties." Since the district courts possessed all the powers of courts of admiralty, the jurisdiction exercised heretofore by the French consul was not so warranted. This decision in effect by denying any extra-territorial jurisdiction on American soil by a foreign power asserted the full sovereignty of the nation in international dealings.

Meanwhile, although Jay as a justice was quite unwilling to involve the court in public matters not represented by cases, he did not feel himself inhibited as a private citizen from taking part in Federalist counsels. He was a constant adviser of Hamilton and Washington, even going so far as to draft a neutrality proclamation when requested by Hamilton to do so. And, in the rising excitement and dissension caused by French agitation for American aid in the war against Britain and her allies, he had a controversy with the provocative French ambassador, Genet, which upset his judicial aplomb and for a time threatened his relations with Washington, who, he felt, had not supported him as he should have done.

That Washington, on his side, was not permanently annoyed was shown well enough when he selected Jay for the delicate task of attempting a settlement with Britain. Ever since the signing of the Treaty of Peace relations between the two nations had been worsening. The violations and repeated provocations on both sides had worked up a readiness among many people on both sides to again go to war. It was Washington's fear that if that happened the nation might not survive, or that, even if it did, its institutions would be deeply impaired. Jay shared these Federalist beliefs; and it was his sense of duty that caused him to undertake the unwelcome task.

He had been defeated for the governorship of New York in 1792 by the Clintonians, old political rivals; and although Jay himself had not campaigned actively, he had been a consenting candidate. That he should have been willing to leave the chief justiceship was undoubtedly the result of several influences. There were the negative ones that he did not like the circuit duties and that his health was very uncertain. But there were also the positive ones that he was more at home in New York than elsewhere; and that his esteem in his own community was immune to the extreme attacks he, along with other Federalists, was suffering from the anti-Federalists led by Jefferson. The New York governorship was not exactly a retreat; but it seemed to offer problems more easily soluble and a base more secure to a tired man.

George Clinton won again; but by a dubious use of technicalities.[27] Aaron Burr played a part, a characteristic one; and so did Jay's erstwhile friend, Robert Livingston.

[27] "The election was stolen under color of law. In Otsego the term of the sheriff had expired. Earlier in the year, when Clinton had been urged to name a successor, he replied that the old one could hold over. The sheriff *de facto* of Otsego deputized a messenger to take the ballots to the secretary of state. The deputy sheriff of Tioga fell ill while en route with the ballots, and turned them over to a clerk. In Clinton County, the sheriff neglected to deputize the messenger. The board of canvassers consisted of four Federals and seven Republicans. Unable to agree, they submitted the question to the two United States Senators. Burr and his Federal colleague, Rufus King, agreed on the law, but differed on its interpretation. King construed the law in furtherance of the privilege of suffrage; Burr interpreted the law literally. By a party vote of seven to four, the board gave the election to Clinton. To prevent a recount, the election thieves burned the disputed ballots." (D. T. Lynch, "The Growth of Political Parties, 1777–1828," in *History of the State of New York*, ed. A. C. Flick [New York: Columbia Univ. Press, 1934], VI, 41–42.)

While the election excitement seethed, Jay went on about his judicial duties as usual; and if he was disappointed at the result he did not show it. He rejected all suggestions that the election should be contested on the basis of the fraudulency involved. But that he had hoped to win everyone knew.

Washington is known to have considered, when he was convinced that American-British relations had reached the breaking point, the names of Adams, Hamilton, Jefferson, and Jay for a mission to attempt a peaceful settlement. That Jay should have been preferred shows not only that the President had confidence in him, but that the country generally had a similar confidence. For Washington cannot have expected any very favorable settlement, the British advantage being what it was, and his envoy must be one whose efforts would be regarded as the best that could be expected whatever the result. As it was to turn out, not even Jay's reputation would survive the negotiations. He would be a sacrifice to Federalist unpopularity.

As on a former occasion, Jay had instructions to guide his forthcoming talks with Grenville in London; but this time they were ones to which he did not object, or which, at least, he considered relevant to the task ahead. It was inconsistent that he should be told to see that peace was maintained at almost any cost, and, at the same time, warned that he must not jeopardize any considerable American interest. But he understood that it was the peace aim that was paramount. The Federalists knew that they would have to agree to British treatment of American commerce at sea in ways which were humiliating and which France and other nations had abandoned in treaties already made with the United States. Only two items of his instructions left him no freedom: he must not impair American obligations to France; and he must not allow American ships to be shut out of the West Indies trade. The main business, of course, would be to settle the controversies that had arisen under the treaty of 1783; these were many and complex; and American grievances were no more just than those of the British. On the whole it was a mission bound to have a politically unsatisfactory result.

There is no really convincing explanation of Jay's acceptance. True, Washington, Hamilton, Rufus King, Oliver Ellsworth, and other Federalist leaders implored him to undertake the task; but he must have felt that a chief justice ought not to undertake extrajudicial duties; and on all personal grounds he is known to have been reluctant. It must also have been a serious consideration that in consenting he made the most serious of all political sacrifices. It is not too much to say that he might well have been Washington's successor as President in 1796 if he had not deliberately exposed himself to bitter criticism over the result most likely to be reached. It must be that he was actually convinced that no one else had so good a chance of averting the war that seemed almot inevitable and that would be so disastrous to the country.

That the treaty would not be received happily he had ample warning before he left for London. The furor in the opposition press was a sufficient preview; it was said elaborately and repeatedly by the opposition that the intention was to give in to the British, that American interests were to be sacrificed, and that France was to be betrayed.[28]

The treaty he negotiated was published in June, 1795, and from that time Jay was ruined as a national political figure. It

[28] The British, too, were by no means satisfied with the treaty. Jay's friend, the British economist James W. Anderson, informed him, "Here as well as in America, there are innumerable persons, who according to an old, and a very expressive adage, *to have an inch of their will would give an ell of their purse*, and who are of course continually for running their heads against any obstruction that comes within their reach." Letter of Anderson to Jay, March 14, 1795, Jay papers, Columbia University Libraries. The collection also contains letters from other British economists including Patrick Colquhuoun, Sir John Sinclair, and Jeremy Bentham, who gave him information on manufactures, agriculture, roads, etc., that might prove of use to the new nation.

is true that his negotiation had kept war from breaking out; moreover, the minimum demands of his Federalist colleagues were met. These included the evacuation of the border posts the British had gone on holding since the war, and the assurance that existing commercial relations would be maintained. But, aside from a promise of compensation for British spoliations of American property, nothing else of importance was favorable.[29] The British would go on seizing American ships under a definition of neutral rights which she stiffly refused to modify; and none of the concessions asked for by Jay in his first exchange with Grenville were made.

Not until the end of May, 1796, did Jay arrive back home in New York. On June 24, by a party vote, the treaty was ratified. It was not until then that the furor over its provisions really reached a climax. It would be impossible to exaggerate the extravagances of denunciation to which Jay was subjected. He was accused of treachery; the lowest motives were ascribed to him; and even those friends who had urged him to undertake the mission gave weak support. He was a man discredited and politically abandoned. Washington, without making any defense of Jay or of himself, signed the treaty in August in a nationally riotous atmosphere; there were marching crowds, endless demagogic denunciations and, in many places, uncontrolled riots.

But by now Jay was governor of New York; he had been elected while he was at sea, and had been inaugurated before the worst of the vituperation had occurred. He spoke of fortitude and of the faithful discharge of his duty to his country; and he quietly abandoned any expectation—if by then he had any—of succeeding to the Presidency.

[29] Samuel F. Bemis in his classic study, *Jay's Treaty* (New York: Macmillan, 1923), has pointed out that the Federalist leaders, especially Hamilton, felt that war or even commercial hostility with England would by cutting off the national government's almost exclusive revenue, import duties, destroy national credit. They held that peace and commercial expansion for some time were essential, to strengthen the new government and place it in a position to assert fully its rights.

In a career such as Jay's the governorship of New York might be thought of as anticlimactic; but probably Jay did not think of it in that way. He was a thorough New Yorker, and living at Government House, which was a fine mansion standing where the Custom House later stood, near the Battery, he was at home. The duties he had had as ambassador and even as chief justice, had not held the same satisfactions as the more intimate ones involved in governing the state. What he had to do was always within his competence; it seldom involved policies the end of which were indeterminate; the results of his industry and judgment were immediate and well understood. He was an excellent executive; and was easily reelected.

Some idea of his interests as governor can be had in a few quotations taken from his annual opening addresses to the legislature. In his first in 1796, he granted that every locality should provide for its own poor, "but by the events . . . of the desolating war between many of the European powers and the advantages which this country offers to immigrants, a great number of persons are induced to come to this state, without other resources than what the benevolence of our citizens or other adventitious circumstances may furnish. As these people do not properly belong to any particular place in this or the neighboring states, would it not be right to consider those of them who may be real objects of charity, as the poor of the state and to provide for them accordingly."

Reflecting the advice of James W. Anderson on the advantage of public construction of canals, Jay contended that "the ultimate connection that subsists between our agriculture, commerce and navigation strongly recommends the policy of facilitating and multiplying the means of intercourse between the different parts of the state." He warned that the task of improving the state was one that could not be performed "without much time, application and well digested information, for it will always be found more difficult, and also more useful to legislate well than to legislate much."

In his next address, he pointed out that in their deliberating on the means of maintaining and increasing the public welfare many interesting subjects would enter into view: "Such as . . . the manner in which its [state] salt springs may be rendered more useful, and the woods in the neighborhood best preserved; the facilities and encouragement that may be proper to obtaining an accurate map of the whole state, the necessity of rendering the laws respecting roads and bridges more effectual, and of revising and amending those which . . . direct the inspection of certain of our staple commodities."

He declared in his address of 1798 that "in a state so progressive as ours, new cares and exigencies will frequently arise and require legislative provision." He closed with an earnest recommendation to the legislature's "notice and patronage," the state's institutions for the education of youth, the common schools and especially the two colleges in the state, Columbia and Union. "Our ancestors have transmitted to us many excellent institutions matured by the wisdom and experience of ages. Let them descend to our posterity accompanied with others, which by promoting useful knowledge, and multiplying the blessings of social order, and diffusing the influence of moral obligations, may be reputable to us and beneficial to them."

In his 1800 address he complained of "all the small proportion which our important public statutes bears to the numerous private ones passed for individual or for local and particular purposes." He asked: "Might not the claims of individuals for the most part be heard, examined and ascertained in some mode more easy to them and to the state than by the legislature; and ought not business of great and general moment to precede that of less and limited importance." Frequently too much of the earlier part of each session was consumed in debating, preparing, and passing on these relatively less important matters; consequently much important public business was either hastily disposed of at the end of the session or left unfinished. "The frequency of acts for private incorporations and the difficulty of afterwards restraining or correcting the evils, resulting to the public from unforeseen defects in them, lead me to advert to the prudence of passing them only under such circumstances of previous publicity and deliberation as may be proper to guard against the effect of cursory and inaccurate views and impressions." He regretted in his address of 1799 that "many of our citizens seem to have inadvertently flattered themselves that unlike other people past and present, they were to live exempt from taxes. To the influence of this error is owing, that the state is at this moment in debt, and paying interest for money it would have been more wise to have collected by a tax, than to have obtained on loan. Whenever our necessary expenses exceed our income, the discrepancy should be supplied by taxes judiciously and impartially imposed." But he made a significant exception for "great and urgent occasions." [30] The quotations, it will be seen, reflect the experience of a judge, an estate holder, and a humanitarian. Jay was all of these.

But when in 1800 the question of a third term came up, he refused. He also refused when Adams appointed him again to the chief justiceship of the United States. Instead he carried out an old project; he built the house at Bedford in which presently his wife would die but in which he would go on living quietly through a long old age. The years of retirement were years of deepening religious contemplation, of mild participation in local affairs, of counseling those who asked to share his experience, and of enjoying the small affairs of the estate he had accumulated around the homestead. He outlived most of those he had worked with so closely; he had many sorrows; but he was sustained by that belief in a hereafter

[30] *The Speeches of the Different Governors to the Legislature of the State of New York* (Albany: Van Steenbergh, 1825), pp. 47–67.

which was the heritage of his training and which had never left him. He had many memories of great occasions; he often talked of them; but he never wrote any account of his experiences. His retreat from public life, after having been so long at the center of affairs, and having as nearly missed the Presidency as anyone could do, was complete.

THE REVEREND JOHN MC VICKAR

The Reverend JOHN McVICKAR: CHRISTIAN TEACHER AND ECONOMIST

New York was a small town in the late eighteenth century and as in most small towns there were a few good families. John McVickar belonged to one of them by birth and to several others by marriage. And not only by belonging to the right family—but by belonging also to the right school and church—he found his attitudes and ways of life forecast from the very first. But then, too, he seems to have been that sort of person: a little stiff, a little of the martinet, a little impatient with democratic notions. He grew up normally, and with an air of fitness, into an upright, handsome vicar, quite as much at home in that little young New York and that valley of gentlemen's estates—the Hudson—as he might have been in an English cathedral town. Class and caste, in spite of those revolutionary struggles which he almost could remember, were far from being suspect; democracy was a word he rarely used, an idea he rarely entertained. A churchman could be a gentleman, too; in fact, he had to be; and he went his Christian way, chin somewhat in air, in full consciousness of the need there was to set a good example.

It was quite normal and right that a handsome man of the church, learned in learned things, should become also a professor in that school for gentlemen's sons which was the Columbia College of those days. And it was inevitable that such a professor, aware of his dignity and his responsibilities, should become a lecturer who taught all the right lessons, used the correct language, and insisted to the full on the disciplines which were orthodox then. We should expect to learn, from the study of such a man's career, what the times were like to the cultivated view; but we should not expect to discover prophecy or creation. Not prophecy, because the sense is lacking of what things are dying and what are growing; not creation, because talents are restrained to the pace of moderation. And, indeed, there was no breathless curiosity in John McVickar, no sense of struggle for definition.

There were, however, numerous virtues of another sort. He spoke of himself always as a man of moderate abilities. This in a sense was true. He generated no new ideas, he was excessively sound, he seldom went in for intellectual adventure. But he was, within limits, supple and clear. If he lacked profundity, he had a certain impressive integrity of thought. Some of these conclusions are inferred. We have a memoir of him written by a moralistic son, the better chapters of which consist of excerpts from the father's letters; we have some published occasional addresses written under the restraints occasions invariably impose; we have his tracts; and we have three series of lecture notes, of students, which have the usual deficiencies of telescoping and occasional misunderstanding.[1] As all historians are forced to do, we are under the necessity of discounting the tone of a book written as "a son's monument to a loved and honored father," of penetrating the glossy sur-

[1] The most comprehensive are those by Wheelock Hendee Parmly, D.D., graduated in Arts at Columbia College in 1840–42 and in Divinity at the Hamilton Literary and Theological Institution (now Colgate University) in 1844. He became a Baptist minister in 1846 and held pastorates in Louisiana, Massachusetts, and New Jersey; he was born at Braintree, Vermont, July 27, 1816, and died in Jersey City, August 1, 1894. His college and seminary notebooks are preserved in the Columbia University Libraries.

Another series of notes available in the Columbia University Libraries is that of Hamilton Fish, who became secretary of state under President Grant. The notebook of James W. Beekman in Political Economy, 1834, is in the New-York Historical Society collection.

face of occasional tracts and addresses, and of looking behind the lecture outlines of students.

With such acknowledgment of our main sources—as to the more important facts—we proceed to two facts, at least, which are unexceptionable, though we might, perhaps, have taken them for granted: he was born, and he grew up rather uneventfully. As to his being born, that occurred in midsummer of 1787, August 10th, to be exact. He liked to say, in later years, that "the Constitution and I are of just the same age," which was quite literally the truth, for among all the New York Federalists, none were more convinced than the McVickars. As to his growing up uneventfully, that was guaranteed by his father's affluence as a leading merchant, his mother's descent from the early English, his attendance, for a time, at a "select school established by a few gentlemen for the benefit of their sons," his later receiving the "exclusive services of a private tutor, a learned Scotch clergyman," and his matriculation at Columbia College in 1800.[2] He was only thirteen; but this was not unusual.

Schooling in those days was still not so prevalent as apprenticeship, even for the professions; and the range of knowledge required for matriculation was confined largely to a good beginning in Latin and Greek imposed on an elementary grounding in the three R's. Columbia, like all colleges, conceived its function to be that of furthering the student's knowledge of the classics, together with an equipment for defense of the scriptures. Charles King in his inauguration as president in 1849 made this quite clear: "Our rock of foundation," he said, "is the Classics." John McVickar, having come through such a college and having become a professor in one, was more than passive in his acceptance of the system. As dean of the faculty,

[2] W. A. McVickar, *The Life of the Reverend John McVickar* (New York: Hurd and Houghton, 1872), pp. 1–6.

he spoke at the inauguration of President King: "What I here stand to praise and plead for," he said, "is . . . the maintenance and advance in our land and wherever decayed the restoration, of what may well be termed the scholar's birthright, the common law of our race, our Anglo-Saxon inheritance—solid, classical, religious training—coming down as it does, from the time of Alfred, bearing as it does, the marks of good King Edward, and standing side by side in English history with the Magna Charta of John and the Bill of Rights of the Revolution."[8] There may be some confusion here of an Anglo-Saxon tradition with a mixed discipline of Greek, Roman, and Hebraic literature, but what he meant is clear enough. The ancient learning and the Bible had been domesticated in England. To English churchmen they were more definitely a point of departure than the rather earthy literature which was more legitimately English. When McVickar mentions the common law of the race and the old kings, he has in mind not Chaucer, Shakespeare, and the rest, but rather the learning borrowed from the Continent at the Renaissance and cultivated with such fervor at Oxford and Cambridge.

The college to which McVickar came in 1800 was devoted to the education of the gentry; but that implied nothing in the way of corporate affluence. There was restriction everywhere, partly as a result of the specific difficulties of educational enterprise in disturbed times, and partly because there were difficulties with a legislature which looked somewhat askance at this kind of Episcopal training. In the year before his entrance the grant which had been depended on for professors' salaries since 1792 (of £750) was withdrawn, and retrenchment was necessary. The trustees appear to have met the emergency by adding the teaching of rhetoric and of belles-lettres, along with logic and moral philosophy, to the duties of the

[8] *Addresses at the Inauguration of Mr. Charles King as President of Columbia College* (New York: Columbia College, 1849), pp. 12, 44.

president. The duties of another professor extended over the whole range of the "Latin and Greek Languages, and Roman and Greek Antiquities"; another taught "Mathematics, Natural Philosophy and Geography." The teaching of "Oriental Languages, French and Law" had to be discontinued; and the professor of chemistry having luckily been elected to the legislature, a successor was found who would not be a drain on the budget; instead of a salary, he agreed to take eight dollars for two years' tuition from each student in his class.

Faced with all these difficulties, perhaps dismayed by the prospect of teaching belles-lettres and logic to a group of boys under twenty, as well as carrying the responsibility for not inconsiderable disciplinary tasks, President William S. Johnson resigned. The two professors who remained carried on the college in McVickar's first year. In his second, the Reverend Charles Henry Wharton agreed to assume the presidency, but after hesitating four months gave it up. In the resulting emergency, the bishop of the diocese became the president and provision was made for a separate professor of moral philosophy, rhetoric, belles-lettres and logic.[4] In 1802 the entire annual permanent revenue of the college did not exceed £1,500, of which £1,477 went for salaries, the New York pound being half the sterling unit. The president received £100 and the three professors a total of £1,300. The college building was not in the best condition. It "consisted of the original pile and that in a very dilapidated state." The entrance examination took place in a "dark confined hall."[5] The professor of moral philosophy, belles-lettres, rhetoric, and logic, John Bowden, was an Episcopal clergyman, who had been an assistant minister at Trinity along with the then president of the college. His previous career had included an army chap-

[4] *A History of Columbia University, 1754–1904* (New York: Columbia Univ. Press, 1904), pp. 82, 85.

[5] John McVickar, *Alumni Anniversary of Columbia College, 1837* (New York: G. & C. Carvill, 1837), p. 9.

laincy and numerous pastorates; and he had been involved in certain bitter theological controversies full-flavored in their time but of little meaning for us. Before receiving his appointment at Columbia he was a teacher in the Episcopal Academy at Cheshire, Connecticut. In 1797 he had unsuccessfully sought the professorship of the "Greek and Latin Languages, and of Grecian and Roman Antiquities"; and in 1801 he had been a candidate for the college presidency.[6] With his professorship at Columbia there closed the "long list of removals in his painfully changeful life." [7] According to McVickar, "He exhibited in his manners, whether as the son of a British officer, or as trained up under a royal government . . . somewhat of that higher tone of courtesy, which, without disparagement to our own republican times, certainly was more marked in those which preceded them." [8] The case of Bowden has this interest: it illustrates how then, and considerably later, college teachers were recruited from the ranks of the clergy, not infrequently those who had broken down under missionary burdens, or who had failed to find preferment in the regular organization of the church. Teaching was a variety of ministerial activity. It was under the influence of such men that John McVickar pursued his education.

In 1804, at the age of seventeen, McVickar graduated from college at the head of his class. It was a stirring occasion. One of Columbia's greatest sons, Alexander Hamilton, a creator of the Federalist party, had just fallen on the duelling field. The eldest surviving son of Hamilton, Alexander, junior, was in the graduating class with McVickar. McVickar, being the "son of a Federalist of the old school," and having worn the Federal-

[6] Columbia University, Minutes of the Trustees, June 9, 19, 1797, May 4, 1801. A typescript copy of the Minutes is in the Columbia University Libraries.

[7] John McVickar, *Alumni Anniversary*, p. 16.

[8] John McVickar, *The Professional Years of John Henry Hobart* (New York: Protestant Episcopal Press, 1836), pp. 412–13.

ist cockade, chose as a topic for his Latin salutatory at Commencement "Eloquence and Hamilton." In this public eulogy it may or may not have been good taste to refer to Hamilton's deathbed repentance: "The boast of our college and the glory of our country has just fallen on the field of mistaken honor; a doubter in the days of a busy life, but a sincere and humble believer on his dying bed." [9] But the orator felt no compunction.

What McVickar was at seventeen he never after ceased to be. If it has been intimated that he was a little withdrawn, a little aristocratic, it should not be inferred that there was any lack of fire or vigor. The fervor may have been lighted at respectable fires, the zeal directed toward orthodox aims; but it burned brightly enough. McVickar's working life was long and arduous; he shirked none of it; and the burdens he carried would have broken a man sustained with a less unwavering faith in their righteousness. No doubter could have found the sources of strength he had at command. And they made his life crowded if not rich, and his career useful if not prophetic.

It is not surprising that McVickar decided within three years of graduation, to enter the ministry. He had spent a year abroad with his father, a year which brought him into touch with a wider clerical and academic world. There is no reason to believe that the poignant sufferings of the Napoleonic period much impressed him. There was some gaiety, but more busy pursuit of learning. His father's business apparently failed to offer the necessary alternative attractions to a career in the ministry, and in 1812 he was ordained. Immediately afterward he was elected first rector of the Church of St. James, Hyde Park, New York, founded and erected by his distinguished father-in-law, Samuel Bard. McVickar had married Eliza Bard in 1809. Doctor Bard, who had been physician to General Washington, was at the time dean of the Medical Faculty of

[9] W. A. McVickar, *Life*, p. 10.

Columbia College. In 1813 this faculty was absorbed by the College of Physicians and Surgeons, and Bard became president.[10] By marriage, then, McVickar was linked to another distinguished family. Two of his brothers had married daughters of the great merchant, William Constable; another brother married a daughter of the celebrated Judge Brockholst Livingston; and a fourth married a daughter of Isaac Lawrence, president of the New York branch of the Second Bank of the United States. His younger sister had married the son of Governor John Jay, and his father's brother had married a Goelet. It was natural, therefore, that he should expect a certain dignity to be maintained both in church and in school—the aristocratic attitude was fostered by all his connections. It is something less than startling to discover that his reaction, as a result of participation in one of the celebrated church trials of his time, was wholly orthodox. Proceedings were instituted for the suspension of a fellow minister, by name Timothy Clowes, who had become "democratic" as McVickar afterward described it; at Clowes's church, "the wealthy and respectable have been put out and the rabble brought in. Mr. Clowes on going there found this democratic spirit existing, and not being much of a gentleman, either in manners or feeling, he fell naturally into their society. . . ." The same attitude appeared when McVickar later visited the German universities in 1830. He noted that "when the professor enters, the students, being all seated, neither rise, nor show any mark of respect." [11] He never afterward had a good word to say for German education. Things were done with more dignity at Oxford, and he took care that Columbia should follow the better example.

McVickar was not only very active in his pastoral duties,

[10] The first comprehensive life of Bard was written by John McVickar, *A Domestic Narrative of the Life of Samuel Bard* (New York: A. Paul, 1822). See also Milton Halsey Thomas, "Doctor Samuel Bard," *The Columbia University Quarterly*, XXIII (June, 1931), 114–30. The College of Physicians and Surgeons became a part of Columbia in 1860.

[11] Cited in W. A. McVickar, *Life*, pp. 42, 191. Clowes was a B. A., Columbia, 1808.

but also willing to accept a good deal of responsibility for the community's guidance. He felt that drunkenness was the cause of whatever wretchedness existed among the lower classes in this prosperous country. In an address, which has what seem now to be rather curious economic implications, before the Christian Association of Dutchess County, in 1815, he declared that in America:

> wretchedness is but the shadow of vice. The demand for labor is so great and the wages of it so high that the means of comfortable subsistance are never wanting to the industrious and the sober. The money spent for spirits needlessly drunk in this neighborhood would support its poor twice over. It is the heaviest tax we pay, and costs the country more than all its other taxes besides. It cuts off its industry, weakens its strength, debases its morals, corrupts its principles and, in the loss of virtue, paves the way for loss of liberty.[12]

In this speech McVickar uses the kind of argument which, growing through the century, provided the rationale for the prohibition movement. It was moral indignation of this sort, and a conviction, spreading out from church circles, which finally became irresistible. It is easy enough to point out now that expenditure for consumption is not generally called a tax, and to say that it is a specious argument which presupposes the alternatives all to be, in an economic sense, better; but this is to overlook the goals sought. There is sufficient evidence of widespread habitual drunkenness and of the intemperate use of spirits in early America. It is not difficult to forgive an early economist—who considered himself first of all a teacher of morals—for a certain overemphasis in the cause of moderation. It is a little more difficult to overlook his opening dictum that "wretchedness is but the shadow of vice." McVickar was not unique in this. He simply, as in so many other instances, made over into characteristically forceful statement what was one of the prevalent doctrines of his time.

[12] W. A. McVickar, *Life*, p. 38.

The life of a practising minister was not altogether pleasant for McVickar; his sense of duty frequently ran beyond his strength. Then, too, his salary was only $250 a year, and his position required a standard of living rather higher than this allowed. At first he had been receiving an additional allowance from the Trinity Corporation, but in 1815 the corporation informed the country ministers that "the enhanced prices of the necessaries and comforts of life, and the depreciation of money" made it necessary to increase the salaries of their own clergy, thus leaving nothing for the outside parishes.[13] Consequently, although his parish was a rural one, the demands of a growing family with aristocratic connections made his situation one to which considerable worry attached.

Fortunately for the future economist and theologian, an appropriate vacancy occurred in his alma mater. Bowden died in 1817, and the chair of moral philosophy, rhetoric, and belles-lettres was open. Six candidates sought the post, with the consequence that there was very active soliciting of the trustees by the friends of various candidates. McVickar's father-in-law was an influential figure in the college, and thanks to him, McVickar, on November 3, 1817, was declared elected after a second ballot. On the first ballot he had received the highest number of votes, but not a majority.[14]

With a salary of $2,500 and a residence with a rental value of $500 McVickar now began a career which occupied forty-seven years of active service during which he was twice acting president. When he began his teaching the faculty was composed of the president, three professors, and one adjunct professor. The student body numbered one hundred, an increase of thirty over the previous year. So numerous were the subjects taught by McVickar that in some of his writings he gave his title as "Professor of Moral Philosophy, etc." [15] He

[13] *Ibid.*, p. 31. [14] *Ibid.*, pp. 48–49.

[15] See, for instance, his *Address on the Death of William Moore De Rham* (New York: Protestant Episcopal Press, 1834).

varied his designation from book to book. In the life of his father-in-law, *A Domestic Narrative of the Life of Samuel Bard* (1822), he called himself "Professor of Moral Philosophy and Rhetoric"; in his *Outlines of Political Economy* (1828) and in the *Introductory Lecture to a Course of Political Economy* (1830), he styled himself "Professor of Moral Philosophy and Political Economy"; in his edition of Samuel Taylor Coleridge's *Aids to Reflection* (1839) and his *Alumni Anniversary* address in 1837, he adopted the simplification, "Professor of Moral Philosophy"; in his *First Lessons in Political Economy for the Use of Primary and Common Schools* (1835), he again called himself "Professor of Political Economy"; in his *Early Life and Professional Years of Bishop Hobart* (1838), he used the more resounding title, "Professor of Moral and Intellectual Philosophy and Political Economy."

All of this variation is to be understood as part of the early educational scheme. McVickar's duties, like those of others, were actually spread over all these fields—as we know from notes taken in his lectures. There is a summary also in the report of the president written in January, 1818:

> With the Professor of Moral Philosophy & Belles Lettres, the Freshman class studies English Grammar explained on the Principles of Universal Grammar, and illustrated by a comparison with the Grammar of other languages, especially of the classical tongues.
>
> With the same Prof[essor], the Sophomore Class, for the first session, studies a course of Ancient History and Chronology, and is instructed in the Data on which Ancient chronology is founded. In the 2d. session the Class studies a course of modern History with leading views of the rise and progress of Art, Arms, & Commerce, in the different Quarters of the world.
>
> . . .
>
> With the same Prof[essor], the Junior Class studies Belles Letters & Rhetoric. 1st, Considered as a Science; its history and state among the classic Nations of Antiquity and the most distinguished among the Moderns. 2dly, Considered as an Art, The practical

Rules of good writing illustrated by examples, and applied in the critical examination of the best writers.

. . .

The Senior Class, for the first session, studies a course of Moral Philosophy, History of the Science and comparison of the most celebrated systems both antient and modern. Application of the science to the various duties of life.

2d session—Analysis of the Intellectual Powers.

The Principles of the Law of Nature & Nations.

The Principles of Political Economy.

The Principles of Logic & Moral reasoning.[16]

Since the second term had not arrived at the time the report was submitted it is difficult to say whether economics was actually taught in this year. However, in the revised statutes, which were adopted by the trustees on March 24, 1821, it was provided that the course in the senior year should include "History of Philosophy—Intellectual and Moral Philosophy, and Political Economy," and in the 1826 catalogue the subject was mentioned in his title—"Professor of Intellectual Philosophy, Rhetoric, Belles Lettres and Political Economy." It seems clear enough that Columbia was among the earliest colleges in the country to direct that "Political Economy" be taught; and this is perhaps all historians are justified in claiming.

The years 1828–30 were interesting and decisive ones in McVickar's life. He had now been teaching at Columbia for ten years and was just over forty years old, the most active and prominent person connected with the college. The venerable President Harris was beset with a long illness which

[16] Columbia University, Minutes of the Trustees, February 2, 1818.

McVickar's offering seems to have been suggested by his father-in-law. In 1817 Dr. Bard wrote him, "Your belles lettres course I think shd be that you begin with, because that will be the most popular, but never give up the moral philosophy, for there you will do most good; and I still think that the general plan I ventured to speak out to you for that course has its peculiar advantages as it will lay the foundation of a religious as well as a moral Education." (J. Brett Langstaff, *Doctor Bard of Hyde Park* [New York: Dutton, 1942], p. 270.)

proved to be fatal. McVickar's leadership was acknowledged by his appointment as acting president; and when in October, 1829, the president died, naturally McVickar was prominent among the candidates to succeed him. He was not, however, elected; he lost by one vote. What seems to account for this reversal is something in his personality which repelled rather than attracted popular approval, an excessive correctness and frigidity, a certain removal from human sympathy. His son explains the matter in a significant passage:

> His devotion to the interests of the college, his high standard of excellence in all that pertained to university education, and his acknowledged ability, all pointed him out as one peculiarly fitted for the post. But his decision of character, firm administration of discipline, and, above all, his earnest Churchmanship, created a strong counter-influence out of those elements which, both among the undergraduates and trustees, would be found naturally antagonistic to such characteristics. We find evidence of this coalition of opposing influences, even before President Harris' death, in a paper presented to the board of trustees on the morning of Commencement Day, in the name of certain members of the graduating class, remonstrating against Professor McVickar's appointment to confer degrees on that occasion. It failed of its object, and though its influence was greatly lessened when among its prompters were found at least one offended father, himself a trustee, and his lately disciplined son, still it was not without its effect in giving color and form to an opposition which was the more unreasonable from the fact that it was doctrinal rather than personal.[17]

In spite of his son's statement that these differences were doctrinal, they seem in fact to have been highly personal, and they sufficed to defeat him for the presidency. It is sometimes difficult to draw the line; but much of McVickar's meticulous doctrinal soundness seems to have come from an insistence, in all his relationships, on a similar literal correctness. In church and college alike he was quick to scent the odor of change, and

[17] W. A. McVickar, *Life*, pp. 101–2.

to rebuke sharp departure from established precept. He had a penchant for being right, because he was a wide and persistent student; but this very rightness explains, doubtless, the existence of a certain jealousy among the less endowed, and even, perhaps, a certain distrust of a too insistent literalness.

It is easy to understand the keen disappointment which ensued upon failure to attain what must have become the central ambition of his life. He did, indeed, fall into deep despair. He had worked incredibly hard, had lived without blemish, was held in universal esteem for his qualities; and yet the obvious reward was withheld and the post he coveted most was given to a person whose academic qualifications were inferior to his own.

It was in these circumstances that he petitioned the trustees for leave and, when it was granted, set off with his family for a second visit to Europe which took him, in the interesting year of 1830, to England, Scotland, the Low Countries, Switzerland, and France. By far the most interesting—and revealing—literary remains of McVickar consist of letters written home during his journey.[18] He must have carried a notable collection of introductory letters, for he visited numerous prominent people and was entertained with uniform hospitality; when it came to traveling on the continent he was even loaned a nobleman's barouche. Among the famous writers to whom he paid visits were Wordsworth, Southey, and Scott. He left New York much worn and in apparent ill-health, but after six months of constant travel, under the usual difficult conditions, and with the added discomfort of getting about in a year of revolutions, and even with a stormy fifty-eight day

[18] McVickar in January had been successful in having the duties of the rhetorical professorship transferred to the president (Minutes of the Trustees, January 16, 1830), but President William Alexander Duer began complaining in March that this arrangement was in ill keeping with his presidential duties and was the outcome of a misunderstanding. (Minutes of the Trustees, March 3, 1830.) McVickar took leave in April. These circumstances may point to some irritations within the faculty which were perhaps as wearing as actual hard work.

passage home, he arrived reconstructed and fit for further decades of wearying labor. All this creates an impression that his illness on leaving was a sickness of the spirit consequent on his great dissappointment rather than an actual physical breakdown. In fact, he seems to have had an extraordinarily tough constitution, and he lived through all the vicissitudes of nineteenth centry New York life to a really ripe old age. He did not die until the Civil War was over and Reconstruction, with all its troubles, was well under way.

What other fruits, besides health, there were from his European adventure it is difficult to say; but there is ample evidence of renewal of faith in his particular attitudes. Among churchmen and academic folk he found similar tastes and beliefs, and he found them more commonly accepted. He records, also, having visited the economist James Mill at India House, and he met John Ramsey McCulloch, the other outstanding disciple of David Ricardo, who so convincingly advocated free trade.[19]

[19] It is interesting that in his manuscript diary, McVickar referred to Mill as "the writer on India, etc.," and not as the economist. He strongly disapproved of the demands of Mill and his fellow Benthamites or "philosophic radicals," including Ricardo and McCulloch, for political reforms and disestablishment of the Church of England. But he had a high opinion of Mill's *Elements of Political Economy* (1821), an opinion shared by American Ricardians in general. Vice-president Philip Lindsley of the College of New Jersey (now Princeton), in a letter to McVickar on December 19, 1822, expressed the hope that an American edition would be forthcoming as a substitute for J. B. Say's *Treatise on Political Economy*. "The work of Mill is almost too concise, dry and abstract; still it may serve as a very convenient syllabus of the lectures to furnish the pupil with such outlines & principles as will enable him to listen with profit to the remarks of his teacher & to extend his researches, as future opportunity may permit." (For the diary entries and the Lindsley letter the authors are indebted to the Reverend W. Brett Langstaff of Morristown, N. J.)

While in England, McVickar described the organ of the philosophical radicals, *The Westminster Review*, as "Jacobinical," and he thought that the Whig organ, *The Edinburgh Review*, had fallen very low. He admired the Tory *Quarterly Review*, which was edited by Scott's son in law, J. Gibson Lockhart. He wrote in his diary an incident illustrative of its sturdy independence:

"In the last number [October, 1930] the [review] article on [Charles] Babbage [*Reflections on the Decline of Science in England*] was shown at the [Privy] Council to [the prime minister] the Duke [of Wellington] on

He also visited the eminent Scottish Presbyterian and economist, Thomas Chalmers. Perhaps he was most excited by his visit to Scott's home at Abbotsford. Scott was then a kind of patriarch, full of years and honors, and McVickar was deeply impressed with the great man's affability. He was deeply impressed, too, by that strange and hardly orthodox Tory Samuel Taylor Coleridge, whom he described as that blend of "a poet by nature and a scholar by education—with a vein of piety from early instruction—yet in some sense an infidel by long habit of presumptuous reasoning—an Oxford student and a German mystic." [20]

As a professor, McVickar lectured for many years on belles-lettres and it must have been a rare experience for a provincial academic man to visit, in middle life, and to be entertained *en famille* for considerable periods, at the homes of these men of reputation. McVickar's view of literature was so restricted that he could whole-heartedly admire most of these nineteenth-century figures. Scott died two years after McVickar's journey, and we have a forty-two page oration on him delivered at the Merchants Exchange by McVickar at the request of New York's leading citizens. It shows, as do notes from

---

the day before publication. He found fault with it and sent for [John Wilson] Croker [Tory politician and literary critic], who threw the responsibility on [John] Murray [the publisher]. Murray was sent for and threw it on Lockhart, but Lockhart when applied to, refused to alter." (Cited in W. A. McVickar, *Life*, p. 230.)

[20] [John] M[cVickar], "Visit to the Residence of Mr. Coleridge," *The Churchman*, April 7, 1832, p. 218. McVickar later became a staunch advocate of Coleridge and also of John Ruskin.

His former student George Templeton Strong, a trustee of Columbia, recorded in his diary on March 10, 1855: "Discoursed with the Rev. Dr. McVickar, who is strong on Ruskin. He talks to his classes about Ruskin; and does not hesitate to tell them that in the combination of aesthetic and spiritual perception and so on, Ruskin is the greatest man since Plato." (*The Diary of George Templeton Strong*, ed. Allan Nevins and Milton Halsey Thomas, 4 vols. [New York: Macmillan, 1952], II, 259.)

Strong thought that Ruskin's works would on the whole "exert vast influence for good. . . . His keen knife seems to dissect and lay bare the internal ulcers, tubercles and 'fatty degenerations' that make our life in the nineteenth century sick and sorrowful. But we want a physician, not an anatomist." (*Ibid.*, p. 258.)

his literature course in 1841, that the clergyman was always uppermost. Scott was approved not only because he gave pleasure but also because he could always be trusted to find moral lessons in his materials. One or two amusing passages from the classroom notes of Parmly betray the same standards. Speaking of English literature, in general, as compared with the literatures of the continent, the notes say:

> Most moral. Beyond any other Literature either ancient or modern. That which is not pure in English Literature is like a blot on the fair page. Compared with Continental Literature. The greatest names on the continent are the most impure. In English Literature it is the reverse. In England that extreme license marks youth. On the continent it marks age. The same poets that indulge in freedom in youth write with purity as they advance.

It is almost possible to see the clerical lecturer hesitate at this point as exceptions occur to him. Still he returns to his thesis with determination. Anglo-Saxon ideals must be churchly ones; bawdy old Hogarthian England must be concealed. So he goes on in this fashion: "Byron is almost the only exception to this, and he had lived so much in the South of Europe that he had almost ceased to be an Englishman. He was more of an Italian."

There was little hope that the undergraduates of 1840 would fail to discover Byron, but so far as possible their professor would prepare them to explain him away. Later on, as the lectures develop detail and reach further back there are other difficulties. For instance, there is the Restoration, when Buckingham and Rochester must be mentioned, even though Milton, Isaac Barrow, and Jeremy Taylor can be made to overshadow them. Still, it could not be denied that a "low tone" prevailed; and McVickar accounted for it thus:

> 1. In French Influence. The King and Courtiers were most of them educated in France.
> 2. In the natural reaction from the strictest Puritanical Princi-

ples to Immorality. Move a Pendulum from its ordinary place on one side and it will return just as far to the other.

3. In the Influence of a material and base philosophy. Hobbes . . . was the Great Apostle of it. Charles protected him and gave him a pension of £100 a year. Hobbes distinguished for great acuteness, confidence in common sense, and a disposition to under-rate the opinions of others. The causes of the Low Tone were also the causes of the High Tone for Clarendon, Cudworth and others came out against Hobbes. Cudworth shows by *Reductio ad Absurdum* that Right and Wrong cannot proceed from Man, which was one of Hobbes' doctrines.

McVickar was first of all a churchman. It was the church which had all his best efforts, and what teaching he did was less in the interest of expanding knowledge than in that of conveying moral precepts and raising up good young men. As a professor, he was still vicar. This was true, in only a slightly different way, with his economics. As an economist he was interested in public morality and sound social practice; and his conception of the way to achieve these ends was by the inculcation of received truths. One cannot hope to understand McVickar's economics without keeping in mind his consistent theological interest. In these respects he departed very little from the prevailing tradition. Teachers of economics, as in other subjects, in those days, as for long afterward, were almost invariably of the cloth. Theology in one form or another was their pervading interest, and economics quite naturally was made to conform to their dogma. There was something almost revealed in their statement of it, or, if not quite revealed, at least axiomatic. But it was an academic discipline also, and so it needed the simple kind of expression youths could understand. If the exposition was sound and simple, the world had a good chance to be bettered through the putting into effect of teachers' maxims. There was therefore a moral and even a religious consequence from the teaching of the subject. McVickar declared that the "German Universities" are "not examples for us" for "they are mere seats of learning." Investigation was not enough. Moral truths ought to be imparted, and for McVickar the study of "revealed religion" was primary and it colors all his work. He said in 1830, "my most agreeable course . . . is the course of Evidences."[21] One of the things he said in this course, at least in the year 1841, according to a student's notebook, was: "The Mosaic account was peculiar in that it taught that *Light* existed before the sun or moon or stars were created. Now in the nineteenth century, that which has always seemed before an absurdity, is explained by the Nebular Theory." Then he asked, "Who taught Moses what phlosophers have never learned until now?" From such "facts" as these he gave as his "conclusion: That there is higher wisdom in Christianity than man can teach."[22] So fundamental did he make "revealed religion" that he insisted in the preface to his edition of Coleridge's *Aids to Reflection* (1839) that Coleridge's philosophy could only be understood in the light of the Anglican faith; whereas Coleridge, as well as Professor James Marsh of Vermont, who had prepared the first American edition of the book, felt that philosophy was needed to explain the faith.[23]

McVickar was always deeply interested in founding a chair of theology. Even as early as 1820 he prepared a "Plan of Theological Professorship to be attached to Columbia and other colleges." In 1837 he pleaded with the alumni to estab-

[21] W. A. McVickar, *Life*, pp. 240, 342.

[22] From the notebook of W. H. Parmly, in "Evidences of Christianity," 1842.

[23] *Aids to Reflection, by Samuel Taylor Coleridge, with the author's last corrections . . . to which is prefixed, a preliminary essay, by John McVickar, D.D., Professor of Moral Philosophy in Columbia College, New York* (New York: Swords, Sanford, & Co., 1839).

McVickar became involved in some difficulties with the friends of Professor Marsh, who complained that the title pages and advertisement of the McVickar edition gave the misleading impression that this edition was also published in London and had the sanction of Henry Nelson Coleridge. (*The New York Review*, VI [April, 1840], 477–79.) See also R. V. Wells, *Three Christian Transcendentalists* (New York: Columbia Univ. Press, 1943), pp. 156–58.

lish an appropriate chair of "evidences of religion." He said, "Let us . . . no longer leave our educated sons to grow up, rich in science, but beggars in better knowledge. Let us, at least, lay the foundation of Christian truth in their minds, by their being well instructed in the evidences of natural and revealed religion." The college had already made this subject a part of the senior course, "but being thrown on an already overloaded professorship, it is evident that it cannot receive the time and attention it deserves." He closed his address with a peroration worthy of his time:

> To place Columbia College on this high, as well as holy ground, by an adequate endowment for religious instruction, and thereby to make it one of the guardians of that living temple which is the true palladium of our national liberties—this, gentlemen alumni, were a worthy and a noble deed, coming from any hands; but from yours—from those of her sons—those who in youth have drawn from her breasts the nourishment of life, this were a boon such as grateful children can alone bestow and a grateful mother alone can estimate.[24]

McVickar, throughout his whole career, was active in religious affairs. He often preached in the local churches as well as in the college chapel. In 1835 he issued, anonymously, *Devotions for the Family and the Closet, from the Manual of a Country Clergyman*, which had been begun while he was in his first pastorate. He took a leading role in the meetings and conventions of his faith. In view of his reputation as an economist, all societies "having funds seemed glad to have him as a trustee," and he was consequently a leading figure in ten important religious organizations.[25] In 1862 he was elected president of the Standing Committee of the Diocese of New York. On several occasions his name was suggested as bishop. For twenty-six years he was superintendent of the Society for Promoting Religion and Learning, and for forty-five years he

[24] John McVickar, *Alumni Anniversary*, pp. 28, 40.
[25] W. A. McVickar, *Life*, pp. 247–48.

was a trustee of the General Theological Seminary. In 1850 he became president of the New York Ecclesiological Society which was an Episcopal organization for the improvement of church architecture.

He also helped to lay the foundations for the permanent chaplaincy at Columbia. In the interval between the resignation of President Nathaniel Fish Moore and the election of Charles King in 1849, McVickar, while acting president, introduced "a short responsive service." He later wrote, "Although Mr. King does not conform to it, I shall use it whenever called on, and thus, not improbably, lay the foundation for the chaplaincy."[26] McVickar also took a leading role in the establishment of St. Stephen's College at Annandale on the Hudson (now Bard College), as a training school for the Episcopal ministry; and he presented the case for a training school in the annual reports to the convention of the diocese, as the superintendent of the Society for Promoting Religion and Learning in the State of New York. At the convention of 1856 he pleaded for a "Church Institution or training school, in which, as a nursery for the Ministry, the destitute sons of our poorer Clergy might find a Home under Church influences, as well as the sons of zealous laymen—a Church School, leading to the Ministry, adequately endowed, Episcopally governed and annually reporting to the Convention, its condition and its progress."[27] He repeated the plea at the conventions of 1857 and 1858. Finally, in 1859, McVickar's efforts bore fruit. He obtained an endowment and a charter.

It was McVickar's ideal of a college:

The period of peril is that of college life. To preserve that pure is the great problem of education. Corruption of morals, perversion of principles, seeds of infidelity begin in those years, and this

[26] *Ibid.*, p. 341.
[27] *Journal of the Proceedings of the Seventy-third Convention of the Protestant Episcopal Church in the Diocese of New York, . . . 1856* (New York: Dana, 1856), p. 38.

more especially in our land, where collegiate teaching and Christian training are so rarely or fully united. To supply that want for those intended for the sacred ministry of our Church, to fill the vacuity that intervenes between youth and manhood, safely as well as wisely, to sanctify classical studies, to Christianize physical science, and make Christian faith the golden thread that runs through all studies and sanctifies all attainments—this is the single yet all important end which "Training Schools" seek to gain and the one before us professes to give—the precursor, as we trust, of many more in our church and in our land—the honor of the age in which they arise, and the source of increasing blessings, under God, to all that come after them.[28]

McVickar became chairman of the Committee of Trustees. He remained a trustee and warm advocate of the interests of St. Stephen's up to the time of his death. By his will, he left the school three thousand dollars and a portion of his library.

In 1844 McVickar became chaplain of the army post at Fort Columbus in New York Harbor. Here he built a small chapel [29] to which he became so attached that, in 1849, when the presidency of Columbia fell vacant, he declined to be a candidate because "it would have . . . cut me off from my little church." [30] At first objections were raised of the meetings of

[28] *Journal of the Proceedings of the Seventy-sixth Convention, . . . 1859*, p. 56.

[29] "The Chapel of St. Cornelius owes its existence to the zeal and liberality of the Rev. John McVickar, D.D. . . . At first, services were held in one of the larger rooms at headquarters. The exigencies of public service sometimes interfered with this arrangement. . . . Dr. McVickar, therefore, in the early part of his Chaplaincy, determined to erect a suitable Chapel, provided any agreement could be made with the Government, by which it should be held for religious uses only. He was happily aided in his efforts by Gen. Scott, and a personal lease for a plot of ground in the southern part of the island having been procured, he had the satisfaction of completing, A.D. 1846, a very neat and tasteful building, expressive as he says of humility and reverence. The funds were either given or collected by Dr. McVickar himself. In consequence of an order from the War Department requiring Chaplains to reside at their posts, which seriously interfered with his other duties, Dr. McVickar resigned the Chaplaincy in the fall of 1862." (*Year Book and Register of the Parish of Trinity Church, 1880*, pp. 48–49.)

[30] W. A. McVickar, *Life*, p. 338.

the Board of Trustees to McVickar's holding this post concurrently with his professorship. According to the statutes of 1821, "The officers of the college who have the charge of its course of instruction and discipline, shall not be engaged in any professional pursuits from which they derive emolument and which are not connected with the college." But McVickar declared that he would resign his professorship rather than the chaplaincy "with its hard work among the soldiers and its seven hundred dollars a year salary." [31]

So deeply did McVickar believe in the efficacy of an avowal of faith that during the Mexican War even regiments made up of adventurers were the recipients of his earnest attentions. There was a regiment camped at the government post which was known as the California Regiment of Colonel Stevenson. Although "he knew they were mostly adventurers," McVickar persuaded them "to elect a chaplain, determine on daily prayers on shipboard and take the nominal position of a God-fearing body." Every member received a Bible and every one who desired it a prayer book. Before they departed he exhorted them in a speech which was "earnest and powerful throughout, and in part . . . rises to eloquence:" [32]

Even while I thus speak do I see her, the venerable Genius of our Anglo-Saxon land, the common mother of us all. I see her rise up from this her watery throne, where she sits embosomed amid the peaceful fleets of an unbounded commerce, to bid you, her armed sons, farewell. I see her followed in dim procession by a long train of patriots, and heroes and Christian men. Men who not only here but in older lands have toiled and fought and bled, not for conquest, but for right; not for license, but for law, and that they might build up for posterity that which we here enjoy, a fair and (I trust) an enduring fabric of constitutional freedom. . . . I see her form, I hear her words, and mine, believe me, are their faithful echo.

"Go forth," she says, "my well armed sons—the sword in your

[31] *Ibid.*, p. 309. [32] *Ibid.*, p. 316.

hands, but peace in your hearts and justice in your deeds. Go forth as Apostles from this, my favored land, to teach and to bless those to which you go. Remember that you bear a widely honored name. It has ever been a lineage of faith and virtue, of courage and gentleness, of peace, of order and of religion. Such has it been in the old world, and in the heroic times of the new. Let not its fair fame be tarnished or its Institutions defamed by unfilial hands, or unworthy tongues. As you bear your country's ensign, so, remember, do you, your Country's honor. Let not the name of American Citizen ever receive a blot through you. Let it not be said, that with Americans, might was the measure of right, or that gold outweighed justice, or that the soldier's sword made heavy the scale of a vanquished enemy's ransom. Rather let that name be known as one of blessing wherever it is heard even as that of a Teacher appointed of Heaven to instruct the nations of the earth—to exhibit to the world the living proof how Liberty may dwell united with law, how individual freedom may stand linked together with Public order, and Christian faith in the nation walk hand in hand with an unfettered private conscience. . . ." [33]

And he proffered the scriptures as a guide in the creation of social institutions in the west:

And that you may perform well all your parts, whether as soldiers or Colonists, as Citizens, or as private men, go forth as CHRISTIANS, and take the Blessed Book I now proffer to you, the gift of your Christian Country as the sum and substance of her farewell. Take it as the best Charter you can draft of your public liberties; the surest safeguard you can have of private virtue and the only enduring basis on which your Social Institutions can grow up. Believe me—believe the voice of history, that Society without Religion is a rope of sand, and government without the fear of God is but tyranny under the name of law.

McVickar's textbooks and his articles on economics had perhaps less of this eloquence, but still are plainly by the same hand as the oration to the departing soldiers. The *Outlines of Political Economy* was actually, as an inside page

[33] *Rev. Dr. McVickar's Address to the California Regiment* (New York: privately printed, 1846), pp. 6–8.

OUTLINES

OF

POLITICAL ECONOMY:

BEING

A REPUBLICATION OF THE ARTICLE UPON THAT SUBJECT CONTAINED IN THE EDINBURGH SUPPLEMENT TO THE ENCYCLOPEDIA BRITANNICA.

TOGETHER WITH

Notes Explanatory and Critical,

AND

A SUMMARY OF THE SCIENCE.

BY REV. JOHN M'VICKAR, A. M.

PROFESSOR OF MORAL PHILOSOPHY AND POLITICAL ECONOMY IN COLUMBIA COLLEGE, NEW-YORK.

New-York

WILDER & CAMPBELL, BROADWAY.

1825.

TITLE PAGE FROM COPY IN COLUMBIANA COLLECTION, COLUMBIA UNIVERSITY

The young man being disciplined in the student's drawing of a classroom scene is Robert LeRoy, of the Class of 1841.

states, the famous article of McCulloch in the *Encyclopaedia Britannica*—with acute and extensive notes by McVickar. The volume was praised by such statesmen as ex-President Thomas Jefferson, who wrote: "I thank you, sir, for the treatise of McCulloch, and your much approved republication of it." [34]

It would not be altogether inaccurate to say that the "notes" were written between prayers, but even the writing of these could consume time. He wrote his daughter in 1825:

> Since my return I have resumed my Notes on Political Economy, perhaps for the press. To these I devote all my leisure time after college duties are over and domestic arrangements attended to. Till nine A.M. is fully occupied, after prayers, with breakfast and a short chat around a warm fire and a long walk to a cold market. From nine to half-past twelve, college lectures which fatigue me sufficiently to send me out of my lecture room for half an hour. . . . Thus strengthened . . . I return to my room, whence I am called to dinner, and generally again after dinner till summoned to tea. After that hour "*vive la bagatelle*," down with the Political Economy,—up with family amusement; at half after nine Aunt S. and I wind up the pleasures of the evening with one or two hits at backgammon . . . and the day closes with prayers, which arise from, I think, not unthankful hearts.[35]

There was in McVickar, in spite of his aristocratic bearing, a becoming humility toward his God. There is something less Episcopalian than Scottish in his submission to reverses. They must, he felt, be a part of a plan, and somehow intended for

[34] W. A. McVickar, *Life*, p. 86.

Jefferson, it should be noted, like his political opponent, ex-chancellor James Kent, was skeptical of the "Ricardian" doctrine of rent which McVickar accepted. This doctrine as interpreted by McVickar traced rent to the diminishing productiveness of the soils successively brought into cultivation with the increase of population and capital—in other words, to the need to resort to soils of inferior quality; but it would not exist where only the best soils were cultivated. Kent, who admired McVickar and the *Outlines*, wrote in his copy (now in the Columbia University Libraries) that McVickar's exposition of the doctrine was "the most dry, dull, obscure and uninteresting portion" of the book.

[35] *Ibid.*, pp. 82–83.

his benefit. When he lost the election for college president by one vote, he "considered it a dispensation of Providence for good." [36] Whenever his investments failed, he attributed it to a punishment for wrongdoing. The son wrote of his father that he was "remarkably practical"; but his business ventures seldom prospered. At the time of its laying out, he purchased the whole north side of Union Square. But taxes and assessments forced a premature sale. The difficulties over this transaction and some speculative losses in the west caused him to write, at the closing of his account book in 1845:

> I am glad to be able to close my eyes, not, I trust, my penitential thoughts, on this long arrear of worldliness and grasping desire of wealth, by transferring to a new book the few accounts that yet remain unsettled. The most of them, after tantalizing for a while with a restless show of profit, terminated in disappointment and some in law suits. All the sorrows of my life from all other causes have not, I think, equaled those from this single source, namely, the speculative purchases into which I was led by persuasion, or perhaps self-prompted, in the years 1835, 1836 and 1837; as I verily believe they have brought upon me deeper guilt than any or all other temptations united. God be thanked that I have survived the shock, the trial and the disgrace, and that a remnant of days is yet spared me, with an humbler mind and higher hopes, and that God has at length called me to a spiritual charge wherein I may show the sincerity of my faith and repentance. Through Christ may that call be blessed to me and those to whom I minister. Amen. So be it.[37]

This was strictly in accordance with his economic and moral principles, for "the will of that wise and good Providence . . . makes virtue our wise choice even in a world of evil." [38] It was a very simple matter. In the light of this theological or moral attitude, McVickar's economics and philosophy are to be understood.

[36] W. A. McVickar, *Life*, p. 111. [37] *Ibid.*, pp. 312–13.

[38] John McVickar, *Introductory Lecture to a Course of Political Economy; Recently Delivered at Columbia College, New York* (London: John Miller, 1830), p. 9. The lecture was originally published in the American free trade organ, *Banner of the Constitution*, in 1830.

To McVickar and to his generation economics was a branch of moral philosophy; and what distinguished moral philosophy from physical science was that the one was "an inquiry into what is," while the other was an inquiry "into what ought to be." [39] Moral philosophy was divided into three branches:

1. Intellectual philosophy or that which elevates man in the scale of reason.

2. Ethical philosophy or the sense of duty.

3. Political or economical philosophy which regards man as a social being.[40]

Thus political economy was the study of proper conduct in economic affairs, "analytically pursued with large reference to authorities." Appropriately enough, the lectures in this subject were allocated to the last two months of the senior year, following intellectual and moral philosophy. The aim of this "moral and intellectual course is training to settle in the mind great principles of truth, and to train the mind to their quick perception and their satisfactory defense." [41] This had a theological reference. It was necessary to understand what the laws of economics required to be done; conforming with them would be rewarded as virtue always is; and punishment would follow violation. Adam Smith had settled the difficulties arising from questions of economic statesmanship, by removing them with qualifications from the social to the individual field where self-interest furnished guidance. Statesmanship consisted largely in arranging for the free functioning of self-directed individuals. In all this McVickar, following McCulloch, concurred; and his teaching of economics was directed to revelation of these truths for the benefit of the rising generations.

This is the way McVickar discussed controversial economic questions, as reported by a student in his notebook:

[39] Notebook of W. H. Parmly in "Moral Science," 1842.
[40] Notebook of Parmly in "Intellectual Philosophy," 1841.
[41] W. A. McVickar, *Life*, p. 344.

Nature of Rent

Smith: It has been maintained by Smith that "Rent is the payment demanded by the Landlord, in return for his Monopoly Right."

Ricardo: On the other hand, Ricardo maintains that "Rent grows up with, and arises from the Wants of Society."

Decision: Ricardo is without doubt Right.

The Relation Between Capital and Labor.

Smith: "Capital and Labor are distinct and opposed in their Nature and Laws."

Ricardo: "Capital is only Reserved or Dead Labor."

Decision: The Analysis of Ricardo is Correct. Capital is only Reserved Labor.

In a further discussion of this question, McVickar stated that the elements entering into the price of grain were wages, average profit (including interest) of capital employed, and the rent of land. After noting that the rent did not appear as distinctly in the United States as in England, he pointed out that according to Adam Smith the price must include all these elements, whereas Ricardo and his followers held that rent had nothing to do with the price. If the landowners in England gave up their "monopoly right," there would still be no difference in the price. "Decision: The Latter [Ricardians] are unquestionably Right."

On interest, McVickar had this to say: "Interest in every instance has its own elements of risk, uncertainty and trouble. . . . Interest is regulated by what can be made with the money, i.e. by profits."

McVickar's discussion of "gluts" as it appears in Parmly's notebook of 1842, shows some confusion which may be due to the reporter, but it does indicate a certain uneasiness with the accepted Ricardian doctrine.

Nature and Origin of a glut in Market.

The fact is clearly seen that whenever the price of an article falls below its Remuneratory Value there is a Glut.

The Cause of Glut

Smith says there is too much made or raised of it, and this appears conclusive. Here again Ricardo says Smith has looked only on one side. The Demand of Society is unbounded for everything. The Cause of Glut is only a misdirected production [and] not too much [production]. If therefore all productions are advanced equally there would be no glut.

Decision: The Latter speak true, but the Truth is metaphysical or more than practical.

On wealth and value, McVickar was reported in students' notebooks as holding that "the essence of wealth is utility," that "utility is the measure of the increase of wealth," that the "criterion is exchangeable value, the sources [are] labor, both mental and manual; the material [is] the elemental powers of nature." Parmly recorded in 1842:

Value

Scarcely any two writers agree in defining this.

Three meanings may be given:

1. Value in Use or Rational Value
2. Value in Cost or Real Value
3. Value in Price, or Market Value in Exchange

All authors agree that [the] first or Rational Value had nothing to do with Science. Of the Second and Third there are various opinions, but properly speaking the Third or Exchange Value, is the proper meaning in Political Economy.[42]

McVickar showed a certain acuteness in his discussion of what he called "appropriated or immaterial wealth," which was ignored by the main British classical tradition. Appropriated capital consisted in mental requirements, such as knowledge and skill. It was appropriated in that it could never be transferred. The question was, how could its value or price be determined?

[42] McVickar was aware of developments of mathematical economics at least as early as 1834. Then, while discussing in class the limit to the division of labor, he said:

"1. Limit of capital—poor countries do not subdivide.

2. Limit of market—or demand must equal supply. All these analyses involve high[er] math[ematics]—quest[ions] of max[ima] & min[ima]." (Notebook of James W. Beekman, 1834, in New-York Historical Society collection.)

The natural price [cost of production] is determined by the time and money spent in acquiring that learning and in cultivating those talents, and the support necessary until they become a source of profit; their market price [exchangeable value] is that which will purchase an annuity equal to the salary received from the application of that learning, skill or talent, subtracting the loss that would arise from sickness, etc. The inhabitants of a country then form a part of the capital in proportion to their physical powers, manual skill and mental acquirements, not in proportion to their numbers. It is this portion of capital and thus estimated [that] has elevated England above the rest of the countries of Europe, & Europe above Asia.[43]

McVickar thought that the Malthusian doctrine of population pressing closely on the means of subsistence was painfully relevant to England's situation, and he hailed its English advocates for urging as the only permanent cure for the increasing degradation of British labor, that the laborers refrain from "early and imprudent marriages"; Malthus's principle, however, could only be "theory and science" in the United States. Unless the rapidly increasing amount of pauperism in England was speedily checked, it threatened "to bear down by the mere instinctive impulse of hungry mouths, all the barriers of law, property and social order," but "of this our wide fertile, and therefore prosperous country" knew nothing.[44]

McVickar viewed with approval the spread of producers' voluntary cooperatives for the relief of the "labouring poor" in England, for they promised to "afford more relief to their starving population, than all legislation has hitherto effected," but "the easy condition of the labourer with us, renders such plans in general unnecessary." He enthusiastically urged the spread of savings banks. "To the economist, they present a double aspect; first on their influence on the poor; and secondly on the accumulation of capital. In this latter point of view, they have become in England, a great financial question, and even

[43] Notebook of Hamilton Fish, "Political Economy," 1827.
[44] [John] M[cVickar], review of Thomas Chalmers's *On Political Economy*, in *The Churchman*, Nov. 10, 1832, p. 242.

in some of our own cities, especially Boston, they are not without their influence."[45]

The connections between economics and religion were quite obvious in McVickar's mind. In his admonition to children, in *First Lessons in Political Economy*, he has this to say:

> I do not ask you of what use is the clergyman, for you know well that he teaches you the way of salvation. Without clergymen, therefore, to teach and explain the WORD of GOD, Christians would by degrees become as ignorant and wicked as the Heathen now are.
>
> . . .
>
> Nor would this be all: If there were no clergymen to preach to men their duty, men would be less honest and less diligent and less sober: there would be more thieving and idleness and drunkenness in a country; and if so, there would be less work done, and even that, less well done; there would be less food to eat, and clothes to wear and houses to live in.
>
> . . .
>
> Now if all this would be the case, as it plainly would, who, I would ask, are they that prevent this effect taking place? Whoever they are, they certainly are productive laborers. Now it is through the labors of Christian teachers that these evils are prevented. So that we conclude that the clergy are helpers to do the work of the country; and that some of it would not be done but for their teaching.
>
> . . .
>
> The greatest use of the Christian clergyman is that he teaches us how to be happy after this life, and to have true comfort when we come to die—when the riches of this world shall be of no more value to us than the dirt we now tread on. But this is something better than Political Economy.[46]

The principles of economics came close, it will be seen, to being "revealed" truths, just as were the religious truths of

[45] John McVickar, *Introductory Lecture to a Course of Political Economy*, pp. 26–28.

[46] *First Lessons in Political Economy* (Boston: Hillard, Gray, 1835), pp. 5–7. This was modeled on the immensely popular English work by Archbishop Richard Whately, *Easy Lessons on Money Matters; for the Use of Young People* (London: Parker, 1833).

which they were counterparts; they all followed from the fundamental principle of virtuous conduct. The clergyman and the economist had very similar expository duties. Once the truths of their discipline were thoroughly impressed upon plastic humanity, harmony would supervene. This world would become more like the next. As he put it in the *Outlines:*

> The high principles which this science teaches, entitle it to be regarded as the moral instructor of nations. To them that will give ear it demonstrates the necessary connections that subsist between national virtue, national interest and national happiness.
>
> It is to states what religion is to individuals, the "preacher of righteousness"—what religion reproves as wrong, Political Economy rejects as inexpedient—what religion condemns as contrary to duty and virtue, Political Economy proves to be equally opposed to the peace, good order and permanent prosperity of the community. Thus slave labour is exploded for its expensiveness—non-intercourse is condemned for its extravagance—privateering for its waste of wealth—and war for the injury sustained even by the victor; and thus freedom of person, friendly intercourse between nations, kindness even in hostilities and, if possible, universal peace, which are the highest blessings as well as the greatest virtues, are supported by the all powerful considerations of self-interest.
>
> This picture, however, presupposes virtue in the people. Political Economy is a science which guards against involuntary, not voluntary error. It enters into harmonious alliance with religion, but cannot supply its place. It must find public men true to their trust.

Political economy demonstrates that virtue is the best policy. In 1830 McVickar, appearing as what later would have been called an extension lecturer, set out for the New York public the merits of the moral science:

> Though it be but the science of wealth, yet does it shew *that* wealth to be the result of the moral and intellectual, as well as the physical powers of man. It demonstrates that to man, ignorant and vicious, there is no road of wealth. Allow that, in the language of this science, man is but a machine for the creation of value, yet still is that machine shewn to be perfect in proportion to skill,

knowledge, temperance, industry and the whole train of personal virtues. Destitute of these, man is a machine out of order—irregular in its movements, performing but one half of its rightful task, and perhaps, as may be said of the idle and vicious, not paying the cost of keeping in motion. . . . National prosperity at all times may be said to find its roots in wisdom, science, and virtue. And is not all history a proof of this?

There had been those who had objected that the pursuit of wealth, which was admittedly the guiding principle of the science, could not be called a virtue. But McVickar earnestly defended its moral character:

Its *pursuit*, in a national point of view, is decidedly favourable to the formation of moral character. In the mass of men it is the only security. In the best of men it is a guard not wisely dispensed with. . . . Where do you find the sober, industrious, moral part of our community? Where do you find the quiet and good citizen? Where do you find domestic order and peaceful subordination, and a careful training of youth in the paths of virtue? Where, but among those engaged in this stigmatized pursuit? And, where, on the other hand, do you find the crimes and vices of society? Where do you find the turbulent agitator, the domestic villain, the disturber of public and private peace, the candidates for prisons and penitentiaries? Where, but among such as have never engaged in the steady pursuit of wealth, never realized its pleasures, never felt its cares—men reckless of the morrow, and caring for nothing but the gratification of the passing hour? And where would you find a surer corrective for such errors than in the pursuit of wealth? When does such an one begin to reform? Is it not so soon as he begins to accumulate, or rather to desire it? It is the pursuit of future independence that first raises him above present temptation.[47]

Shortly afterwards, McVickar summed up this view by saying that if political economy were concerned only with wealth, it could not be the "science of national prosperity" (the nineteenth-century term for economic growth), and "must not pretend to dictate to Government." The intellectual,

[47] *Introductory Lecture to a Course of Political Economy*, pp. 5–7.

moral, and religious interests of society must also be considered, for they were " 'part and parcel' of the science." [48]

McVickar was aware that the founders of the science of political economy could hardly be called believers in orthodox religion; but he acepted a reconciliation which was most concisely expressed by the Reverend Francis Wayland, president of Brown University: "This science [of political economy] has been, to say the least, most successfully cultivated by men who held no belief in the Christian religion. And yet, reasoning from unquestionable facts in the history of man, they have incontrovertibly proved that the precepts of Jesus Christ, in all their simplicity, point out the only rules of conduct, in obedience to which either *nations or individuals* can become either rich or happy." [49]

To McVickar, according to one historian of early teaching of economics in America, the diffusion of a knowledge of political economy was "a source of safety for existing institutions." [50] Moreover, its diffusion should not be a difficult task. So simple and obvious were its fundamental principles that, as we have seen, he prepared a textbook on the subject for primary and secondary schools. In the introduction to *First Lessons*, he took occasion to say:

The first principles of Political Economy are truisms which a child may understand, and which children should therefore be taught. In the last century they were among the speculations of the learned; they have now become the heritage of the nursery; and the only difficulty in teaching them in after life arises from a suspicion excited by their very simplicity. They are so obvious, that men are apt to think, if true, they would not have then, for the first time, to learn them. That this stumbling-block may be removed from the path of the next generation, we must now in-

[48] M[cVickar], review of Thomas Chalmers's *On Political Economy*, in *The Churchman*, Nov. 10, 1832, p. 342

[49] *Encouragement to Religious Effort* (Philadelphia: American Sunday School Union, 1830), p. 17.

[50] E. V. Wills, "Political Economy in the Early American College Curriculum," *The South Atlantic Quarterly*, XXIV (April, 1925), 136.

corporate these truths into the studies of children, in order that they may become, as it were, "part and parcel of their minds."

As a result of thorough schooling in childhood "men in high and responsible stations would then no longer be found engaged in learning principles where they should be occupied in applying them, nor in discussing theories when they should be directing practice." Political economy, because it offered simple and invariable rules for proper conduct, was also pre-eminently a practical science. When McVickar took his short vacation in Europe in 1830, he arranged for "a practical man" to handle the lectures in the subject. At that time a former student, "W. B. Lawrence, Esq., late Chargé d'Affaires at the court of London . . . kindly undertook and most ably fulfilled the duties of the Professor of Political Economy." [51]

The McVickars had been a commercial family; it was natural that the son who was a teacher should take a very deep interest in the financial issues of the day. The elder McVickar was a general merchant receiving vessels and cargoes from all parts of the West Indies and Europe. He was a large shipowner and one of the earliest in the direct trade with China from the port of New York. Besides, he was a director of the Bank of New York, of the Mutual Insurance Co., and of the United Insurance Co.

A still younger McVickar commented that:

> the subject . . . of political economy was one very congenial to my father's mind. But not theoretically alone. It, like every other subject in which he interested himself, must have its practical applications in the wants of the hour, or else, except so far as duty required, his interest flagged. His mind, though analytic to a high degree, was remarkably practical.[52]

McVickar wrote anonymously a number of practical pamphlets which were highly praised. During the existence of *The New York Review*, from 1837 to 1842, he was a constant

[51] John McVickar, *A Biographical Memoir of the Rev. Edmund D. Griffin* (New York: Protestant Episcopal Press, 1832), p. 95, note.

[52] W. A. McVickar, *Life*, p. 87.

contributor; but his articles, like those of the other contributors, were unsigned. The banking community expressed deep admiration for his abilities. The president of the Metropolitan Bank, Mr. John Earl Williams, wrote McVickar's son:

To a practical man of business, an every-day banker, it really seems wonderful that a scholar, investigating the subject of Political Economy on purely scientific principles, should be able to see, not only the practical workings of existing laws, but should also be able to foresee and foretell what changes are necessary to produce the highest prosperity and secure the greatest safety to the community.[53]

In 1826, one year after the publication of the *Outlines of Political Economy*, McVickar republished another of McCulloch's *Encyclopaedia Britannica* articles, *Interest Made Equity*, with an editorial preface by himself. This was a demonstration that so-called usury laws were a hindrance to trade.

The views expressed in his pamphlet, *Considerations upon the Expediency of Abolishing Damages on Protested Bills of Exchange and the Effect of Establishing a Reciprocal Exchange with Europe* (1829) were held to be sound not only by leading New York financiers but also by such eminent London bankers as the managing partner of Baring Brothers, the American born and trained Joshua Bates. The chief cities of the United States, McVickar wrote, should become the money centers of the western continent and the great settling houses for the balances of the new with the old world. The means of achieving this role was to remove all artificial impediments, and "time and self-interest, with our natural advantages, will do the rest."

The influential New-York *American*, edited by Charles King, praised the pamphlet for leaving no room for the common although not rational objection of its being "mere theorizing." It pointed out that McVickar had prepared the essay "at the particular request and with the sanction of several

[53] *Ibid.*, p. 409.

highly reputable merchants. The practical knowledge of these gentlemen had satisfied them of the oppression and unjust character of our existing laws in relation to Bills of Exchange, and they put into the hands of the author part of the details of which he has so skillfully availed himself to sustain their views and his own." This, the newspaper thought, should exonerate the author "from any imputation—if indeed it could be made an imputation, of *volunteering* in the discussion of a question which is much mooted among practical men." McVickar was also praised for providing in an appendix a "concise and clear exposition of the nature and operations of bills of exchange, for those unfamiliar with the subject." [54]

In the area of banking, McVickar did his most constructive work. He sharply criticized the banks for "discounting freely and inviting speculation & then taking fright, they suddenly cut off discounts," and bankrupt merchants. The evil could not be completely eliminated, for, as recorded by James W. Beekman in 1834, "the root of the matter lies much deeper; in the very speculative turn of Americans," a boldness that had the characteristics of a trait of human nature, and had led to "the distress of 1825 and 1829." Still, much could be done to moderate excesses.

He was a leader in popularizing banking reform, first in the state and then for the nation. In those days bank charters were obtained by special act of the legislature. One group of bank reformers insisted that this system made banking a purely speculative business for promoters without capital, and thus a major source of inflation and consequent "convulsions," that

[54] New-York *American*, February 13, 18, 1829. The appendix on bills of exchange is one of the first, if not the first, systematic presentation of the subject in the United States. (See Appendix I in this volume.) It followed largely McCulloch.

The leading critic of McVickar was Ferris Pell, who published under the pseudonym of Publicola *Strictures on Professor M'Vickar's Pamphlet . . .* (New York: Elliott and Palmer, 1829). Publicola referred to himself in the preface as having been a "junior schoolmate" of McVickar. He received his B. A. from Columbia in 1806, two years later than McVickar.

is, panics and depressions. A prominent leader of banking reform in New York, the financier Isaac Bronson, recognizing McVickar's ability and influence, sought his support for a measure that was one of the first steps in establishing sound banking in the state: Safeguarding the issuance of bank notes through the deposit of an equivalent amount of valuable securities with the state authorities. Bronson wrote McVickar in 1827 that the best way to promote "the particular interests of the banks and the general interests of Society" would be "a well-written tract explaining the elementary principles by which banks of discount and deposit should be regulated. Your acquaintance with a science with which the principles of banking are intimately connected and indeed form a part, must eminently qualify you for the task." [55] Bronson's arguments seemed sound, and McVickar published anonymously *Hints on Banking in a Letter to a Gentleman in Albany by a New Yorker* (1827).

The main provisions of the scheme were:

> Banking to be a free trade, insofar as that it may be freely entered into by individuals or associations, under the provisions of a general statute.
>
> The amount of the Banking Capital of such individual or association to be freely fixed, but to be invested one-tenth at the discretion of the Bank, the remaining nine-tenths in government stock, whereof the bank is to receive the dividends, but the principle to remain in pledge for the redemption of its promissory notes, under such securities as to place the safety of the public beyond doubt or risk.
>
> . . .
>
> No notes of denominations under five dollars to be issued by such a bank.[56]

[55] Bronson to John McVickar, Feb. 12, 1827, in Abraham H. Venit, "Isaac Bronson: His Banking Theory and Financial Controversies," *The Journal of Economic History*, V (November, 1945), 203.

[56] McVickar later also advocated the full payment of bank capital and publicity for the statements of banks. (Notebook of Parmly, in "Political Economy," 1842.)

The general principles laid down by McVickar were embodied in the Free Banking Act of New York in 1838, and more strictly in the National Banking Act of 1863, which governed bank note issue for the United States for half a century—until the establishment of the Federal Reserve System in 1913.

McVickar strongly supported the Free Banking Act of 1838, but he felt that such provisions as the one allowing mortgages along with government bonds to be used as security for the notes was dangerous. As he explained in 1839, when bank difficulties stemming from the depression raised questions as to the soundness of free banking: the new banking law "contains sound principles, unsoundly carried out. That the capital . . . of a bank in good credit be . . . loaned out on permanent securities—and making use in banking mainly of its deposits for its discounts—this is a sound principle, but it becomes unsound when such real securities are taken as actual subscription, and without the sound caution exercised by money lenders." Banks based on such securities were associations not of capitalists and money lenders, but of landholders, who are borrowers. The principle of pledging the capital for the redemption of notes becomes unsound when such pledged capital is inconvertible at the will of the holder. Such bonds and mortgages were, therefore, poor security for circulation. "Nothing but market stocks, convertible and unquestionable," was appropriate.

The basic solution for the ills of banking would be a national regulation of note issues by means of a national bank: "Under a national bank, competent to regulate the national currency from its magnitude—its local position, and its privilege of branches—the law of freedom would be operating only for good." A particularly effective argument for a national bank in this land of many legislatures was that only such an institution would "render nugatory all the dangerous and false banking schemes of the states." Under such a regulation credit would be evenly extended: "the productive industry of the country developed—prices become firm and remunerating, and . . . bank notes become throughout the limits of our land, safe counters of their [men's] wealth."[57]

There should be somewhere in the nation adequate controls to regulate all other bank note issues, to keep them within safe limits by collecting and returning to all local banks those surplus issues into which their individual interest as coiners of money constantly and unsuccessfully led them. A national bank would perform central bank functions, which he described as maintaining a safe, uniform currency, with a maximum of steadiness in its value and in regulating all exchanges, both domestic and foreign, so as to maintain bills of exchange at a steady price and that price as near as might be at the real par for the safety of the merchant and the security of sound commerce. More concretely, a central bank seemed desirable. It might well resemble the second Bank of the United States the recharter of which President Jackson had successfully opposed in 1832, and which had gone out of existence at the end of its twenty-year term in 1836.[58]

Although McVickar did not approve of President Jackson's "ruthless war" on the Bank of the United States, he still felt

[57] John [McVickar], "Money and Banks," *The New York Review*, V (October, 1839), 347–48.

[58] In 1832 McVickar had sent the secretary of the Treasury a proposal for a new national bank, and he had been asked to advise on a new national banking system by a congressional committee. (W. A. McVickar, *Life*, pp. 243–44.)

This committee seems to have been the powerful House Ways and Means Committee. Its chairman, Churchill C. Cambreleng of New York City, who was leading the Jackson opposition in the House to the Bank, was an admirer of McVickar as a monetary and banking expert. In 1831 he asked his friend Isaac Bronson to pass on to McVickar a pamphlet he had just received from Nassau Senior, presumably *Three Lectures on the Cost of Obtaining Money and on Effects of Private and Government Paper Money* (Cambreleng to Bronson, Feb. 26, 1831, in Venit, "Isaac Bronson . . . ," p. 206). The following year Cambreleng forwarded to McVickar the list of questions that his committee had asked Nicholas Biddle, president of the Bank.

that the bank had not been completely innocent. He pointed out that in its last four years it had, in attempting to save itself from Jackson's onslaughts, forgotten its duties and used "its power in desperation, as a tyrant over the currency, rather than its regulation." Furthermore the bank had been unable to maintain complete steadiness of the value of the currency. Serious and frequent fluctuations of the currency had occurred, "even under the fullest action of the late United States Bank, as for instance in 1825 and 1826, the very central period of its power." [59] McVickar also contended that the bank with its headquarters in Philadelphia, governed by Philadelphians, had been subject to local influences at the expense of the country.

In 1841 he presented a plan for a national bank that was prophetic of later developments. He published his scheme in *The New York Review*, and the article proved so popular that it was quickly reprinted as a pamphlet under the title of *A National Bank: Its Necessity, and Most Advisable Form.* He strongly urged the principle of "separating altogether in banking the making of notes from the loaning of notes—thus constituting the national bank the only issuer and leaving to local banks the safer and more rightful business of the banker—discount and deposit." [60]

The new national bank, as a part of its regulating function,

[59] [John McVickar], "Money and Banks," p. 340.

[60] The desirability of a single issuer of bank notes was long debated in England as well as in the United States. In 1833 the famed governor of the Bank of England, J. Horsley Palmer, in seeking the support of Albert A. Gallatin in the bank's struggle for recharter, explained to Gallatin that until there was a sole issuer of paper money, "all the evils arising from competition of issue must exist, both in currency and prices. . . . The difficulty seems to be to make the public understand that the creation of paper money is not the legitimate business of a Banker; Sir Henry Parnell [who was a leader in the House of Commons and considered himself a follower of Ricardo] would have them believe that the trade of coining ought to be as free, as the trade of sugar and coffee." Palmer explained that it would be extremely difficult to bring about the reform without first obtaining "the concurrence of the general Banking interest, through whom that one issue must be negotiated. We must therefore wait the change of public opinion before a measure of that kind is extensively attempted." Meanwhile, he would greatly appreciate Gallatin's "opinion upon the propriety of attempting the measure," for he had derived, he said,

would also engage in the purchase and sale of exchange, both foreign and domestic. Its operations in exchange should be strengthened by a:

heavier capital, and a more determinate occupation of it, so as to be always in the bill market, both buying and selling, and thus determining the price of all drafts at home and abroad, conclusively and definitively . . . By its intervention the exports and imports of the country come to know each other, and thus become self-regulated; by it, is the domestic currency enabled to value itself with foreign currencies, and contract or expand as needful; by it is the home demand for money regulated, as well as the foreign, and the debtor and creditor sides of international accounts balanced. The price of bills is therefore the commercial barometer, and on it, as the most delicate criterion of all coming changes of weather, will the experienced seaman fix his eyes and sail by it.

The source of inability of the Second Bank of the United States to maintain the currency at a steady value, McVickar asserted, lay in the inconsistent duties of the bank's governing

---

from Gallatin's *Considerations on the Currency and Banking System of the United States* (1831) no small portion of his present opinions. (Letter of Palmer to Gallatin, Dec. 12, 1832, in Gallatin papers, New-York Historical Society Collection.)

Gallatin, after much prodding, in his reply four months later pointed out that Parnell's opinions were "entitled to the highest respect," and went on to say: "No legislation was better than a bad, and, on most subjects connected with political economy, than any legislation. Yet, with respect to currency, to the power of issuing that which is the standard of the value of every other commodity and regulates every contract, our experience in the United States is decisive against allowing the privilege to every one indiscriminately." The evils of that system were such that every state had passed restraining laws, and despite the imperfection of many of them, the current situation was much better than "when everyone issued paper as he pleased." He said that he had always considered "a single Bank of issue . . . as . . . the *beau idéal*." In the United States, however, "it would be impossible . . . to separate entirely a bank of issue from ordinary banking business, viz., discounting private paper and receiving private deposits. But if the Bank of England can do without either, it would be a great improvement, remove many well-founded objections, lessen the great power which must necessarily be given to the bank and leave the Banking business proper where it ought to be,—to the natural competition of private Bankers." (Letter of Gallatin to Palmer, May 1, 1833, in Gallatin papers. The letter as printed in Henry Adams's edition of Gallatin's *Writings* lacks "political" in front of "economy" in the first paragraph.

board of directors. These had led them "to have one interest as issuers and an opposite interest as regulators of the currency." The remedy was to separate these incongruous interests—the interests of the stockholders and those of the public. McVickar in his scheme assigned to "distinct boards and different hands the task of supply [of currency] and the higher task of regulating that supply." To the central bank, as the governing body, the regulation of supply would alone belong.

The members of the board, he suggested, should be few and be elected by the stockholders (except its government directors); it would be salaried and have powers of visitation over the branches, and issue weekly or semimonthly public statements of its financial condition, "with such details as its charter may designate."

To improve the bank's efficiency over that of the Second Bank, he proposed to reduce the amount of specie required as reserves, by making the bank's notes payable at only one point—its own counter, or what is equivalent, at that of its central branch. To eliminate the danger of the bank becoming a prey of speculators as had the Second Bank in its first years, he proposed to limit its dividends to 6 percent (5 percent, if the general government guaranteed them). The annual surplus, if any, would be distributed among the states.

The board would make an annual report to Congress "and, as a farther bond of unanimity of action between government, the bank, and the public, . . . its notes should be receivable in all dues to government, until otherwise ordered by Congress."

To prevent such protracted controversies over renewals of the charter as had occurred in the case of the Second Bank two reforms were proposed.

The charter ought to be for a much longer period than the usual twenty years, say, fifty, but subject at all times to the action of Congress for necessary modifications. He preferred that the charter be of indefinite duration, but subject every ten years to the prospective action of Congress, upon its continuance, to take effect at the end of the ensuing ten years; that is, it would become a tenant at will every ten years, but would have ten years' notice to quit. This would remove from the bank all dangerous independence without subjecting it at the same time to "temporary or capricious executive or party will."

The second change proposed was the establishment of headquarters in New York, and not in Philadelphia, which had been the location of the two former banks:

> The regulator of the national currency and the equalizer of its exchanges should *there* sit, where the currency is in truth measured, and its exchanges in fact equalized; at the point where the two extremes meet, of foreign and domestic exchange—that point of contact where they are to be made by touching to sympathize with each other. The national bank is that connecting sympathizer; in its right hand, it holds the one, and in its left the other; and this it can do nowhere but in the city of banks and street of banks, namely, in Wall Street, New York. He who supposes that he thinks otherwise, deceives himself; he does not *think*, but *dream;* for he dreams that it is a matter of doubt, whether the steersman should stand at the wheel or at the windlass; he doubts whether he who holds the reins had better sit on the box or in the basket; he doubts whether the engineer of a railroad train should ride on the locomotive or in one of the passenger coaches; for all these are in fact but exemplifications of the same absurdity, all equivalent to supposing that the national regulator of the currency should be placed anywhere but where the currency is in fact regulated—in the city of New York. It is a case, in short, we again say, not of choice but of necessity.[61]

[61] The New York City banks had from the start, in 1831, opposed the movement for rechartering the Second Bank of the United States. As the president of the New York branch informed headquarters, "Our hopes in the city Banks, petitioning for a renewal of the charter of the Bank of U.[nited] States is . . . at an end." (Letter of Isaac Lawrence to Nicholas Biddle, Jan. 30, 1832, in Biddle papers, Library of Congress.) For an illuminating discussion of the controversy between the financial centers, see Bray Hammond, *Banks and Politics in America* (Princeton, N.J.: Princeton Univ. Press, 1957), pp. 351-56, 392.

At least as early as 1834 McVickar urged that the bank's headquarters

As was characteristic of the time McVickar's chief concern was with bank notes. He paid scarcely any attention to deposits, which have since become the chief element of bank currency. It was still felt in dominant circles that the interference of law in banking was legitimate only in the issue of a bank's promissory notes. Since they served as a substitute for coins they were in effect a form of coinage and therefore ought to be subject to regulation:

> Besides being regarded as money, passing as actual payment, and going into the hands of the poor, the young, and the ignorant, to whom government stands peculiarly in the light of a protector, it is bound to look into, and to regulate what thus trenches at once, on its functions as sovereign, and on its duties as public guardian. . . . As between the bank and the merchant, the laws have nothing to say; their interchange of notes is a matter of mutual confidence—and, if done, it will doubtless be well done; it is as between the bank and the public [third parties] for the safety of those who give not promise for promise, but sweat and toil and real values for them—men who . . . can know nothing of the source or the security of the means, or the morals of those who sign that promise, which they receive as actual payment.[62]

On the matter of the desirability of a public debt, McVickar departed from the Ricardian view, which held that public debts were an unmitigated evil, so much so that Ricardo favored a capital levy in order to eliminate completely once and for all England's huge debt. Writing in *The New York Review*, in the depression year of 1840, McVickar criticized President Jackson's administration for paying off in 1834 the last installment of the national debt.[63] This action, McVickar contended, increased the necessity of the country for new

should be New York, "the center of the commercial exchanges of the country" (Notebook of J. W. Beekman, 1834).

[62] [John McVickar], "Money and Banks," p. 342.

[63] The controversy over rechartering the Second Bank of the United States had involved among others the question of the redemption of the federal debt (which was largely held abroad), because one of President Jackson's criticisms of the bank was that it had refused to cooperate in making available funds for redemption.

loans from Europe and on more expensive and less available securities, and with more questionable credit; furthermore, it meant the loss from the national money market of the nation's only unquestioned stock, whether for domestic or foreign investment, a loss of incalculable magnitude from a financial point of view, and one for which no substitute was practical. This loss outweighed the only "European reputation it purchased, that of more wealth than wisdom."

Without such unquestioned monied securities as federal bonds, no "great enterprising commercial nation" could remain either safe or prosperous. For confidence both at home and abroad, there must be a safe, profitable, national receptacle for the large amount of floating capital which for financial safety in every department of productive industry "should be kept floating, waiting investment, or standing ready to meet emergencies." In the absence of such a receptacle, capital would float elsewhere. "It will not stay at hazard; it will not stay without profit. If foreign [capital], therefore it will be withdrawn; if domestic, it will be driven into fixed investments, hastly and therefore rashly." Such conversion, furthermore, would leave no reserves or storehouse for times of need, and would force the national industry to live as it were from hand to mouth, "a condition no more desirable for a nation than for individuals." All this applied against the reduction of the public debt. It would also be economically desirable to have a pub-

---

At the height of the struggle over recharter, in 1831–32, only a few leading economists (notably Albert Gallatin) did not believe that the redemption of the federal debt was an evil. George Tucker of the University of Virginia expressed the general sentiment of the profession. He wrote in 1831 that "It is now a favorite object of the people and the government to pay off the national debt; and from the novelty of the phenomenon it must give great *eclat* to the administration in which it takes place." But every good economist would say yes "to the question whether the money that would have to be exported to pay the foreign debt had better remain here." ([Tucker], "Bank of the United States," *The American Quarterly Review*, IX [March, 1831], 281–82. For Tucker's authorship see letter of Tucker to Nicholas Biddle, April 8, 1831, in Biddle papers, Library of Congress.)

lic debt for the purposes of constructing such "public improvements" as canals and railroads, which would meet interest and amortization payments.[64] Such were productive expenditures opening up new avenues to national wealth in contrast to borrowing where the proceeds went off in a flash, or were "squandered on a royal feast—fired away in powder or frittered away in pensions."

The continuous need for public improvements supplied the means of providing investment for generations to come. McVickar denied "that we have now exhausted the means afforded by our country for such profitable investment." At present, the great western areas were to New York what the valley of the Genesee was previous to the Erie canal: "an unlocked treasure-house." The completion of their canals and railroads was "operating . . . and will operate to a similar result." There was a surplus, for the moment, of agricultural products, "then as now, heaped up, and running over, in the eyes of superficial reasoners, to waste, and the extended cultivation counted a mistake. So it was reasoned then as so now, until the results shamed their fears, and not only so but taught them science—how that the means of life bring forth life; and that such products, unlike those of art run on till they force exchange, 'making glad,' wherever they go, the heart of man, giving him 'a cheerful countenance,' and strength to labor and

[64] McVickar in his lectures showed that he had deeply thought about the problem of determining the profitability of state constructed or state aided internal improvements. Thomas Cooper in his popular *Lectures On the Elements of Political Economy* (1826) had argued that the guiding rule for such construction was that, if at an early period of its completion, the project could not earn at least legal interest on the investment, the project should not be undertaken. McVickar's analyses began with the pregnant question: "Are governments to be influenced by the same consideration as an individual? *viz.* that if it be not productive for the first 10 or 15 years, it should not be undertaken?" He answered, "But an individual looks forward but a few years—a government is more permanent. Therefore if a gov[ernment] can clearly see that a public work, is going to pay capital and interest in 15 or 20 years, they are justified in going on with it. True rule, [is] that Capital and Interest must be replaced at some time." (Notebook of James W. Beekman, 1834. New-York Historical Society collection.)

hope in his toil, until they return to the soil that furnished them in all the varied products of human industry."

McVickar's argument (drawn undoubtedly from Malthus) that agriculture faces no problem of "overproduction," because it incites to a greater population to consume it, may be questionable, but there is much to be said for his conclusion at this point. "We cry shame, then, on those among us who would have us stop short in our career of improvement." They fail to distinguish "between the momentary reflux of an advancing wave" and "the fall of an ebbing tide." [65]

To be sure, McVickar, following the Ricardian line, declared, according to Hamilton Fish's notebook of 1827, that the condition of the laboring class would at some distant date be depressed:

> In this country the rate of wages is high; and the rate at which capital increases nearly keeps pace with the increase of population; as long as this continues the prosperity of the country, and the happiness & comfort of the laboring class will continue to increase; but there is a certain course which every nation must run: So soon as all the land owned by a country is cultivated the population increases faster than the capital of the country. Whenever this happens the condition of the lower class gradually grows worse and worse; this leads us to perceive that nations, like individuals, have their periods of increase, maturity and decay. When the latter comes it is not to be assigned to the fault of government, but to the common course of nature. What in this country puts that time off for an indefinite period is the immense tract of country we have; even when a country is fully cultivated this decline may be delayed by a liberal system of freedom and by removing all restrictions.

The eventual outcome did not preclude state intervention to put off the evil day by such means as "public improvements." The basic, technical justification was orthodox—the preven-

[65] [John McVickar], "American Finances and Credit," *The New York Review*, VII (July, 1840), 192, 196, 204. For John McVickar's authorship, see W. A. McVickar, *Life*, p. 409.

tion of the fall in the rate of profit (including interest) which was the source of capital accumulation. In Ricardian terms, the "internal improvements" prevented the recourse to poorer soil. "All national improvements, all scientific discoveries, all improvements in agriculture, canals, roads, bridges, etc., all that tend to open the country, and facilitate transportation must be considered as contributing to produce this effect."

Parmly's notes reveal that McVickar considerably qualified the "system of freedom." He first laid down as foundations of the science "four axioms which are facts in our nature and from which flow the results of political economy." First was that universal desire, "the desire for enjoyment. Men love enjoyment and are willing to barter labor for it." From this desire sprang civilization. Give man a stimulus and he is at once engaged. Second was the "love of accumulation." This was not always true of individuals but it was of nations. From the love of accumulation flowed all capital. "Men love personal pleasure but they fear want." The third axiom was the "desire of competition." This determined and awakened talent and ingenuity. The final axiom was "the clearsightedness of self interest. This if not a universal is a general principle, and from it flow the principles of the free system of political economy."

Taking Adam Smith as the great exponent of the free system, McVickar went on to suggest qualifications. He granted that Adam Smith's view, as he interpreted it, that "individual and national wealth were identical" was valid, but not in "exclusive strictness." The very existence and necessity of government proved this. "Take the case of peace and war." Another great class of exceptions were those cases that he described as involving "prospective interests."

He questioned, too, Adam Smith's argument that government interference in production was unnecessary, because if there be a demand there would be a supply. This, McVickar held, was true for the material products which society demands, but not of "the intellectual and moral wants of man." In the case of material wants, this creates a desire in men for them and a willingness to barter labor or money for the gratification of these wants. The less he gets of material products the more he wants. But in the case of moral and intellectual wants, for example, "the more ignorant a man is the less he desires education. And the less his moral nature is cultivated, the less he feels the want of religion, etc." Similarly, there should be qualification of Smith's principle that individual interest is the only sufficient guide, that "each man knows what his own interest is better than the government can." If this were invariably true, then why government? "Many do not follow their true interest, for the time being. Besides, many who pursue their present interest are blind to their prospective good. Individuals do know their best interests and will pursue them if they are wise and well governed by themselves. But in the present times it would be dangerous to carry this principle into execution."

McVickar proceeded to a more generalized line of argument in his lecture on freedom and the necessary restrictions upon it. The general argument was that "a state of freedom alone, calls for the power and energies of man. It is therefore the only state in which nations must govern wisely." However, since the danger of extremes was great, restrictions were necessary. He repeated that "the impossibility of universal freedom is obvious from the existence of government." There were specific limitations on freedom. There were first financial limitations, that is, government must interfere to obtain revenue. Then there were political limitations, which arise from the relations to foreign countries. "The Science of Political Economy knows nothing of individual and distinct nations, or a State of War. This is a Science of Peace. This view may be considered as at once an eulogium and a discrediting of the

Science." Another class consisted of "municipal" regulations, which referred to welfare. Dangerous trades must be limited and the sale of spirituous liquors regulated. Yet another category was the regulation of professions in order to prevent their degradation. "Thus a particular course is prescribed for the study of law; and also . . . medicine." Government intervention in education, or what McVickar called "educational limitations" on the principles of freedom were strongly endorsed. "The law does not leave it to the people to say whether they will have schools, but it provides for them. The Prussian law says it will no more permit a man to bring up his children, ignorant and uneducated, than it will permit him to throw firebrands among combustibles."

Some restrictions, continued McVickar, were justified on the grounds of public convenience; for example, the government—the "public"—performed the functions of coining money and specifying weights and measures in order to prevent imposition and fraud and "save time in trading." This category also, it appears, provided the rationale for the prohibition of the issue of paper money by individuals (and also of small notes by banks). The dangers to society were "(1) to the ignorant and poor, the very classes which government should protect; and (2) loss of time. . . . The use of money is after all to save time in trade. This is the cause of superiority of coin over bullion and of paper from known sources over that issued by individuals." But of the three functions of banks—deposits, loans, and issue of promissory notes (bank notes)—only the last ought to be regulated. The others were self-regulating, through the operations of the foreign exchanges. The currency of a country, McVickar emphasized, should be controlled by one national bank which would be a connecting link between the business and the currency of a country.

There was one problem which deeply disturbed him even though he could find no place where state intervention could be useful. This is the problem which today is called technological unemployment. He pointed out that it made no sense to talk about giving up machinery, unless one preferred barbarism to civilization, that the products of machinery, being cheaper, come within reach of the poor, and in the long run, and especially through the lowering of prices, there would be sufficient demand to take care of the unemployed, but the introduction of machines would cause temporary distress.[66] The temporary evil involved "should be met by temporary alleviations, e.g., the introduction should be gradual," but it was granted that the question was "popularly and scientifically doubtful" in the sense of being unsettled.[67]

McVickar was an ardent believer in the separation of church and state, but he thought that government could help with information and guidance in church missionary work, especially in "the cause of that much neglected race," the Indian. As chairman of his denomination's Indian committee on the intended exploration of the Indian territory he appealed to federal officials for such aid as they could "expect their church's action in the Premises [to] entitle them both from the Government & the Community." [68]

In 1857 Columbia moved. "The opening of a new street, directly in front of the building, taking from it all retirement and privacy, and the current of trade, which poured steadily

[66] McVickar entertained Robert Owen both at the college and at his home several times, and Parmly's notebook of 1842 has the notation, "Owen remarked to Prof. McVickar that England's distress was owing to her surplus machinery."

[67] It was scientifically a doubtful question, according to McVickar, because men have changed their opinions; for instance, Ricardo's frank admission that the problem was more serious than he had originally thought.

[68] Letter of John McVickar to John C. Spencer, no date, in Historical Society of Pennsylvania collection.

just in that direction," a trustee said, "forced it to retreat." [69] This was the signal for an expansion program which had been discussed for some time and involved postgraduate study and popular extension lectures as well as changes in the courses for seniors. McVickar's chair of moral philosophy, rhetoric and belles lettres was not continued in its inclusive form. He was now seventy years of age. He petitioned the trustees for a "qualified appointment bearing on one or more of the Studies involved in my present Professorship, and which might be considered suitable and profitable for graduate students, or popular as Public Lectures." There followed an "enumeration of the distinct branches" with which "my past duties have rendered me necessarily daily familiar:

The Evidences of Religion, Natural and Revealed
The History of Philosophy
Political Economy
Aesthetics
English Literature
Rhetoric with Logic
English History
The Principles and Practice of English Composition."

The trustees made him professor of the evidences of religion, natural and revealed, with a salary of $2,000.

McVickar replied with deep thanks. The position was "most gratifying" to his feelings. He felt that the position would strengthen within the college

> that element of Christian knowledge, and training, without which no education, however enlarged, can be deemed completed or safe. It is an element, as we all fearfully know, that most needs strengthening in our land, and wherein our greatest peril lies, whether teaching national or individual welfare. To strengthen it then becomes a high duty, as well as a glorious privilege on the

[69] William Betts, "Introductory Address," in *Addresses of the Newly-Appointed Professors of Columbia College* (New York: Columbia College, 1858), p. 4.

part of those in whose hands the interests of education are placed. It is an adage as true as it is old that "the fear of the Lord is the beginning of wisdom." [70]

The rest of his old professorship was distributed between two new chairs, the professorship of history and political science, and the professorship of moral and intellectual philosophy and literature.[71]

While McVickar was professor of evidences he maintained a certain interest in economic matters. He was chairman of a faculty committee in 1864 to prepare a report for the trustees on the subject of an international system of uniform weights, measures, and coins. An international congress was being held on the subject to which the United States was sending a commissioner. In the committee report, as amended by the trustees, which approved of the international measure, there is this passage:

It cannot therefore be deemed presumptuous on the part of this College, the oldest and most influential in the great state of New York, and seated, as it is, in the great commercial emporium of the New World, as well as the center of its financial influence, *directly* to address Congress on a subject so cognate not only to its present studies, but to its past history, familiarizing to its students, as it has done for more than forty years, the fundamental principles of the very science by which this measure is to be judged, and through the growing in influence of which we cannot doubt but it will be continually successful.[72]

[70] Columbia University, Minutes of the Trustees, April 27, May 4, 1857. McVickar on his retirement from teaching in 1864 was made professor emeritus.

[71] Each carried a salary of $3,000, plus an allowance of $1,000 for house rent. (Minutes of the Trustees, May 18, 1857.)

[72] Minutes of the Trustees, June 6, 1864.

This memorial for a universal uniform coinage was probably the first one made by a college on an economic issue. The prime mover was the trustee S. B. Ruggles, who had played a leading role in the development of the Erie Canal and the New York and Erie Railroad. He had been the delegate of the United States to the International Statistical Congress at Berlin in 1863, and would be the prime mover in the establishment of the Faculty of Political Science at Columbia. He originally had the idea that

In 1868, in October, McVickar had visibly begun to approach the final rest from his long labors:

Before the month closed he was at rest. The summer had been spent at Bloomingdale, within a short distance of the old paternal mansion where, sixty years before, as a solitary student, we saw him preparing for that life-work, which, nobly finished, he was now about to lay down. Surrounded by his surviving children, he passed quietly away, in his eighty-second year, with the oft-reiterated words, "Pray," "Prayer," "Praise" upon his lips, and was buried in the grave-yard of his own Church at Hyde Park, beside her whose memory he had so faithfully cherished, and in the grave he had marked for himself thirty-five years before.[73]

Eight years before he had begun to weary a little. He spoke of his life as having been long and as having now become a protracted one, and tried to read its lesson:

Every such life must give its lesson, like a sum worked out, a story fully told. Mine, I think, is this. The power and blessing of quiet perseverance. A feeble constitution thus hardened—a treacherous memory thus made retentive—very moderate talents thus fitted for usefulness—fair scholarship thus gained by quiet industry—college duties an early choice and never changed—and through my whole life an abiding feeling that, in a good cause, rightly pursued, nothing is impossible. The single eye and the unchanging mind governs the world, and in proportion as we partake of them are we successful, and in all good works, both blessing and blessed.[74]

---

the faculty should petition Congress (Francis Lieber to Ruggles, April 10, 1864, Lieber papers, Library of Congress).

Ruggles was a member of the committee which the National Academy of Sciences set up at the request of Secretary of the Treasury Salmon P. Chase, in 1863, to investigate the subject of "Uniformity of weights, measures and coins, considered in relation to domestic and international commerce." The secretary had already, in his *Annual Report* for 1861, called Congress's attention to the importance of "a uniform system and a uniform nomenclature of weight and measures, and coins to the commerce of the world, in which the United States already so largely shares." (*A History of the First Half-Century of the National Academy of Sciences: 1863–1913*, ed. F. W. True [Washington: privately printed, 1913], p. 206.)

[73] W. A. McVickar, *Life*, p. 404. John McVickar died on October 29.

[74] *Ibid.*, p. 405.

HENRY VETHAKE

HENRY VETHAKE: JACKSONIAN RICARDIAN

The influence of David Ricardo on economic thought in the United States of the nineteenth century was enormous. It was felt not only by such native thinkers and teachers as John McVickar, but by most others as well. One of these others, of some importance in the higher learning, was Henry Vethake, who differed in many ways from McVickar but shared with him the Ricardian belief in laissez faire. McVickar was a Whig; Vethake was a Jackson-Van Buren Democrat; but both were free traders. McVickar was an ultra-respectable New York clergyman besides being a professor. Vethake was a professor, but instead of being a clergyman, was an administrator of varied experience in the academic world, his intellectual bent being for mathematics and physical science rather than theology; and, perhaps it should be noted, he was a Presbyterian, not an Episcopalian. Both departed from Ricardian doctrine in certain respects—the American environment had at least some effect—especially in conceptions of public policy.

Perhaps Vethake's admiration for Ricardo was enlarged by the English economist's success in business affairs; at least he spoke of him "as that distinguished political philosopher, statesman and *merchant* who began life with an inconsiderable capital and died worth several millions of dollars." [1] At any

[1] Vethake, "The Distinctive Provinces of the Political Philosopher and the Statesman," *The Merchants' Magazine and Commercial Review,* II (February, 1840), 109–10. Italics are in the original.

rate he must be considered a follower of Ricardo, however striking certain of his departures from the received doctrine. Vethake differed in another way from McVickar. He was not of English but of Dutch Calvinist stock. His parents, who originally came from Germany, had been residents in British Guiana at the time of his birth and he had been brought to the United States as a child.[2] In 1804 he entered Columbia College, where his interest in mathematics and natural philosophy (physics) appeared. These were taught by John Kemp, who was also a teacher of geography. The range of subjects—within his major interest—was surprisingly wide; for example, the courses for seniors included the "General Properties of Mathematics; Laws of Motion, Mechanical Powers, Construction of Machines, Hydrostatics, Hydraulics, Pneumatics, Optics, Astronomy and Electricity." [3] He was graduated, eighth in the class of twenty-two, in 1808, and began the study of law. In 1811 he received an M. A. which, in accordance with prevalent practice and following English precedent, was granted as a matter of course three years after receipt of the B. A.[4] The death of Professor Kemp in 1812, after which the college was headed by the eminent Presbyterian minister John M. Mason, opened for Vethake an academic opportunity.[5]

[2] The year of Vethake's birth has heretofore been given as 1790 or 1792, but in the old family Dutch Bible (*Biblia dat is De gantsche H. Schrifture vervattende alle de canonyke boeken des Ouden en des Nieuwen Testaments*, [Haarlem: John Enschede, 1780], given by a descendant to the Columbia University Libraries, there is on the flyleaf, "Frederick Hendrik Vethake; is geborn d. 26 May 1791."

[3] Minutes of the Trustees, April 9, 1789.

[4] Columbia awarded Vethake an LL. D. degree in 1836.

[5] The college trustees ingeniously solved in Mason's case the problem of meeting the requirement of the pre-Revolutionary War grant by Trinity Church that the president be a communicant of the Episcopal church. They chose as president an Episcopalian, but created a more powerful office for Mason, that of provost. After Mason's resignation in 1816 on grounds of ill-health, the office was abolished.

Largely through Mason's efforts, the state legislature in 1814 gave Columbia the land which is now occupied largely by Rockefeller Center and which was then described as "within a few miles of the city." In 1819 the trustees secured the repeal of the provision made by the grant that the college

He was then only twenty-one years old, but he was given a one-year appointment, at a salary of $1,000, to teach the "mathematical and geographical course." [6] In the following year Robert Adrain of Queen's College (now Rutgers) who was one of the leading mathematicians of his day, was made professor of mathematics, and Vethake went to Adrain's old post at Queens. When the professor of classics resigned in 1815 to take a pastorate, Vethake taught his courses for a term. Financial difficulties soon forced the college to suspend activities.[7]

Fortunately for Vethake, the College of New Jersey was having some difficulty in maintaining discipline. In 1817 a

---

must move to the property within twelve years. They argued that the repeal would enable them to make the land productive towards the support of the college and "remedy the want of fellowships on the European plan, and . . . provision for poor and meritorious scholars." (Minutes of the Trustees, Jan. 2, 1817, Feb. 7, 1818.)

[6] Minutes of the Trustees, Aug. 1, 1812.

Vethake in his report of the year's work suggested that his chair should be divided into two—mathematics and natural philosophy, including geography—and be taught by separate professors. The relations between the two areas were close, yet "they are . . . in their nature very distinct and the powers and habits of mind which qualify for eminence in the one are very different in the other. There are very few whose minds are habitually exercised in the rigid and (if I may use the expression) unbending accuracy of mathematical science [who] possess much taste or satisfaction in the experimental investigation of nature's laws." An alternative division, he said, would be for one professor to teach pure mathematics and the parts of natural philosophy which were "least experimental, namely mechanics and astronomy" and another to teach experimental philosophy. This would include geography, hydrostatics, hydrodynamics, pneumatics, electricity, magnetism, galvanism, optics, "and the general outlines of chemistry, particularly the subject of heat." (Vethake's report is in the Columbia University Libraries.)

[7] Vethake's first salary at Queen's was $800 and a house. He received $100 extra for teaching the classics courses; and when the college suspended he was allowed to continue occupying his house. Information is from Rutgers University, Treasurer's Records.

Vethake always retained a warm feeling for the college and, after its permanent revival in 1825, publicly recalled how the trustees and the leading citizens had cordially welcomed him on his arrival and continued to treat him with "a kindliness, a hospitality, and a consideration, not to have been expected by one who had very limited claims to such attentions—attentions deserving of this public acknowledgment." (Vethake, *An Address before the Literary Societies of Rutgers College* [New Brunswick, N.J.: Mosher, 1854], p. 6.)

series of riots occurred, during which, "after fastening the doors of the Tutors and of sundry students, the rioters set fire to the outbuilding in the rear yard and began to ring the College bell, with shouts of fire and rebellion." [8] After the suppression of the riot, when the vice president heard that he "had been sharply criticized by certain trustees following his undignified antics during the riot, he handed in his resignation." Vethake was chosen to teach his courses as professor of mathematics and natural philosophy. In addition to introducing "fluxions"—differential calculus—at the college, he also began giving the seniors lectures on political economy in 1819.[9]

In 1821 an opportunity arose to improve his situation. Dickinson College, in Carlisle, Pennsylvania, after a few years of suspension, was being revived by a grant from the state legislature of $6,000 and, in addition, $2,000 a year for five years. Vethake's old Columbia chief, the Reverend John M. Mason was made principal; [10] and he offered Vethake the professorship of mathematics and natural philosophy.[11] From

[8] John Maclean, *History of the College of New Jersey*, II (Philadelphia: Lippincott, 1877), p. 167; Thomas Jefferson Wertenbaker, *Princeton: 1746–1896* (Princeton: Princeton Univ. Press, 1946), pp. 170–71.

[9] In 1819 Vethake's title became professor of mathematics and mechanical philosophy.

[10] Mason in his inaugural *Address* expressed concern over the lack of "subordination to authority." He said regretfully "that in all the departments of society, from the parental control to that of the government, this is held by our youth in too little esteem . . . Such a temper . . . militates alike against the very constitution of our nature—against the most express commandments of God and against those principles of action, which at all times and in every place, but from peculiar causes, in the present day and in our own country, are necessary to the order of society and the happiness of individuals." A resolution was passed by the trustees at the same time, resolving "that no student shall recite any speech embracing political or national subjects, which might have a tendency in any degree to excite party feelings." (*A Narrative of the Proceedings of the Board of Trustees of Dickinson College from 1821 to 1830* [Carlisle, Penn.: Board of Trustees, 1830], p. 5.)

[11] At a salary of $1,500 and residence. A first offer of $1,250 had been refused.

Besides Vethake, Mason appointed the Reverend Joseph Spencer, who also became the local Episcopal minister, as professor of languages (classics), the start he taught economics to the seniors.[12] The character of Vethake's economics at the time is indicated by the reference to the subject in an oration delivered before the college's two student societies. The speaker, after referring to Political Economy as "the philosophy of national interest and the science of wealth," declared that "the burden of its exposition is the complex harmonies of the association of men." Although in the older works it concerned itself primarily with controversies over the important matter of nomenclature, recent speculation concerned itself more with the no less important aspect of inferring principles "of sound prudential & lucrative policy. It is the associate of the moral science of government, and is emphatically the study for Republics, whose peculiar and consummate aim, & natural beauty, is to unite efficiency with economy, and to whom profuse experiments in finance cannot be allowed." [13]

Another and more direct indication can be got from a letter

---

and the Reverend Alexander McClelland of the Dutch Reformed Church as professor of belles lettres and history of the human mind. In consideration of the Synod of the German Reformed Church establishing its seminary at Carlisle, the principal of the seminary became professor of history and German literature—with house rent paid by Dickinson—and students of the seminary were gratuitously admitted to the lectures on moral philosophy and chemistry.

When Mason resigned on grounds of ill-health he was succeeded by another Presbyterian, the Reverend William Neill, who took charge of the "religious training of the young men in Natural Theology, the Evidences of Christianity, and . . . Bible instruction on the Sabbath." (*Autobiography of William Neill*, ed. J. H. Jones [Philadelphia: Presbyterian Board of Education, 1861], p. 50.)

[12] The trustees' minutes of Dickinson definitely recognized that Vethake was teaching political economy by 1826. In that year they authorized certain theological students being trained in Carlisle "To attend lectures *inter alia* in 'political economy,'" and "Resolved that to the professorship of Mr. Henry Vethake be added that in political economy." (Cited from letter of J. H. Morgan to E. R. A. Seligman in Seligman, "The Early Teaching of Economics in the United States," in *Economic Essays Contributed in Honor of John Bates Clark*, ed. Jacob H. Hollander [New York: Macmillan, 1927], p. 310.) His title became professor of mathematics, political economy, natural and experimental philosophy.

[13] Charles F. Mayer, *The Second Annual Oration, Delivered Before the Belles Lettres and Union Philosophical Societies of Dickinson College* (Carlisle, Penn.: privately printed at the Herald, 1827), p. 8.

from Vethake to Mathew Carey in 1825 asking for statistical information needed to determine the relative costs and benefits of turnpikes, railroads, and canals.

His pragmatic attitude was, for his time, unusual. He expressed little concern as to whether the construction was undertaken by the state, by private capital, or by a mixture; the question of most importance, so long as the costs would be covered by revenue, was which mode of transportation would be cheaper and bring the most pecuniary gain, including a rise in the most important business asset of the day, land. But the letter also illustrates the difficulties, of which McVickar was well aware, of determining the economic desirability of public works in the era of tremendous expansion of transportation.

Carlisle, January 26th, 1825

Sir:

A meeting of the citizens of Cumberland County a few days since was held in Carlisle to consider the propriety of petitioning the Legislature "that during the present session an act may be passed for the construction of a complete water communication for boats of burden between the Susquehannah and the Allegheny, at the expense of the state." The meeting was convened in consequence of a communication made by the acting committee of the "Pennsylvania Society for the Promotion of Internal Improvement" of which committee you are a member, to A. Carothers Esq. of this place. After this communication had been read, a committee, of whom I am one, was appointed to obtain information on the important subject of the proposed canal, and more especially as to its relation to the prosperity of our own county, when the meeting adjourned to the 9th of February. If you could conveniently furnish me before that date with information on the following points you will much oblige me.

1st. In what manner has the construction of the turnpike road from Philada. to Pittsburg and of the Cumberland road to Wheeling, affected the comparative prosperity of the counties more or less remote from Philada. and Baltimore. I wish more particularly to know if it be possible to procure any where a comparative contemporary view of the prices of land for a series of years, before and after the construction of the roads, along these lines of communication.

2dly. The like information respecting the state of New York before, during and after, the construction of the Erie and Champlain canals.

3dly. The comparative expense of the construction of canals and railroads, with a comparative view of the expense of transportation by each.

You must excuse my troubling you with this matter, but I am encouraged to do so by your zeal on the subject of internal improvement, and your readiness to labour for whatever you conceive for the advantage of our country.

I have the honour to be

Very respectfully,

Your obt. servt.

Mathew Carey, Esq. Henry Vethake

P.S. Will you be so good as to give me such information as you conveniently can as to the cost of the Pennsylvania turnpike from Philada. to Pittsburg. The amount of the tolls annually received, & the amount and value of merchandize annually transported.

H.V.[14]

Peace and quiet seem not to have blessed the college. The students are reported to have engaged in "repeated attacks on a Professor's room and rebellions were the order of the day. . . . There were endless restrictions but little liberty." The student disturbances and their handling gave rise to the "final explosion" in 1829. At that time the entire faculty, including the principal, resigned. As a historian of the college wrote: "The faculty members were at odds not only with one another, and probably uncertain about their tenure, but they were at odds with the Board of Trustees," which had taken complete charge of disciplinary matters.[15] The trustees the

[14] Letter is in Historical Society of Pennsylvania collection.

[15] J. H. Morgan, *Dickinson College: The History of One Hundred and Fifty Years, 1783-1933* (Carlisle, Penn.: Dickinson College, 1933), pp. 218, 222). The college was later reopened under Methodist auspices.

following year issued a lengthy statement of the case; this was summarized by a student's letter:

They place the conduct of Doct. Neill, H. Vethake and several of the resigned members of their board in a quite disagreeable point of view, and one which is in no possible way enviable. On the other hand it entirely clears the Presbyterian part of the board of the old charge of sectarianism. McClelland appears, through the whole, to have acted his part as a professor ought to have . . . done, although most outragiously persecuted by the other members of the faculty. It is strongly suspected by some that . . . [Vethake] intends relating the other side of the story and I, for my part, sincerely wish he may, for I think, and indeed am certain, that both he and the old Doctor have been seriously misrepresented." [16]

Vethake, not surprisingly, replied to the trustees' statement. When power was vested in the board, he said, it was inevitably seized with a "spirit of legislation"; frequent legislation would "very naturally create a necessity for more legislation," and at length it was "perpetually meddling with the details of college government so as to reduce the Faculty almost to the condition of mere executive officers." Since the faculty tended to become timid and unwilling to act without consulting the trustees, the number of trustees' meetings increased and so did delays and the inefficiency of operations. Worse, the faculty was without the bond of union, that necessary "esprit de corps," which existed where the faculty was not continually interfered with in its appropriate province.

The major source of the ills, he complained, was the lack of faculty representation. Consequently the board must often legislate in the dark or be guided by frequently inaccurate and prejudiced statements of one of its own members who might be supposed to be better informed on the matter at issue than the others. Also, the trustees made a mystery of their proceedings so far as the faculty was concerned, and thus impaired the

[16] C. C. Hames to H. B. Wright, Dec. 16, 1830. Wyoming Historical and Geological Society collection.

mutual confidence that should exist between them. The remedy was to allow a regular representation of the faculty, at least when the discipline or order of the college was involved.[17]

Vethake seems to have had a certain following. On his return from a visit in 1829–30 to the leading mathematicians and physicists in Prussia, one student wrote to another, "Have you heard . . . how he was welcomed by old and young, large and small, literary and unlearned?" [18]

Meanwhile the College of New Jersey was seeking Vethake's services. Just before he had gone abroad he had refused the offer of its professorship of mathematics, because he felt that the salary of $1,000 and a house was inadequate. On his return, in 1830, he accepted the professorship of natural philosophy at $1,200 and a house. Vethake's courses included history for the sophomores, natural philosophy for the juniors, and natural philosophy, astronomy, and political economy for the seniors. The seniors were so impressed with his course on political economy that at their request his first lecture in January, 1831, was published.[19]

In 1830 Vethake became active in the movement to establish a national university in New York City which would resemble the universities on the Continent. Columbia College was con-

[17] Vethake, *Reply to a "Narrative of the Proceedings of the Board of Trustees of Dickinson College from 1821 to 1830"* (Princeton, N.J.: privately printed, 1830).

[18] J. F. Latta to H. B. Wright, July 19, 1830. Wyoming Historical and Geological Society collection.

[19] Vethake, *An Introductory Lecture on Political Economy, delivered at Nassau Hall, January 31, 1831* (Princeton, N.J.: W. D'Hart, 1831). It was reprinted in the influential free trade organ *Banner of the Constitution*, II (March 9, 1831), 113–15.

The editor of the *Banner*, Condy Raguet, had praised Vethake's performance with the statement that "the reputation of the professor for deep erudition in the mathematics is extensive, and the influence of his name, in connection with the lecture cannot fail to produce an accession of strength and numbers to our [free trade] cause" (*ibid.*, p. 119). The Carlisle *Republican* in an editorial hailed the lecture as presenting "the orthodox system of the economists" founded by Smith and Ricardo (*ibid.*, March 23, 1831).

sidered by critics to be too closely allied to the Episcopal Church, especially the "high church" element, and too much devoted to the classics and the cultivation of "gentlemen." As John McVickar's son and biographer put it, "the closeness . . . and conservative character of her corporation, her high appreciation of classical training and her churchly origins, created enemies and at this time they all combined in the attempt to give her a secondary position, by establishing, in New York, a great university which should unite in itself all the literary and scientific bodies in the city." [20] The chief promoter of the new institution chartered in 1831 was a Columbia trustee, the Reverend James M. Mathews, pastor of the South Dutch Reformed Church, who became its first president with the title of chancellor. The University of the City of New York (later New York University) was, like the recently established University of London, organized as a joint stock corporation with shareholders each entitled to one vote for every $100 of capital stock in choosing a governing board. A $10,000 subscription entitled its purchaser to nominate a professor, subject to the approval of the administration. A somewhat novel feature of the new institution was an embryonic fellowship system, which allowed large subscribers to send a pupil without charge.[21] It was voted that no "one religious denomination should at any time have a majority on the governing board." Albert Gallatin was chosen president of the university council.[22]

A call had been issued to prominent figures in the academic

[20] W. A. McVickar, *The Life of the Reverend John McVickar* (New York: Hurd and Houghton, 1872), p. 122.

[21] *The Constitution and Statutes for the present Government of the University of the City of New York* (New York: Mercein, 1831), pp. 4–5. Vethake attempted to use this provision to enable one of his able College of New Jersey students "to meet the *additional* expense of going to the University (board included) instead of continuing at Princeton." (Letter from Vethake to James M. Mathews, April 16, 1832, in Historical Society of Pennsylvania collection.)

[22] *New York University, 1832:1932*, ed. Theodore F. Jones (New York: New York Univ. Press, 1933), p. 17.

world and in cultural and business affairs to meet in New York City in October, 1830, to give advice on policy for the proposed new university. This three-day Convention of Literary and Scientific Gentlemen was the most impressive assembly of leaders in education that had as yet been held in the United States. Vethake took part. In fact, his was the first main address; and he used it to say that the existing colleges were "for those only who have the wealth necessary to enable them to consume many years of their lives in the exclusive, or nearly the exclusive, occupation of learning two complicated and difficult languages, very imperfectly, in most cases, if at all." He went on to advocate abolition of the Bachelor of Arts degree and the substitution for it of the French practice of alternate degrees, one in literature, which would require Greek and Latin, and one in science, which would not require the two dead languages, but would demand that the student make "a certain progress in *some* of the sciences, as, for example, in mathematics and natural philosophy, or in chemistry and natural history." He suggested that for the class system which was responsible for student solidarity and consequent riots, there should be substituted a curriculum with elective features. If these changes were made, "sons of persons in moderate circumstances—of our farmers and mechanics"—would be induced to enter the colleges; this would uplift the moral tone of the higher institutions of learning. Gallatin expressed a similar view. He thought that the proposed university should be a graduate school and at the same time should "diffuse knowledge and render it more accessible to the community at large." [23]

[23] *Journal of the Proceedings of a Convention of Literary and Scientific Gentlemen* (New York: Jonathan Leavitt and G&C&H Carvill, 1831), pp. 23, 35, 40, 170.

In the course of pointing out the advantages of a great university in New York, George Bancroft, the eminent historian and Jacksonian leader said something of importance:

"On men of letters the great commercial city would exert a favorable

Others expressed the hope that the new institution would give particular attention to many important branches of knowledge to which professorships were almost unknown in American colleges, notably: history, political economy, geography, statistics, agriculture, the principles of legislation, comparative anatomy, and the fine arts.

Vethake, whose address had deeply impressed Mathews, served from the start as a chief aide to the chancellor in the planning of the curricula and the selection of the faculty. It was natural that he should be among the first to be offered a major post. Residence in a big city was a major inducement to Vethake; he expressed a willingness to teach either mathematics or natural philosophy. In conformity with his wishes he was originally to be appointed professor of mechanical philosophy and astronomy. But on second thought he found fault with the title, because its lack of sufficient definiteness made it subject to misapprehension. He informed the chancellor that he intended to teach the various branches of natural philosophy as commonly understood. These were "Statics, Dynamics, Hydrostatics, Hydrodynamics, Pneumatics, Acoustics, Heat, Electricity, including Galvanism, Magnetism, Optics, Astronomy; to which it may be added as a separate branch, Meteorology." But mechanical philosophy was usually restricted to what was called mechanics. This included "Statics, Dynamics, Hydrostatics, Hydrodynamics, Pneumatics," with the latter term embracing the remainder of natural philosophy except astronomy, under the designation of "physics." Consequently, except for its length, the title

---

influence. The habit of the place is industry; and the literary man, partaking of the general excitement, is led to form habits of profound application. So, too, the varied intercourse with men of all nations, stirs the stagnant pool of superstition and prejudice. The immense movements in business, the daily spectacle of crowds of sail from every quarter of the world, the frequent presence of minds, which have been developed in the most diffused pursuits, or ripened under every sky, gradually yet surely tend to promote intellectual freedom, and to do away that narrow mindedness which is the worst enemy of improvement" (pp. 51–52).

professor of mechanics, physics and astronomy would be satisfactory. The most desirable title would be the one used at London University, that of professor of natural philosophy and astronomy.

Vethake's concern over a precision in the title of his chair involved a much more constructive matter; namely the prevention of a rigid boundary between the fields of chemistry and physics—areas which only recently had been separated and which were both undergoing substantial changes. The matter of title, as he explained, was of no consequence, provided the professor of chemistry who, besides chemistry proper must necessarily give instruction also in heat, electricity, and galvanism, understood that he did not have the exclusive right of instruction in those branches, but that they were equally open to both professors; that is, the professor of chemistry could take up anything in natural philosophy that would make his course more efficient and interesting, and vice versa. Vethake pointed out that he would find himself quite crippled if he could not take up certain aspects of chemistry. Both professors and courses would gain substantially by this mutual borrowing. Students in natural philosophy would be incited to cultivate chemistry, and students in chemistry would find their interest stimulated in natural philosophy. The arrangement would work well at the new university, he predicted, because the prospective professor of chemistry, his friend and colleague at the College of New Jersey, John Torrey, as a man of "liberal views," was taking the same attitude.[24]

Before the title of his chair was definitely settled, however, the authorities found it difficult to fill the chair of mathematics. Vethake searched for an appropriate person; but as he ex-

[24] Letter of Vethake to Mathews, March 10, 1832, in Historical Society of Pennsylvania collection. Torrey's full title was professor of chemistry, mineralogy and botany. He became a famous botanist; Asa Gray was his student and collaborator.

plained to the chancellor, the task was hard, because pedantry was a characteristic failing of mathematicians. Furthermore, there was need to consider the candidate's "religious or moral *tone*." [25]

The result was that when the first professorial appointments were made in July, 1832, he became, at his own suggestion, professor of mathematics and astronomy.[26]

At the same time, Vethake urged that the social sciences be given an important role in the university. He called attention to the need of history, especially the philosophy of history. This, as he put it later, should be "of the kind which has given origin to some of the best histories in the German language, and to which in France, we owe the celebrated work of the eloquent and philosophic Guizot on the civilization of modern Europe." [27] At his suggestion, the authorities also appointed him lecturer on history, and he scheduled a course of public lectures on the French Revolution of 1789.

Vethake was naturally anxious that there be a department of political economy, but barriers to its achievement were more than the difficulty of obtaining sufficient funds. This was indicated by Vethake in his suggestion to the chancellor in August, 1832, that the one temporary exception to the rule that a candidate for the B.A. should be examined by all the professors should be in the case of political economy, for while the subject was to be taught by a "*professor* and not by a lecturer [still] on account of the relation of the subject to party politics, and the peculiar jealousy entertained regarding it by the majority of the community, I would by all

[25] Letter of Vethake to Mathews, February 3, 1832, in Historical Society of Pennsylvania collection.

[26] Letter of Vethake to Mathews, July 3, 1832, in New-York Historical Society collection.

His salary was $2,000 plus the fees from his public lectures. In 1833, "natural philosophy" was added to his teaching load and title.

[27] Vethake, "The Distinctive Provinces of the Political Philosopher and the Statesman," p. 117.

means *not* make that subject essential to the obtaining of a diploma. To do otherwise might make enemies most unnecessarily of some, who might be conciliated by the course suggested." [28]

Vethake was disappointed to find a month later in the announcement of the university's opening that political economy was among those departments that would not be started at present, but would be added shortly.[29] He was concerned that at least a lecture course should be given. He had been asked by the authorities even before the university formally opened to give a series of lectures on "politico-economical subjects." Vethake was glad to give them, but there was then one fly in the ointment. They could only be three or four instead of a full series of ten or twelve if the auditors, he said, were of both sexes. As he informed the authorities, "If *ladies* are expected to be present (which I hope will not be the case) I shall find it very difficult to treat the subject at all on account of the manner in which the theory of *population* is necessarily involved in it." [30]

The problem was solved eventually by having Vethake deliver the lectures in the winter of 1832–33 in the same hall that housed the university, but under the auspices of the New York Young Men's Society. His listeners—like the

[28] Letter of Vethake to Mathews, Aug. 2, 1832, in Historical Society of Pennsylvania collection. Vethake thought the B.A. should be temporarily retained because some able students might otherwise be attracted to the older institution.

[29] Vethake had expected that his friend and fellow Columbia alumnus William Beach Lawrence would be appointed to the professorship. He wrote to Mathews on September 2, 1832 that he had missed, in the chancellor's public announcement, the appointment of Lawrence. (The letter is in the Historical Society of Pennsylvania collection.)

Lawrence had delivered in December, 1831, two lectures on political economy under the auspices of the Mercantile Library Association of the City of New York, whose building, Clinton Hall, was the temporary home of the university. He is discussed in the following essay.

[30] Letter of Vethake to John Delafield, Nov. 15, 1831, in Historical Society of Pennsylvania collection.

seniors of the College of New Jersey—considered them "eloquent and profound" and caused the opening address to be printed.[31]

Soon, however, Vethake was involved in difficulties with the administration. That the university would have a stormy beginning had already been foreshadowed by Gallatin's severance of all connections with it before it actually opened in the fall of 1832. As one of his biographers has put it, Gallatin felt that "none of the goals he thought desirable had been adopted." [32] It had been in operation only a little more than a year when it was "convulsed" by a series of "explosions," involving the faculty and the chancellor. These culminated in the resignation of three of the five members of the regular faculty, including Vethake. They presented their case to the public in a pamphlet. It was their contention that the chancellor had acted as though the university was only an ordinary college and that he viewed its operations from the standpoint of their publicity value. They accused the university council of being "blinded by the fact that the university needed money and that Dr. Mathews was particularly valuable to them as a procurer of that indispensable commodity." [33]

A year later Vethake, so often in disagreement with other

[31] Vethake, *An Introductory Lecture on Political Economy delivered in Clinton Hall before the New York Young Men's Society, Dec. 21, 1832* (New York: Moore, 1833).

[32] Raymond Walters, Jr., *Albert Gallatin: Jeffersonian Financier and Diplomat* (New York: Macmillan, 1957), p. 351.

Walters has pointed out that the university "in the course of several decades, adopted Gallatin's principles of scientific and English instruction to serve the people of many stocks in the city, and of graduate training" (p. 351).

[33] Henry Vethake, John Mulligan, and John Torrey, *An Exposition of the Reasons for the Resignation of Some of the Professors in the University of the City of New York* (New York: Van Norden, 1833).

For an illuminating discussion of the early difficulties of the University see Richard J. Storr, *The Beginnings of Graduate Education in America* (Chicago: Univ. Chicago Press, 1953), pp. 33–43.

administrators, found himself faced with the same difficulties. He had in 1834 been appointed to the presidency of Washington College (now Washington and Lee University), where he also served as rector of the board of trustees and professor of mathematics and moral philosophy. He had obtained the post through some friends at the College of New Jersey.[34]

In his inaugural address, after noting that it was of primary importance that every student should receive religious instruction, he denounced the "rigid conservatism" of instruction and curricula in the colleges. He pointed out that "there are . . . many quack teachers, who . . . have no other guide but a routine to which they were accustomed when they themselves were pupils, or which they have borrowed with little or no alteration from other teachers who have preceded them." He deprecated the characteristic method of having students recite the precise contents of the textbook. This precluded, he said, any questioning, any curiosity, any "spirit of independence" among them. When a vacant professorship occurred in "metaphysical, ethical, and political science it was not surprising that a multitude of candidates presented themselves. And, were we to judge simply from the number and very limited qualifications of the candidates, we would conclude that moral or political philosophy instead of being fitted to exercise to the utmost the powers of the human intellect, is a mere bundle of truisms, obvious to the comprehension of the dullest and most unlettered of men." He noted that "the sciences [both moral and physical] are of course intended to be taught as extensively as the time appropriated to them by the student will admit." He showed

[34] The salary was $1,000 and a house, plus an equal share with the two professors of the tuition fee of thirty dollars a year per student. He was told frankly that the stipend was not as high as at some institutions, "but considering the cheapness of living here, the salubrity of our climate, and some other advantages, the salary will we hope be deemed not inadequate." (Letter from committee to Vethake, Dec. 4, 1834, in Washington and Lee University, Treasurer's Office.)

his respect for economics by referring to it as the "modern science of political economy." [35]

Vethake did little teaching in the moral sciences. As a colleague, the Reverend Henry Ruffner, noted, "very few of the students were sufficiently advanced to study them." Ruffner thought his mathematics teaching was done with much ability, but that he showed some strong peculiarities. At examination he was heard to ask one astonishing question: "If 20 turkeys cost 50 cents apiece, what would be the cost of a hogshead of tobacco?"

Ruffner's son has left an excellent portrait of Vethake during this period. "He was a man of dignified appearance and manners, reserved yet cordial. He was perhaps six feet in height, with somewhat heavy features, round in body and limb without being fleshy." He seemed to be "disconnected from surrounding objects" and given to exercising "his reflective rather than his perceptive faculties. He showed in his teaching that besides a little dry humor now and then he was capable of profound and long sustained trains of thought. This he showed in another way. Chess was the gentleman's game in Lexington." The leading player admitted that Dr. Vethake not only went far beyond him, "but he introduced a style of playing that had not been known here previously, to-wit, the excogitation of a complete campaign down to the checkmate as soon as three or four opening moves had been made." [36]

Vethake soon again had difficulties over discipline. In 1836 a student who had been suspended assaulted him. As he lay prostrate, the professor of chemistry came to his rescue with a pair of tongs. The student summoned a party of his friends

[35] Vethake, *An Address Delivered at His Inauguration, as President of Washington College, Lexington, Virginia, February 21st, 1835* (Lexington, Va.: Baldwin, 1835).

[36] W. H. Ruffner, "The History of Washington College, 1830–1848," in Washington and Lee University, *Historical Papers*, No. 6 (May, 1904), pp. 26–27.

and attempted to waylay the rescuer. The participants were taken to court.

After this experience Vethake began looking for another position. It was necessary. He was recently married. While he was away on a trip in the northwest to see what there might be in the way of lands for speculation, he received notice of his appointment at the University of Pennsylvania as professor of mathematics.[37] There he became known, in the words of the future president, James A. Buchanan, as "one of the most learned, respectable and esteemed citizens of Pennsylvania." [38] In 1846 he was made vice-provost and eight years later provost of the university. In 1855 he exchanged the professorship of mathematics for that of intellectual and moral philosophy.[39]

[37] University of Pennsylvania, Minutes of the Trustees, August 23, 1836. (The minutes are in the secretary's office.) His salary was $2,300.

The chair of mathematics included "Algebra, Geometry, Plane and Spherical, Trigonometry with applications to Surveying, Navigation, etc., General Theory of Equations, Analytical Geometry including Conic Sections. Differential and Integral Calculus [and] Analytical Mechanics."

Vethake had declined the professorship of natural philosophy at Pennsylvania in 1828. (Letter of Vethake to Nicholas Biddle, August 24, 1828, in University of Pennsylvania collection, Office of the Archivist. Biddle was chairman of the Committee of the Trustees that was reorganizing the staff.)

[38] Notation by James A. Buchanan, dated April 27, 1848, on letter from Henry Vethake, dated April 22, to General Henderson, in the Historical Society of Pennsylvania collection.

[39] While provost, Vethake taught seven hours a week, spending four hours with the seniors, and three hours with the juniors. In his major course, the textbooks were *Elements of Mental Philosophy*, by the professor of mental and moral philosophy of Bowdoin College, Thomas C. Upham, and *The Elements of Moral Science*, by Francis Wayland, president of Brown University and author of the most popular treatise on economics, *The Elements of Political Economy*. Vethake used William Paley's *Natural Theology* and *Evidences of Christianity* in his courses on religion. Beginning in 1852, Vethake also lectured on the Constitution of the United States and used as the textbook Mordecai McKinney's *United States Constitutional Manual* (1845); 2d ed., titled *Our Government* (1856).

During his first year as professor of intellectual and moral philosophy, Vethake also taught history via Georg Weber's *Outlines of Universal History* (translation by Francis Bowen of Harvard) and logic from Archbishop Whately's *Elements of Logic;* but on October 9, 1855, the trustees decided that the professor of English language and literature should teach these subjects.

From the beginning of his tenure at Pennsylvania, Vethake lectured on political economy, but it was not until 1854 that the discipline was recognized as a part of the fixed curriculum and subject to examination.[40] The trustees on March 20, 1855, accepted the report of its committee on alterations of the Collegiate Department, which recommended among other things that political economy be a part of a provost's duties. The minutes of the board of trustees, of October 2, specifically speak of "Lectures on Political Economy every Wednesday at the fourth hour." In the minutes of February 5, 1856, political economy acquired more dignity. It was the regular subject for the seniors, and the provost's *The Principles of Political Economy* (1838; 2d edition, 1844), was specified as a text. This, like the manuals prepared by McVickar, followed in general the British classical school, but was more comprehensive and systematic, so much so that one college acquaintance was led to say that it was "better suited to interest political economists than college students." [41]

Vethake insisted that he did not treat political economy as being a "science only of hypothetical description," without any "necessary connection with . . . public affairs." The science included "the laws which regulate the production, distribution, and consumption of wealth"; in order to ascertain what course individuals and government should pursue or avoid in disposing of the wealth under their control, so as to maximize the happiness of mankind.

Vethake in his published introductory lectures had already elaborated on methodological issues. In his New York lecture, following a Newtonian model, he explained that to achieve

[40] Printed circular letter, University of Pennsylvania, Department of Arts and Letters, Dec. 13, 1854, addressed to Committee to Attend the Examination. Copy in minutes of the faculty, in the office of the archivist, University of Pennsylvania.

[41] W. H. Ruffner, "The History of Washington College, 1830–1848," p. 25.

a perfect theory in science, "we should know first all the causes which actually conspire to produce the phenomena to be explained," and second, "we should be able to determine accurately the effect produced by each separate and independent cause." Thereby prediction was possible. But the sciences centering in the human mind generally lack the necessary exact information and must often deal with probabilities, sometimes slight ones.

He cited three barriers to the progress of political economy even though its practitioners might possess an unquenchable love of truth: (1) the influence of their feelings and motivations in diverting them from properly estimating the relative importance of the manifold considerations involved in the phenomena; (2) the "undue weight attached by the mind to arguments that from the circumstance in which the individual is placed, are more frequently the object of attention than others, perhaps of equal comparative moment"; (3) the vagueness and ambiguity of language used in discussing the subject, which often led to confused and circular speculations.

Despite its limitations, continued Vethake, political economy contained the promise inherent in every science of a cumulative development. "Those limits which at one period task the power of the strongest minds for their discussion constitute in a subsequent age the inheritance of all, and come to be regarded . . . as so many elementary steps to a further advance, . . ."

In his published lecture at the College of New Jersey especially he had sought to overcome the suspicions directed against this new science and to show its usefulness to clergymen, lawyers, merchants, legislators, and statesmen. He recognized and countered several familiar criticisms: that political economists did not agree on the fundamental terms; that the study was new, metaphysical, and abstract; that its adepts were theorists with little practical sense; and that its conclusions conflicted with the precepts of religion, in particular with "respect to pauperism and its relief."

He felt it necessary to meet the argument that political economists were unnecessary since "nations have prospered from the beginning of time to the present" without their assistance, and that anyway their conclusions ran contrary to the wisdom of the ages. His answer was this:

> Now as regards the setting up of his [the political economist's] conclusions in opposition to the wisdom of the ages, everyone who has ever been guilty of expressing an original thought has done the same thing, and it is only by such "setting up" that there has been . . . an improvement in the condition of mankind, physical, social, moral or political.

He argued further that since other changes that were continually occurring were acknowledged to be beneficial,

> why should the changes proposed by the political economist alone be considered injurious to society? And without any mention of nations which, instead of advancing in prosperity without the aid of political economy, have declined without the like aid, are we to take for granted *a priori* that because a society enjoys a certain degree of prosperity, the counsels of the political economist would have no influence to augment that prosperity? The causes that conspire to produce the actual condition of a people, are manifold, some of them operating advantageously, and others disadvantageously. Will not, then, the science that comprehends within its scope the discovery of these causes, together with the means of giving additional activity to the former description of them, and of removing or weakening the energy of the latter, have a natural tendency in favor of the public welfare? . . . National prosperity, as the expression is generally employed, is perfectly consistent with a vast amount of misery. The condition of the great majority of the people, for example, in many European countries, which no one hesitates to denominate prosperous, cries aloud for improvement; and such improvement . . . is one of the principal objects of political economy.

He felt the need of empirical research throughout the economic world and made a contribution by editing an American version of McCulloch's *Dictionary, Practical, Theoretical and Historical, of Commerce and Commercial Navigation* (1839). His preface stated that "there is, generally speaking, an extreme difficulty in the United States of procuring statistical information, which may be depended on for its accuracy."

Vethake's *Principles of Political Economy* began with a comprehensive discussion of the theory of value. His sophisticated analysis of the mechanics of supply and demand in the determination of the exchange value of a commodity has a modern ring. He defined the supply of a commodity as

> the quantity of it which comes into the possession of the sellers and is offered by them for sale, during a given portion of time. This must be distinguished from the amount or stock of it [the commodity] which the sellers may think it for their advantage to keep on hand, in order to atttract purchasers to their respective stores or warehouses. . . . The demand is to be estimated by the number of offers to purchase made in a given time, at any given rate, and when more offers are made to purchase a commodity at its existing price than before, the demand is said to have increased, while the contrary will take place when the number of similar offers is diminished.

He pointed out that "in like manner, the demand for money is correctly said to become greater when people generally are more disposed than they previously were to retain it in their possession for future use." He examined in succession "the different modes in which variations in the relation between the supply of, and the demand for, commodities, can influence their prices." In the case of demand for a commodity remaining the same, but supply becoming more abundant, sellers must lower the price to avoid an accumulation of stock, which would be so much "dead and unprofitable capital." Many previous purchasers would buy larger quantities; and some who had refrained from buying would now become purchasers. The price would cease to fall when the "quantity disposed of is just equal to the supply."

If supply is reduced, while demand remains the same, "the interest of sellers will prompt them to raise its price, until in consequence of the corresponding diminution of the amount of sales, the quantity disposed of will . . . be just equal to the diminished supply."

In the case of the supply remaining the same, with increased demand, Vethake pointed out that

> we can suppose that an increase of demand to arise, either from a change in the fashions of the day, or from some new use to which the article in question is capable of being applied. But whatever the occasion of it may be, the sellers will be induced to raise prices; for by doing so, while they make greater profits, they can at the same time, dispose of the whole supply.

Last, he explained that a "diminution of demand" would obviously produce an effect directly opposite to that resulting from an increase of demand.

He also noted that prices were affected not only by actual

> variations in the rates of supply and demand but also by every expectation of the imminence of such variations at some future time. . . . Every expected future change in the rate of supply or demand will have an influence on present prices, so much the less in proportion to the *remoteness of the expectation*. . . . The degree, too, of that influence will depend, in some measure, on the *nature of the commodity*.

Notable was the inclusion of a chapter on "Effects of Monopolies on Prices." [42]

[42] Vethake did not make explicit use of mathematical economics; but he was a mathematician and was well acquainted with the works of men who were prominent in the development of that area. His library contained, e.g., Cournot, *Traité élementaire de la theorie des fonctions* and Charles Ellet, *Essay on the Laws of Trade*. Evidencing Vethake's interests in economics beyond the familiar standard authors was his possession of such

There was a sharp questioning of the doctrine, identified with Ricardo, that the price of a commodity was in proportion to the "amount of *labour* necessary from first to last to produce it." Since the theory was a "favorite one with some political economists of the highest order" it was worthy of examination, but it seemed to Vethake that no significant practical consequences depended upon its validity. The other element determining price, besides the quantity of labor in producing a commodity, was the "time that elapses from the application of the several portions of labour until the production of it is in its complete state." He conceded, however, that the prices of goods were more frequently lowered by a reduction of the quantity of labor necessary for their production, or

> what is the same thing, by a given quantity of labor having been rendered more productive, than by a diminution of the time required in production. Improvements of the latter description we know from experience to be confined within comparatively very narrow limits; while, on the other hand, improvements of a labor-saving nature have been introduced more especially in our own age, with extraordinary rapidity, and to a prodigious extent. Hence I would not object to the language of those writers who, when speaking generally, regard all improvements in the arts as resulting from a greater productiveness of labor.

Vethake most strongly and systematically attacked the view of the British classical economists, that only the labor directly applied to the production of material commodities should be classified as productive; in fact, he did this so

---

books as Karl H. Rau, *Finanzwissenschaft;* Simonde de Sismondi, *Nouveaux principes d'économie politique,* P. J. Proudhon, *Système des contradictions économiques, ou philosophie de la misère;* H. D. Macleod, *The Theory and Practice of Banking;* Thomas Hodgskin, *Popular Political Economy.* (*Catalogue of the Valuable Private Library of Henry Vethake to be sold at Auction . . . February 26, 1872, and following day by Bangs, Merwin & Co., New York, Charles C. Shelley, Printer.*)

For an interesting, recent account of Rau, see Z. Clark Dickinson, "The Library and Works of Karl Heinrich Rau," *Zeitschrift für die Staatswissenschaft,* Band 114, Heft 4 (1958), pp. 577–93.

forcefully that one of his former Dickinson students, the prominent minister the Reverend George W. Bethune, exclaimed in a public address at Pennsylvania: "God bless him for rescuing the physician, the jurist, the divine, the man of letters, and the man of science, out of the same category with jugglers and opera dancers, where previous economists had placed us as unproductive consumers." [43]

Vethake agreed that there could be "unproductive *consumption*" in the sense of wealth not designed for use as capital, but there could be no unproductive labor except when more labor than necessary was used to produce a particular good or when more of a commodity was produced than was required by "the comparative wants of the community." Whether the product be material or immaterial, the labor is productive, for the "*ultimate* product" of both is "*agreeable sensations*" of consumption. He thought that if the political economist succeeded in banishing from popular language such phrases as "the productive classes and the unproductive classes" the result would be a great political and moral advantage; it would be the most effective way of preventing "the 'workmen' . . . from esteeming themselves to be the only *useful* portion of a society."

He believed that "free competition between employers and employed" was an essential element of that "natural course of things" which was most beneficial to the interest of both rich and poor. Accordingly, he held the customary view that "trades' unions" were an "unmixed evil." At best they could succeed only temporarily, since their success would retard the rate of capital accumulation and this would be "accompanied by a less rapid increase of population and a diminution of the rate of wages." Similarly, Vethake gravely doubted that the adult laborer would benefit from a legis-

[43] *An Address Before the Philomathean Society of the University of Pennsylvania* (Philadelphia: John C. Clark, 1840), p. 24.

lative reduction of the work day. The leisure time to which he was not accustomed might "contribute to deteriorate instead of improving his condition, by being spent as often in dissipation and vice, as in the business of acquiring knowledge or exercising his mental faculties."

In the question of relief to the unemployed Vethake held views that were somewhat in advance of dominant opinion. These he had originally expressed in an essay which was designed to show the usefulness of political economy to the ministry.[14] He had begun with a radical thesis. "Improvements in machinery, and in the various arts of life," he said, "seem everywhere—under differing forms of government, and different modes of administration—to have been chiefly instrumental in improving the condition of the already more privileged and prosperous classes of society." But this situation was neither the exclusive consequence of vicious political institutions, nor the inevitable lot of humanity. The explanation lay in moral causes: the lack of foresight, thrift, and prudence, which resulted in an undue increase of population. Here, following Malthus, and casting the inquiry into mathematical form, he began with "Let us now suppose the population to be on the increase." The answer was to retard the increase by "all *proper* means," that is, the measures taken should voluntary. But Vethake differed from Malthus in favoring public poor relief.

There are those . . . who have been led to proscribe, as it were the wretchedness around them, and to look upon him who is reduced to beggary, very much in the light of one whose employment is to prepare the way for the reduction of many others . . . to the same wretched condition with themselves, and who should

[14] "An Essay on the Moral Relations of Political Economy" in Presbyterian Church in the United States, Board of Education, *Annual 1835*, ed. John Breckenridge (Philadelphia: privately printed, 1835), pp. 117, 143. Breckenridge, who was also recording secretary of the board, had been a student of Vethake at the College of New Jersey.

be dismissed without ceremony on that account, as *hostis humani generis*.

However, it was necessary to help those who "from infirmities, old age, or extreme youth, are unable to gain a livelihood, and such of the able-bodied labourers as having been thrown out of employment, cannot readily find employment again." He granted that such aid weakened the motive for the accumulation of wealth, but in the choice of evils people could not "put aside the sympathies of their nature or the precepts of the Bible."

For the involuntarily unemployed, Vethake proposed that work be provided in workhouses, or in their own homes, every such person to receive "less than the ordinary rate of wages, or what amounts to the same thing, . . . being systematically rendered less comfortable than . . . the independent labourer."

Vethake was among the first American economists to discuss systematically the economic effects of immigration. Immigrants of superior intelligence, or skill in any of the arts, or any superior qualifications were, he granted, a national gain. Other immigrant labor would not be a national benefit, if it did not bring capital sufficient for the employment of labor to an equal extent with the labor which it added to the existing working force, for the rate of wages would fall.

Speaking of government aid to religion, Vethake asserted that religion was the one great exception to the doctrine that what was, generally speaking, the duty of an individual in reference to the national welfare was also the duty of the government. "We are unanimous in thinking that the cause of religion is impaired . . . by an alliance with men in power, and that an entire equality of privileges on the part of the different religious sects [is best adapted] . . . to turn them from vain speculations and fruitless controversies with each other to the exercise of a practical piety."

It was different with education. Legislative appropriations for the common schools were proper in order that children might be prepared to become useful citizens, and public money should also be given to colleges and universities. Opponents of public aid for higher education, he pointed out, contended that since colleges were places for the education of the rich, the rich should bear the entire cost. There was a ready remedy: increase the public contribution to the institutions of higher learning. This would enable them to provide training at comparatively small expense. Since the public contribution would make possible a greater number of highly educated people, a taste for knowledge would be more surely and rapidly transmitted through the successive gradations of society. The resulting rise in the character of the laborer would increase his command over luxuries and necessaries. Similarly, there ought to be public support for science, literature, and the fine arts, and especially for the "useful arts" (which he felt was a misnomer since the "fine arts" were equally useful).

The ultimate justification for government aid for these "intellectual products" was that people could not estimate as accurately their relative advantages as they could material products, and if they had to depend on a "pre-existing demand," mankind would advance very slowly, if at all.

Government regulations to prevent persons not properly qualified from belonging to any of the learned professions, or from engaging in any other employment, should gradually disappear. They were based on the supposition that a "considerable portion of the community are not sufficiently well informed to be able to form a proper judgment concerning the qualifications of the professional man, or other *labourers*, for whose services he may be disposed to apply." Vethake predicted that, with the diffusion of knowledge, first one, and then another, of these restraints could be removed to the public advantage.

A class of government interferences with men's liberty of action was fortunately on its way out. This included government inspection of the quality of certain goods and the restriction of transactions in certain commodities to particular times and places. These annoyances to both buyer and seller were unaccompanied by compensatory advantages, and served merely to supply the occasion of "creating a number of offices for partisans or creatures of the administration."

But Vethake approved state regulation of railroad (and also canal) rates. Such enterprises were either legal or *de facto* monopolies. An existing railroad could prevent the rise of a competitor by virtue of its possession of the field. Should news of its extraordinary profits lead capitalists to consider promoting a competing enterprise, the old company could often postpone or even prevent its construction, by temporarily lowering the rates. The railroads should be built by private individuals or companies, under legislative authority; the rates should be fixed by government at a level that on the one hand would not raise undue obstacles to the "progress of improvement, and, on the other, secure the country the benefit of an interested agency in the superintendence of that progress, without making too great a sacrifice to the grasping spirit of monopoly"; but at the end of a given period the public should acquire the property at "original cost, or at any other stipulated price."

He felt that the law on the subject should be as general as possible in order to provide the maximum degree of impartiality toward every individual and every district of a country, both as to benefits rendered and as to damages to property inevitably suffered. He suggested that a "tribunal" should be established to decide on the expediency of proposed roads or canals. The commission would be guided by principles formulated by the legislature with the objective of determining how far the public good, viewed on the most extensive scale, justified an interference with private property without prior consent of the owner.

In the case of the post office, Vethake made a modification. After warning that a government should never view it as a source of revenue, he added: "I might, perhaps, with propriety, go even farther, and maintain the expediency, in so far as newspapers and periodicals are concerned, of making some *sacrifice* to promote by their circulation the diffusion of knowledge, political and literary, among the great body of a people."

Vethake devoted much more space to taxation than was customary. He thought that in principle much could be said for the view that the first source of taxation should be rent "wherever this may be paid, be it in agriculture, manufactures, or commerce; or I may say simply a tax upon the rent of *land;* considering land . . . as the representative of all the situations or sites in which there is a return of rent, to the proprietor, over and above the ordinary profits of the capital invested by him." Before any other taxes were levied, according to this principle, this source should be fully exhausted. Such a tax, he pointed out, was justified on the Ricardian doctrine that rent was conferred "*gratuitously* on the owners of the land" and that the owners could almost always calculate upon obtaining a continually increasing revenue with the country's growth in wealth and population, "and all the while without any sacrifice on their part." But there were insuperable objections, also Ricardian, to be made on grounds of both practice and equity. It was impossible to distinguish in practice between rent and profits (which included interest), especially in agriculture. Second, such a practice would be equitable only if it had been enforced in a country from its original settlement, for then every person who at any time possessed the land would know that it would now yield greater return than the ordinary profit of the capital he invested in it.

But in the actual state of things the case is very different. The possession of lands of a country has been passing, it may be for many centuries, with more or less frequency, from individual to individual, every new purchaser having as entire a reliance on the secure enjoyment of the produce, or advantages generally to be derived from it, as he could possibly have in the possession of any other kind of property. Hence . . . it would be quite as unjust, and therefore inexpedient, to tax exclusively or in an extraordinary degree the owners of the soil, as it would be to tax exclusively or in an extraordinary degree any other class of the community.

Vethake expressed qualified sympathy for an inheritance tax, but more enthusiasm for a tax on collateral inheritance. The best tax would be a uniform direct tax on property. Next would be an income tax, but this was less desirable than a property tax because the incomes of individuals could not be estimated as accurately as their property "or the amount of what they are at any time worth." Such a tax on every man's property in the same proportion "would be a refinement on the doctrines of free trade. It would be proclaiming to the world that the government is in no case instituted for the purpose of discriminating between the different classes of society, according as they are rich or as they are poor; and that where the public good requires a certain amount of the wealth produced to be taken by the government, every portion of it should be affected exactly in the same way as if the productiveness of labor were proportionally diminished." He was aware of the view that the tax should be progressive rather than proportional; for example, that "a man owning property to the value of $100 is less able to bear the loss of a dollar than another worth $100,000 is able to bear the loss of $1,000; and that to tax them proportionally is therefore in fact to do injustice to the former." But he thought that the advantage of a proportional property tax in reducing much of the jealousy between the rich and the poor overbalanced any "temporary inconvenience." In fact, a progressive tax would be inexpedient and unjust: for government to take from the wealthy more than their proportional share meant that government would be sitting in judgment on the distribution of wealth, and determining at pleasure how much of it should belong to the rich and poor. Vethake, like Jefferson, contended that governments "travel out of their province" and invade the right of property when they interfere with the distribution of wealth. Taxation of the wealthy, that is, depriving them of their property, should be done only "when it can be shown to be ultimately advantageous to the rich themselves, to an extent more than equivalent to the loss incurred by them in the first instance." On this basis, interestingly enough, he thought that a case might be made for factory legislation for children. As the "general principles of taxation," Vethake laid down that "the amount of taxation should be as small as is possible, consistent with a due regard to the interests for the protection and promotion of which governments are instituted. . . . The next general principle . . . is that, other circumstances being the same, it is desirable the taxes imposed should be so distributed as to give occasion to as few transfers of capital as possible. . . . Another principle, closely connected with the preceding, is, *caeteris paribus*, that an old tax is preferable to a new one. . . ."

"A tax which will have the effect of lowering the profits received in a branch of industry where the circulating predominates over the fixed portion of the capital invested, is preferable to one which will diminish the profits of capital where this is in a greater degree fixed than circulating. The truth of this proposition follows necessarily from the greater facility, generally speaking, of transferring circulating than fixed capital. Taxes should be imposed rather on a commodity which is prepared for *final* consumption than upon one which is in any degree the material on which labour is still further exerted; rather also upon such objects as cannot easily, on account of their possessing a great value in proportion to their bulk, or for any other reason, be subtracted from the operation of the taxes; and they should be imposed with a view to readiness and economy of collection." [45]

Vethake's views on a public debt were, like McVickar's, hardly the standard Ricardian views. He complained that the supposed evil of a public debt was the subject of as much vague and unnecessary declamation as any other important point of the science: "The evil is often very much exaggerated, while it is sometimes entirely misconceived." The amount of damage depended on the degree to which the borrowed money was unproductively expended. So far as the proceeds were properly expended, as for "national defense or other purposes of public utility," the expenditure was a national good, just as was an individual's debt which enabled him to reap a gain in excess of the inconvenience of paying interest.

To redeem the national debt would not remedy the unproductive expenditure of any portion of the borrowed

[45] Vethake's specific proposals in taxation accorded with those of free traders in general, and were well expressed in the article on "Political Economy" appearing in the opening issue (January, 1833) of the famous New York literary organ, *The Knickerbocker*. The writer offered three alternative methods of providing revenue for the federal government. First, it could be done through the proceeds from the public lands which had been ceded by older states for the support of the federal government. The writer suggested that those lands with "better husbandry may be sold or farmed out," so as to obtain at all times sufficient revenue. The other possibilities were "direct taxation bearing on all the products of industry throughout the country," or a ten percent ad valorem duty on all imports.

The editor stated that "we shall be happy, in the existing curiosity upon the subject of political economy, to contribute all in our power toward arriving at sound principles, by inviting those skilled in 'The New Science,' to unfold their different views in our pages."

money. If the holders of the debt are residents, as in the case of a domestically held debt, redemption would

be equivalent simply to a transfer of the amount of the debt from the pockets of the community in general to those of the creditors; the community, on the other hand, being relieved, in time to come, from the payment of the interest. But to possess a given portion of wealth and to pay the interest upon it, is here manifestly the same thing, in reference to the country regarded as a whole, as to part with that wealth and to be relieved from the payment of the interest.

The only economic gain from redemption of the public debt was merely the avoidance of the cost involved in collecting taxes for interest payments. He granted the moral effect of repayment in confirming the public credit, and the impression it produced on other nations of the magnitude of the national resources.

On the tariff, at that time so important an issue, Vethake had been politically active, especially as a delegate to the great Free Trade Convention of 1831 in Philadelphia, in urging a reduction of duties.[46] He was in principle a free trader, but he recognized a number of temporary exceptions or modifications. The relevant ones in the circumstances of an agricultural country, especially one continually spreading itself over a vast wilderness, were: (1) The introduction of manufactures, even at the immediate national sacrifice implied by tariff duties or bounties, would, by furnishing a greater diversity of occupations, be favorable to the development by the people of greater intellectual and therefore ultimately of greater physical powers. Every individual could then more readily find an occupation adapted to his talents;

[46] Albert Gallatin, who was chairman of the Free Trade Convention, prepared its *Memorial* (1832) to Congress. It proposed that the duties be so reduced as to leave, after the extinguishment of the public debt, only "that amount of revenue which may be necessary to meet the ordinary exigencies of the Government." The average rate, it was held, should be under twenty percent.

and "inventions" in the various arts would be made more rapidly, because "opportunity would be afforded of comparing together, a greater number of the processes actually employed in them"; (2) The population of a country might be diffused over too great an area, when compared with its numbers, and thus be subject to a considerable moral disadvantage. "A greater proportion of the people must then be almost necessarily destitute of the means of education as well as the services of religion, or must possess them to a diminished extent."

There were offsets to these advantages. They were presented with some novel Ricardian twists, going beyond the tariff itself.

> Although . . . every occupation is equally advantageous on the average, to both the capitalists and the labourers concerned—and therefore to the country in general, *insofar as the capitalists and labourers are capable of appreciating the various circumstances of advantage or disadvantage connected with it,*—it is likewise true that men are apt in most cases to exaggerate the prospects of advantage, and to do the reverse of this in reference to those of disadvantage. . . . At every period of life, we perceive individuals speculating in lotteries, in the stocks, and in property of every description, on the same principle; even with a full knowledge of the chances of success being against them, everyone looks with a more or less sanguine expectation to a prosperous result.

Thus capital and labor, relatively speaking, were drawn more to occupations in which the value of the products fluctuated most. In other words, occupations producing luxuries would be more crowded than those producing necessities; manufactures consequently would be more attractive than agriculture.

Another closely related disadvantage of manufacturing was the "sudden declension" to which many of its branches were subject, because of the "diminution of demand"—a reduction that might arise from a change in fashions. This frequently threw a large number of laborers out of employment, who would be forced at least for a time to be content with a reduced standard of living. The lowering of their ideas of a competent livelihood might tend to lead to a permanently degraded condition. This reenforced the arguments for not encouraging manufactures by legislation, before the arrival of "the natural period of their introduction."

Economists were agreed, he said, that the national welfare required that industries called into existence by war, should be given protection, if necessary, in peace time, as long as the threat of war was serious. It would be expedient, he argued, for government to impose a tariff for "the purpose of giving greater stability to the employment of capital." After considering the future prospects of the country in the light of past experiences, and surveying existing international relations, he thought that a tariff of five to ten percent would be reasonable.

Moderate protectionists felt that these views provided a common ground from which both the protectionists and the free traders might start. As the reviewer in the protectionist *North American Review* explained, Vethake

> is in favor of duties . . . sufficient to give stability to the national industry, so that it may not be alternately established and taken up on the succession of war and peace; and he thinks that if a discrimination is made in laying duties, it ought to be made so as to favor the production of articles necessary for national defense.[47]

Both *The North American Review* and the free-trade *New York Review* criticized his acceptance of the Malthusian doctrine of population as not appropriate to America's present condition, but their major criticism was directed to his monetary views.

Vethake agreed in general with the exponents of laissez

[47] "Vethake's Political Economy," *The North American Review*, XLVII (July, 1838), 248.

faire in holding that banks, by their power to expand and control currency, were the chief source of panics and depressions. When the circulating medium was expanded beyond its ordinary amount, "or average or usual state," the merchants not only could punctually pay their debts, but would also be prompt to make new purchases. Relying on the continuance of this state of things, they would extend their credit farther than they were accustomed to do. If the expansion should go on for a time they would be enabled by the corresponding rise of prices to make large profits; "and speculations generally, by whomsoever made and of whatever kind, will eventuate successfully." But reaction was inevitable. In the absence of other causes, the mere increase in the circulating medium would soon bring a contraction; for the rise in prices would result in larger imports and reduced exports; specie would be demanded from the banks to meet the balance, and the banks would be forced to curtail discounts. Money would become less abundant, and therefore more difficult to obtain. But merchants, especially, must obtain funds to meet contracts or suffer the penalty "attached to a failure." Some might be able to meet their engagements by paying high interest for loans, but many others would become bankrupt. "Those individuals who have been relying upon the receipt of the money due to them by others, and who have failed to receive such payment, will in their turn, very frequently, be prevented, in consequence, from paying with puntuality what they themselves owe. The distress . . . will thus be extended through the various ramifications of society, and will be everywhere more or less intensely felt, according to the magnitude of the *disturbance* to which the currency of the country has been subject."

After pointing out that the evils of a contraction of the

currency considerably overbalanced the "advantages or seeming advantages" of the previous expansion, he commented, "I must not forget to add the diminished production which must ensue from the greater number of persons who, at every period of this kind, are thrown out of employment altogether, or are only partially employed."

Whereas in the contraction the wage earners suffered from unemployment, in the expansion they suffered from the lag of wages. "A customary rate of wages, comes, indeed, to be paid in every place and in every employment; which, *because it is a customary rate*, is only slowly alterable."

On monetary policy however, Vethake took a "Jacksonian" position or, more precisely, a modification of the position of Jackson's heir and successor, Martin Van Buren. Like McVickar, he held that there should be only one issuer of paper money, so as to prevent monetary panics—"periodical convulsions"—but, unlike McVickar, he proposed that this power be entrusted not to a privately controlled national bank or national banking system, but to the general government. It would issue non-interest-bearing treasury notes or drafts to the public creditors who would have the option of receiving "hard money" or notes, and the notes would be receivable in payment of taxes.

Until these reforms were achieved, Vethake held, the usury laws should not be completely repealed. He agreed that since there should be "a free trade in money as in . . . every other commodity," all usury laws in principle should be eliminated, but he opposed "absolute repeal, so long as a limited number of banking institutions exist in a country, possessing peculiar privileges, and capable of combining together to diminish unexpectedly the quantity of money in circulation"; that is, the laws should be continued "until the power of regulating the currency of the society by means of an issue of paper money shall be taken from the banks and unrestricted competition shall also be permitted in the business of lending money."

The New York Review complained that, since his monetary scheme was an open approbation of President Van Buren's proposed substitute for private banks of issue, it was a "foul stain" on his economics and constituted "plotting a death blow to political economy." [48]

[48] "Vethake's Political Economy," *The New York Review*, III (July, 1838), 236.

President Van Buren's proposal, which became law as the Sub-Treasury or Independent Treasury System, provided that the government would pay out and receive only "hard" money and only at the Treasury and other places set up as sub-treasuries.

Vethake's scheme was based on that of Secretary of the Treasury Levi Woodbury in 1837. Woodbury based his views on the proposition that "the spirit of the Constitution and the first principles of political economy," require that a paper currency should always be equivalent to specie.

"While chartered and used solely for local purposes, the regulation and control of [banks] are supposed to belong exclusively to the States. But their organization as well as responsibilities and an early reform in both, became questions of great importance to the Treasury when connected with them, as heretofore, in the capacity of either public depositories or the sources of a portion of the currency received for public dues. . . . A wide departure has been made from the original principle of having its issues of paper rest on a foundation . . . of specie alone, and that used in deposite chiefly for commercial objects. [When] the paper issued rests, like mere bills of exchange, almost exclusively on credit, and that credit not always guarded in the best practicable methods, such a currency . . . must become exposed to many of the vicissitudes of commerce, forfeit most of its original character as the actual representative of money and lose its security in a considerable degree as a circulating medium for the use of either the community or the Government. Under such circumstances, that calamity . . . will often ensue which happened during the last spring [of a panic and suspension of specie payments]."

But there was a need of a sound paper currency for large payments, distant remittances, exchange, traveling, and especially in places where gold did not circulate. To achieve it, Congress should authorize the Treasury to issue non-interest bearing certificates "payable in specie to bearer or order as well as being receivable for all public dues." These would be paid to the public creditor when he preferred them and sufficient specie was in the Treasury. "This kind of paper would be very convenient in form, and would differ little from the drafts now in use in the banks, except being drawn on a known specie fund, and expressing on the face not only this, but their being receivable in the first instance for all public dues. It would possess the highest credit attainable in society." The other main provision of Woodbury's scheme brought it close to Ricardo's plan: The Treasury

The North American Review denounced Vethake's modified sub-treasury scheme as being simply government paper money. Nothing in economics, declared the reviewer, had been better settled than that such things must be avoided, but he did add an interesting qualification—"so long as the medium can be maintained any other way."[49]

Vethake acquired a certain disillusionment about the possibility of achieving salutary reform. He voiced it thus:

> Unfortunately for the interests of the community, the questions relating to our circulating medium have been for a long period involved in the contentions of party politics, and so it would seem that they are likely to continue; a most unpropitious condition of things to obtain a proper degree of public attention to the principles on which our circulating medium should be most safely, as well as most steadily, constituted.[50]

But as for political economy as a science, he never lost his conviction of its usefulness. In a lecture before the Mercantile

would invest any considerable temporary surplus or "unexpected excesses" in "safe state stocks [there were no federal securities then] at the market rate," and consequently they could be easily liquidated to meet requisitions when required. (Woodbury, "Report on the Finances," September and December 1837, reprinted in *Reports of the Secretary of the Treasury*, IV [Washington: Rivers, 1851], pp. 9, 25–26, 102–3, 106–7.)

[49] The reviewer approved of Vethake's support of poor laws, but found many serious errors and contradictions in addition to the fatal one on the currency. These included: "regulation of government cannot create capital, but only divert it from one course to another; that the capital of a country is a fixed quality; that the value of the circulating medium, whether greater or less in quantity, and whatever in kind, always bears a certain proportion to the whole capital of the country; that population has a natural tendency to increase more rapidly than food and clothing; that banks can *expand*, that is, *augment* circulating medium at pleasure, though Mr. Vethake says, not indefinitely, that facility of credit is identical with augmentation of the amount of currency, that one employment is as worthwhile to the country as another; that there is a *natural* period for introducing the useful arts into a community."

The reviewer, in amplifying his view that government regulation could increase capital, declared that "not only legislative acts but the judicial administration of the laws, the invention of a useful machine, and a thousand other influences that work through the community, *create* capital by increasing or giving greater effect to industry."

[50] *Encyclopaedia Americana*, vol. XIV, ed. Henry Vethake (Philadelphia: Lea and Blanchard, 1846), p. 615.

Library Company of Philadelphia (1839),[51] he complained that the colleges neglected its study just as they did other social sciences so essential for "the political education of their pupils" who, in many instances, were destined to become the nation's statesmen. And even when these subjects were taught, there was "a timidity in the discussion of disputed points, lest offense should be given to any considerable part of the public." This rendered the instruction uninteresting and futile. The remedy he suggested was that a college appoint two lecturers of political economy, "one of them maintaining and defending the received doctrines of the science, and the other impugning them." If the critic should be so hostile to the received doctrines as to object to being called a political economist, he might be titled "lecturer on statistics or any other title he might prefer." The student or his parent would decide which set of lectures the student should attend, but Vethake hoped that he would desire both. Such a procedure would be better for the cause of truth, the best interests of society, and the exercise of the students' intellectual faculties. It would provide a far more valuable education than that of making them the "passive recipients of the contents of whole libraries, filled with the records of other men's thoughts." [52]

Fifteen years later Vethake again complained that political economy had not been given its rightful place of at least second to "the wider spread of Christianity" as an agent of progress. Because of certain prejudices, it was "*tabooed*" alto-

[51] The Mercantile Library Company of Philadelphia, like the Mercantile Library Association of the City of New York, was an early business school. The audience was composed largely of merchants' clerks.

[52] Vethake, "The Distinctive Provinces of the Political Philosopher and the Statesman," p. 111.

A few colleges zealously pushed political economy. At Brown University, for example, a prize, the Jackson Premium, was awarded in the subject (letter of Francis Wayland to William E. Tolman, July 28, 1849, in Brown University Library collection). Tolman was awarded the prize that year for his "disputation" bearing the title *Libertas.*

gether even in some of the colleges of the United States. Yet it dealt with problems "upon the proper solution of which not the welfare merely, but the stability of society" depended. It aimed, he said, "at advancing no faster than consists with a maintenance of the rights of property . . . and urges a change only after public opinion is fully prepared for its introduction." [53]

He did somewhat change his idea of a university with the passing years. He stood for the old order of the dominance of the Greek and Latin classics in a national controversy that began in 1852. Leading scientists including Alexander D. Bache, Louis Agassiz, James D. Dana, and Benjamin Peirce, in 1851, saw a possibility of setting up a true graduate school in Albany, New York, that would be like the continental universities, notably Berlin. This caused considerable excitement among administrators of the established colleges, and they appointed committees to look into ways of meeting the threat. At Pennsylvania, one of the trustees, the Protestant Episcopal Bishop, Alonzo Potter, who had formerly been vice president and professor of mathematics and natural theology and of moral philosophy and political economy at Union College, strongly supported advanced studies.[54] He declared that "no *city* college in this country has yet reached any considerable magnitude." He thought the University of Pennsylvania should engage in graduate work and thereby be in a position to extend the curriculum. Students should be given an opportunity to pursue their studies further than

[53] Vethake, *An Address before the Literary Societies of Rutgers College*, pp. 17–18.

[54] Potter published a popular manual, *Political Economy* (New York: Harper, 1840). The book was largely a reprint of one by the British economist and member of parliament G. Poulett Scrope, *Principles of Political Economy* (London: Longman, Rees, Orme, Brown, Green, & Longman, 1833). For a detailed study of both works see M. J. L. O'Connor, *Origins of Academic Economics in the United States* (New York: Columbia Univ. Press, 1944), pp. 204–13.

they were able to do at present at any college. More attention should be given to American history, the sciences, and the mechanical arts. There should be freedom in choosing studies and free competition in teaching. Prize scholarships and fellowships should be established.[55]

Most of these statements seem to echo Vethake's former views; but now he defended the established scheme of things: "At twenty-five, an age when according to . . . the new plan . . . students might be supposed to be in attendance . . . there are few who have not an expectation of being heads of families, living in comfort and even luxury." And comparisons with German universities were irrelevant. Scientific subjects, for example (which were being stressed by the supporters of the university), were neither popular nor considered important in the German universities. He had found, for example, at the University of Berlin in 1829–30 that out of 2,000 students only twenty took differential and integral calculus with Öhm, and that Encke had only five persons in physical astronomy. Gauss had informed him at Göttingen, which had 1,700 students, that he had only one student in physical astronomy, and that for some years there had been no demand for his tickets.[56] The few students attending the faculty of philosophy, as distinct from the professional faculties of law, medicine, and divinity, were chiefly persons preparing for careers in teaching, civil service, and diplomacy, that is, persons for whom there were no equivalents in the United States. In the United States hardly anyone deliberately

[55] Printed letter from Alonzo Potter to Joseph R. Ingersoll, July 8, 1852; copy in the University of Pennsylvania Library.

[56] The German professor received a substantial salary and also the fees paid by the auditors for his course. Francis Lieber, who advocated a similar system at Columbia in 1859, asserted, "All German professors, indeed all European professors, receive salary and the fees. Law professors such as Mittermaier, make at times 20,000 guilders a year by their lectures. The more they make the more the governments are pleased, because it shows the flourishing state of the respective university." (Letter of Lieber to S. B. Ruggles, Aug. 31, 1859, in Lieber papers, Library of Congress.)

chose to teach, except under financial pressure and then only as a temporary expedient. As for holding government offices, either by appointment or election, no American "in his sane mind, would . . . set about systematically to make a special preparation for filling them." Fitness was not the basis for government appointments; and victory of the opposite party or the operation of rotation in one's own party might mean loss of a job.[57] Furthermore, the scheme, with its free tuition and more than one professor in a subject, would require a "fund which we may despair of seeing in our day collected and applied to the support of any single college or university."

Four years later Vethake had become so conservative in this matter that he felt free higher education would be the first step toward the "very brink of the worst species of socialism." [58]

He did, however, remain sufficiently true to the spirit of free inquiry to oppose the old view that textbooks should be subjected to a "preliminary" censorship by college authorities. "Which textbooks should be used, ought, I think, to be left very much to the professor," he wrote to a committee of trustees of his alma mater in 1857. Similarly he would leave complete freedom to the instructor as to the modes and means of instruction in his special department. The authorities should only "prescribe to each professor, the general subject and the extent of his course." [59]

Years of strife and loneliness took their toll. Professor Ruffner's son saw Vethake in 1851 in the chess room of the Athenaeum in Philadelphia, "sitting taciturn and wrapt, as if he had never done anything else, and never meant to do anything else, but play a dead game of chess." [60] He had a

[57] Printed letter from Henry Vethake to William M. Meredith, Nov. 27, 1852; copy in University of Pennsylvania Library.

[58] Vethake, *An Address before the Literary Societies of Rutgers College*, p. 22.

[59] Vethake, "Communication, Feb. 27, 1857," in *Statements, Opinions, and Testimony Taken by the Committee of Inquiry Appointed by the Trustees of Columbia College* (New York: Amerman, 1857)

[60] W. H. Ruffner, "The History of Washington College, 1830–1848," p. 28.

difficult course to follow as head of the University of Pennsylvania.[61]

There were controversies not only with trustees, as in the past, but also with faculty members. At times it seemed that some of the trustees were hardly tactful with him. For example, in 1852 there was a move to establish a school of mines, completely separate from the college proper, in the university for training in engineering and allied disciplines and with a bachelor of science degree. Vethake contended first of all that such a development would be prejudicial to the efficiency and prospects of success of the newly established scientific department in the college, for it would entice a good number of able young men who otherwise would be glad of the opportunity to be in the scientific department. There was little reason why they could not take mathematics in the college rather than have their own instructor. Finally, it seemed strange to him that while he was professor of mathematics, the instruction in pure mathematics in the proposed school should be given by the present professor of natural philosophy in the college.[62] As he pointed out, he approved of the objective, but he thought that it could be accomplished without setting up a completely independent school.

As provost, Vethake found fellow faculty members somewhat too individualistic. The one major defect in the organization of the university, he thought, was the provost had too little power. In a *Letter . . . on the Subject of the Duties of the Provost* (1859), he told the trustees that

> Too little importance is attached to the office of the Provost. Although regarded very generally by the trustees, the public, and

[61] H. M. Lippincott, *The University of Pennsylvania* (Philadelphia: Lippincott, 1918), p. 101.

[62] Letter of Vethake to Messrs. J. R. Ingersoll, G. M. Wharton, & T. Wagner, late members of a committee of the Board of Trustees of the University of Pennsylvania, April 30, 1852, in Historical Society of Pennsylvania collection.

the parents and guardians of the students as mainly responsible for the proper management of the institution, he has only an equal vote on the Faculty with every other member. He may be continually, and for years, outvoted on the measures of discipline or of a different nature, proposed by him; and worse than this, all action of the Faculty may be arrested, where there is an even number of members, as is the case at present, by a steady vote of three to three, four to four, etc. The Professors too, who are thus, so to speak, successively triumphing over the Provost will very naturally, be led to treat him with an ever diminishing respect, while the students will do the like, becoming aware of his being unsupported by a majority of the Faculty. To me it seems to be essential for the prosperity of the Literary Department of the University that at least when the Faculty, including the Provost, shall be divided on a question, this shall be decided by another and casting vote of the Provost,—any action being for the most part better than none. But I may mention also, that in nearly all our colleges, especially in those which have flourished most—Harvard, Yale, Princeton, [Union College in] Schenectady, Columbia College in the city of New York, etc. etc., it has been judged expedient to give greater importance and weight to the President or Provost by making him a member of the Board of Trustees. And it may be proper to mention that, in all the institutions just referred to, excepting only Columbia College, the President is *ex-officio* (in the absence of the Governor of the State) the President also of the Board of Trustees. In the Columbia College, he is not necessarily the presiding officer, but simply a member of the board. He is, however, clothed with a veto power on the proceedings of the Faculty.

As in other matters, Vethake's request was in fact a very modest one.

Beyond these difficulties involving more or less personal matters were those broad controversial issues that hardly made Vethake's path a smooth one. With other institutions attempting to become the peers of the leading universities of Europe, the university was bound to appear somewhat behind the times. The failure of those experiments might justify Vethake's view that the time was not ripe for the great venture,[63] but it hardly eliminated the contentiousness that characterized the growth of the colleges of the day. Furthermore, the fact that he was an ardent free trader and prognosticator of the demise of the protective tariff or, as he called it, the "restrictive system," in the leading protectionist state, would certainly have surcharged the atmosphere.[64] But there must have been some satisfaction when he retired, in knowing that among the would-be successors who were seriously considered was George W. Bethune, who had implored the Dickinson students to

> make yourselves thoroughly acquainted with Political Economy; which, despite the abuse that has been heaped upon it, as mere theory, cold, abstract, and uncertain, aims next to Christianity itself for the happiness of mankind. Lay fast hold of the laws God himself has given to the commerce and products of nations, and which like his other laws, can never be violated without a consequence of penalty. And then, stand fast as freemen, as patriots, as men of science and truth, and demonstrate the interests of the people to the American mind and heart.[65]

In 1859 Vethake resigned as provost. He was made emeritus professor of moral philosophy and given an honorarium of

[63] For example, Columbia valiantly started a postgraduate program in 1858, but it soon had to be suspended, for, as one lecturer commiserated with another: "My dear Fellow-Lecturer to many benches and few hearers, had we not better turn Buddhists at once and lecture, in deep meditation to ourselves, on ourselves, and by ourselves?" (Francis Lieber to George Perkins Marsh, Jan. 12, 1859, in David Lowenthal, *George Perkins Marsh* [New York: Columbia Univ. Press, 1958], p. 196).

Vethake explained that he was willing to go somewhat beyond the "existing demand," but if there was practically no demand there was little sense in starting an advanced program.

[64] Vethake's successor, the Reverend Daniel R. Goodwin, used as a text, the moderate protectionist treatise of Francis Bowen of Harvard, *The Principles of Political Economy* (1856).

[65] Bethune, *The Duties of an Educated Man: An Oration Before the Literary Societies of Dickinson College* (Philadelphia: Lippincott, 1843), p. 39. In his *Plea for Study*, delivered before the literary societies of Yale in 1845, Bethune gave a little clearer statement: "That most philanthropic science, Political Economy, which next to the Gospel, whose legitimate offspring it is, will do more than anything else for the elevation and fraternization of our race."

$1,250, and a fund was collected for the painting of his portrait.[66]

After leaving teaching at Pennsylvania in 1860, he accepted the professorship of higher mathematics at the Polytechnic College of the State of Pennsylvania.[67] He died in Philadelphia on December 16, 1866.

Vethake's economic philosophy was well summed up in the hope that through the spread of the science of political economy not only would the masses be taught contentment, but the rich, instead of proceeding on the principles of a "rigid conservatism to oppose every reform would become anxious for the introduction of reforms fast enough to prevent any supposed necessity or pretext for revolutionary action on the part of the multitude." More specifically, he explicitly spoke for the sober mercantile mind of the Jacksonian as the ideal. This he summed up in urging the merchant to follow the maxim of Ricardo, "to be content with small profits upon their goods," and thereby receive the "double advantage of at once acquiring wealth and of earning the approbation of their customers." [68] This tied up with his general belief that

[66] University of Pennsylvania, Minutes of the Trustees, April 5, May 3, 1859.

[67] This school, which was chartered in 1853, "enabled companies engaged in works of improvement to obtain technicians," and thus, as its *Announcement* of 1860 stated, had "become an important agent in the skillful and economical development of the vast resources of the continent, and in the elevation of the industrial professions to the true rank in the scale of human employments."

It was the first American institution offering a curriculum leading to a degree in mining engineering. It appears to have disappeared in the 1890s.

[68] Vethake, "The Distinctive Provinces of the Political Philosopher and the Statesman," pp. 109–10.

As Joshua Bates of Baring Brothers commented to Francis Wayland not long afterward, in the United States there was "a higher *average* of intellectual power, of education, of wealth, of comfort, of temperance, and of religion, than in any other country, and this would soon be apparent could you prevail upon people to look on a dishonest man as a rogue and avoid dealing with him." The big problem was to reason the "trading community" out of the idea that they could gain great wealth quickly by the system of laissez faire would achieve a society where there would not be as now "even in the most progressive communities, the wealthy . . . few, and the many poor," but a sufficiently numerous group of people in any neighborhood who were "not a great deal more wealthy" than the poorer class, for under these circumstances the poor would be stimulated to better their condition.

---

sharp, speculative practice. "The variation in the amount of currency is one chief cause of the uncertainty, and too often failure of success in commercial professions. If you could fix the amount of Bank notes that can be issued as Sir Robert Peel is about to do here, much misery could be saved." (Letter of Bates to Wayland, May 18, 1844, in Brown University Library.)

WILLIAM BEACH LAWRENCE

WILLIAM BEACH LAWRENCE: AMERICAN BENTHAMITE

Like John McVickar and Henry Vethake, William Beach Lawrence was an expositor of free trade thinking; but where McVickar's coordinate if not major interest was theology, and Vethake's mathematics and physics, Lawrence's was international law. All saluted that "acute reasoner," David Ricardo, as the great authority; but it was Lawrence who continually and explicitly proclaimed his economics to be the only sound system. He, more than any other individual, was responsible for the naturalization of Ricardianism in America.[1]

Lawrence was more, however, than merely an influential expositor of economic theory; he was also deeply involved in activities intended to achieve the "salutary reform" required by his economic theory; this, of course, meant politics and propaganda. In sympathy and in his way of working he might have been an American member of the British movement known as Philosophic Radicalism, which took its inspiration from Jeremy Bentham. Ricardo and Bentham—this was a formidable intellectual affiliation; but it was one that Lawrence was proud to expound.

His theoretical interests must be understood in the context of his family, his education, and especially his continuous

[1] Many others, however, including originally Jefferson, deprecated "the exquisite subtlety of the speculations . . . of the school of Ricardo." Cf. the review of McVickar's *Outline of Political Economy* in *The United States Literary Gazette*, Sept. 15, 1825, p. 451.

activity in business and politics. He was born in New York on October 23, 1800, the son of Isaac and Cornelia A. Beach Lawrence. Isaac was a member of the "real aristocracy," with lineage going back to English families who had come to the Plymouth colony as early as 1635. He was a wealthy New York businessman and landowner, and was prominent in Wall Street as president of the New York branch of the Bank of the United States, a station which from "the controlling influence possessed by the parent institution over the currency . . . was regarded as the most honourable distinction that could be conferred on a retired merchant." [2] Young Lawrence's maternal grandfather, Reverend Abraham Beach, was assistant rector of Trinity Church and a member of the boards of trustees of Columbia and Queens.

For a while Lawrence attended the school of the Reverend Edmund Drienan Barry (Hon. A.M. Columbia, 1804) in Thames Street. In 1812, while living at the Abraham Beach estate on the Raritan River in New Jersey, he entered nearby Queens College, where he may have begun his friendship with Henry Vethake.[3] After two years at Queens Lawrence returned to his father's home in New York and matriculated at Columbia College. In his senior year, 1817–18, John McVickar became professor of moral philosophy and belles lettres. The records of the courses are rather uncertain; but it is possible that Lawrence was among the first to receive formal instruction in the principles of political economy at

[2] W. B. Lawrence, "Introductory Remarks," in Henry Wheaton, *Elements of International Law*, 6th edition, ed. W. B. Lawrence (Boston: Little Brown, 1855), p. xiv.

[3] Vethake in his *Address before the Literary Societies of Rutgers College* (1854) recalled that Lawrence's father and maternal grandfather had been among those prominent in the affairs of Queen's, who had treated him so generously. Lawrence's copy of Vethake's *Principles of Political Economy* carried the inscription, "William Beach Lawrence, esq., New York, from his friend, the author," in *Catalogue of the First Part of the Library of the Late William Beach Lawrence . . . to be Sold at Auction . . . , George A. Leavitt & Co., Auctioneer* (New York: privately printed, 1881), p 114.

Columbia.[4] In July, 1818, he was graduated from Columbia, second in his class.

Lawrence's family intended him for the public service, according to that gossipy historian of old New York merchant families, Joseph Scoville.[5] The road to such a career lay through the law; and after graduation and a summer trip through the west, he began his studies in the office of the leading New York commercial lawyer, William Slosson. He continued his education at the famous law school at Litchfield, Connecticut, where Tapping Reeve and James Gould taught the common law as the perfection of reason and denounced Jefferson as a Jacobin. When he heard the results of the election of 1800 Reeve pictured "the horrors of the French Revolution . . . in vivid colors, as the probable result of Democratic success." [6] Young Lawrence, however, like his father, who was a Democratic presidential elector in 1820, was a Jeffersonian. He had visited and won the friendship, to use his words, of "this ancient chief of the republic—than whom no sovereign ever possessed more influence over the minds of an entire nation." [7]

In 1821 the young man, after marrying Esther Gracie, a daughter of the great merchant Archibald Gracie, began a two-year visit to Europe. There, among others, he met Albert Gallatin and George Bancroft. In Paris, he studied at the Sorbonne and the law school (École de Droit) of the University of Paris, where he attended the lectures on political economy of J. B. Say, who was the outstanding continental

[4] It was scheduled to be taught for the first time in the second semester of his senior year. In later years Lawrence thanked McVickar for having excited his interest in international law.

[5] [Joseph A. Scoville], *The Old Merchants of New York City* (New York: Carleton, 1863), II, 67.

[6] S. H. Fisher, *The Litchfield Law School, 1775–1883* (New Haven: Yale Univ. Press, 1833), p. 21.

[7] W. B. Lawrence, *An Address Delivered at the Opening of the Eleventh Exhibition of the American Academy of Fine Arts, May 10, 1825*, 2nd edition (New York: G&C Carvill, 1826), p. 45.

exponent of the free trade tradition. This was the beginning of studies which Lawrence pursued throughout his life.[8]

Lawrence returned to the United States in 1823 and soon passed his examinations for the bar. He continued his legal education by attending the lectures of James Kent at Columbia College. Kent, who as chancellor had been head of the state's equity court and the most powerful judicial officer for many years, enjoyed a tremendous scholarly reputation after the publication of his *Commentaries on American Law* (1826–30).[9]

The influence of Kent in the education of Lawrence was apparently considerable. His teaching began with international law—very necessary not only to lawyers "practicing in our commercial courts but to every gentleman who is animated by liberal views and a generous ambition to assume stations of high public trust." This might have been a description of young Lawrence. That his ambitions disposed him to listen respectfully as Kent enlarged on his views we can be sure. The disquisition went on to stress the rights of property. No state could exist, Kent said, without a separate property law. There were theorists who viewed:

separate property and inequalities of property, as the cause of injustice, and the unhappy result of government and artificial in-

[8] C. H. Hart, "William Beach Lawrence," *The Penn Monthly*, XII (June, 1881), 431–32; J. G. Wilson, "Gov. William Beach Lawrence," *The New York Genealogical and Biographical Record*, XIII (April, 1882), 56. Say's popular *A Treatise on Political Economy* had almost as many English and American editions as French ones, and was hailed by the American Ricardians for its "popular style and great clearness of illustration." ([Gulian C.] V. [erplanck], "Error in Mr. Say's Political Economy," *The Atlantic Magazine*, I [June, 1824], p. 129.) Harvard as well as a number of other American colleges began its first formal teaching of political economy with the use of Say's *Treatise* after it became available in translation in 1821.

[9] These were his lectures in expanded form. Kent was a strong, cultured Federalist. In a list of readings which he carefully prepared at the request of the Mercantile Library Association of the city of New York, he included the sociological novel *Caleb Williams*, by William Godwin, who believed, contrary to Kent's views, that men's vices arose from the institutions of society and not from human nature. (James Kent, *A Course of Reading* [New York: Wiley and Putnam, 1840], p. 63.)

stitutions. But human society would be in a most unnatural and miserable condition, if it were instituted or reorganized upon the basis of such speculations. The sense of property is graciously implanted in the human breast, for the purpose of rousing us from sloth, and stimulating us to action, and so long as the right of acquisition is exercised in conformity to the social relations and the moral obligations which spring from them, it ought to be sacredly protected. The natural and active sense of property pervades the foundations of social improvement.

This was doctrine congenial to a young man of Lawrence's bent. Teacher and student saw eye to eye. In fact, Lawrence had hardly finished his studies when he joined those who were working to make New York a cultural as well as an economic and a financial center. All his early publications, for instance, stressed the importance of commerce, which for him not only produced wealth and prosperity, but also diffused intelligence and encouraged the arts. This appeared sharply in the first of his literary efforts, *An Address*, before the American Academy of the Fine Arts, in New York in 1825.[10]

He contended that those objects which "conduce to intellectual and moral culture and which tend to impress an honorable character on the state," such as architectural embellishments, painting, and statuary, were only possible in the centers of commerce—large cities—for only in such places

[10] He delivered the address at the request of his fellow Columbia alumnus, Ricardian, prominent politician and literary figure, and professor of the Evidences of Christianity at the General Theological Seminary, Gulian C. Verplanck. (Letter of Verplanck to Lawrence, March 25, 1825, in New-York Historical Society collection.

Verplanck constantly urged the claims of political economy in all his activities. In 1840, while chairman of the New York Senate Committee of Finance, he informed fellow senators in a speech, later published as *Finance and Policy of New York*, that "the science of Political Economy is indeed 'the Master Science of civil life' " and he particularly praised "the analytical acuteness and unrivalled original sagacity of David Ricardo."

Verplanck, in the name of equal justice to all parts of the state, vigorously advocated the expansion of New York's canal system. In his report as chairman in 1839, he had presented as a "self-adjusting" check a suggestion that the interest payments for the resulting increases of state debt should be met not from an increase of taxation but from the increasing revenue from the canal system.

were there great private fortunes and accumulations of wealth capable of supporting artists. He went on to point out that an "America extending from the Atlantic to the Pacific," and constructing "artificial communications where navigable rivers are wanting" as settlement proceeds, promised to have a great foreign commerce and internal trade. And glancing toward "the greatest commercial power of Europe," he saw the dominant Tory party moving toward free trade under the guidance of William Huskisson, and envisaged the day when "an universally free trade will be recognized as an axiom in political science."

It seemed to later observers that Lawrence, like so many others, was over-sanguine about the opportunities opened to the "enterprise of our merchants" by the recent independence of Latin America from Spain. But there was much to be said for his observation (more relevant much later) that Americans had ceased to be merely the carriers of the productions of other countries. The nation's manufactures were known in the new republics. In useful knowledge American schools and academies were training a substantial number of the future legislators of South America. There would be a demand for the creations of artists, especially in New York City which he spoke of as that "emporium of America—at once the entrepôt of foreign merchandise and the point at which terminate all channels of internal trade."

Free traders praised this early exposition very highly. *The United States Literary Gazette* (published in New York) was impressed with the reference to the arts and their relation to political economy. The *New-York Review*, of which William Cullen Bryant was an editor, praised the address for showing "the dependence of all liberal institutions upon the freedom and activity of commerce," and for advocating obedience to "the great maxim of modern policy, *laisser-faire, et pas trop gouverner.*"

Encouraged, evidently, by the reception of his ideas, Lawrence began writing and lecturing more directly on economic problems, especially financial ones, from the standpoint of expanding commerce. The first essay of this sort appeared anonymously. It was called "Restrictions on Banking," [11] and was occasioned by a legislative investigation into corruption in the securing of bank charters and the demands of influential merchants and bankers for more freedom. There was especially a demand for the repeal of the Restraining Act of 1818, which forbade individuals and companies not chartered for the purpose by the legislature to engage in the banking business—not only note issue but also the making of loans and the receiving of deposits. Transcending and giving economic point to the charge of corruption was the complaint that the excessive issues of state bank paper were responsible for money panics. Although there was general agreement among the economists on the cause, there was controversy as to what would be desirable reforms of the banking structure.

It seemed to Lawrence that a banking system based upon the precious metals was the most efficient, because specie like other commodities obeyed the great Ricardian law of exchangeable value as interpreted by McCulloch: unless monopolies prevailed or temporary causes made exceptions, the general rule was that commodities were to one another as the quantities of labor used in their production. The existing state legislation, Lawrence thought, had the laudable objective of preventing unsound banking; but it had in fact established a monopoly. It had also made possible extravagant issues of paper money.

[11] [W. B. Lawrence], "Restrictions on Banking," *The Atlantic Magazine*, II (January, 1825), pp. 165–81
For Lawrence's authorship see S. Austin Allibone, *A Critical Dictionary of English Literature* (Philadelphia: Childs & Peterson, 1858), I 1068.

He contended that originally the state legislatures had been suspicious of charters conferring limited liability, because of their effect on the currency. The banking privilege became exceedingly difficult to obtain; but there had been surreptitious grants. For instance the Manhattan Company had secured a charter in 1799 through "an Act for supplying the city of New York with pure and wholesome water." [12] Similarly, such banks as the Phoenix, Chatham and Chemical obtained charters for some useful purpose never intended to be carried out. "Bridges, canals, etc., appear in bold letters in the bills of incorporation. The legislative assent obtained, the engraver, not the *architect* or *engineer* is put in requisition."

To prevent these abuses, continued Lawrence, the New York Constitution of 1821 required the assent of two thirds of the members of each branch of the legislature for the issuance of charters. But the greater its attempt to maintain a strict monopoly, the greater had been the corruption. Lawrence proposed first of all that the Restraining Act be repealed and that a free banking system (substantially similar to that proposed by McVickar) be established. Merchants, he said, no more require that "aid of an *immaculate* and enlightened legislature" to determine when they need an increase of bank capital than they need Congress to tell them whether they should continue to import cloth or should purchase it from domestic manufacturers.

[12] A clause was inserted which read that "it shall and may be lawful for the said company to employ all such surplus capital as may belong or accrue to the said company in the purchase of public or other stocks, or in any other monied transaction or operation, not incompatible with the constitution of this state, or of the United States, for the sole benefit of the said company."

Later, Lawrence asserted that one incidental advantage of the great credit expansion that had culminated in the panic of 1837 was that it had led to numerous "permanent works of art and utility." For example, it had enabled the city of New York to construct the Croton aqueduct to supply water, "one of the most obvious of municipal rights and duties." ("The Croton Aqueduct," *The Merchants' Magazine and Commercial Review*, X (May, 1844), 434–35.

Besides lifting the Restraining Act, the state should allow banking associations the privilege of limited liability and should not follow the English precedent of unlimited liability. There were in the United States different "habits of conducting business" and a smaller "number of individuals possessing great capitals." He proposed that the general incorporation act of 1811 for manufacturing purposes be extended to all joint stock companies.

Lawrence was aware that Ricardo and his leading British followers had proposed another solution of the problem of note issue. Claiming that the Bank of England has issued excessive notes to secure profits and that this had caused depression, they had proposed that all notes should remain convertible into specie but should be issued by a government institution. The profits then would go to the public and not to private interests.

In a following article, Lawrence argued that Ricardo's scheme was fatally defective, because government instead of maintaining convertibility would, whenever faced with the need of meeting extraordinary expenditures, resort not to increased taxation but to more notes and cause inflation, financial collapse, and ultimate suspension of specie payments.[13]

The New York banks, he granted, profited from the absence of a free banking system, but still the competition among existing banks, the settlement of balances among themselves, and above all the enormous means possessed by the Second Bank of the United States, were effective preventives of excessive issues.

One of the most interesting of Lawrence's essays in this period had to do with national policy. After repeating the familiar "laissez-faire" dicta that "the wealth of the nation is the aggregate of that of individuals," and that money is

[13] [W. B. Lawrence], "Money," *The New-York Review*, I (September, 1825), 264–83. For Lawrence's authorship see Allibone, *A Critical Dictionary*, I, 1068.

seldom as productively employed by governments as by individuals, he went on to argue that it was possible for a nation in certain cases to gain by sacrificing a part of its national wealth.[14] For example, if $1,000,000 of property be seized by depredations every year, the expenditure of half that amount for "warlike measures" would be a clear saving of national wealth.

Of more importance were his views on the public debt. He did not approve of public borrowing; but he held that the outstanding bonds should not be redeemed, at least not immediately. The evil of the public debt, as McVickar had argued, was done when it was created; it represented unproductive consumption of wealth; but repayment of the $24,000,000 foreign debt (the total federal debt was $90,000,000) would mean a reduction of the nation's "efficient capital," because the foreign holders were not likely to reinvest in other American securities, especially bank stocks. Unlike the public debt, these lacked acceptability on the leading exchanges of Europe ("near money" in modern terms). Foreign holders, ignorant of the nation's monied institutions, would hesitate to use these basic facilities for reinvestment and economic expansion.

Lawrence also agreed with Hamilton that, from a political point of view, repayment might weaken the Union. Widespread investment in the federal debt tended to attach men to the existing order of things by considerations of individual interest, "the most powerful motives that can govern the actions of men."

These articles doubtless were the core of the series of lectures that he gave the following year at the Athenaeum, which were devoted to making "the application of Pol. Econ. to the ordinary affairs of life as apparent as possible." In

[14] [W. B. Lawrence], "Financial Policy of the United States," *The Atlantic Magazine*, II (February, 1825), 307–12. For Lawrence's authorship see Allibone, *A Critical Dictionary*, I, 1068.

preparing these he followed Verplanck's suggestion that he read the works of Colonel Robert Torrens, basically a Ricardian, who he found had made "a great addition to our stock of economical learning." He also informed Verplanck at the time that "I have been reading [the Russian economist, Heinrich von] Storch [*Cours d'economie politique*, 1815] & have derived much information from him. He is much more profound than Say, & although he does not cite the recent English writers, his opinions on many important questions approximate to the principles of the Ricardian School." [15]

Lawrence was not only a publicist in this phase of his career; he still had in mind some sort of public service. Of some importance in this was a lifelong friendship he had formed with another future outstanding student of international law, Henry Wheaton, who was the son of the president of the Providence branch of the Bank of the United States. They had been brought together not only by their common intellectual interests, but also by their joint efforts on behalf of Calhoun for the presidency in 1823–24. Their interest in the southern statesman, Lawrence said later, was caused by his view that the Supreme Court should be the expositor of the Constitution.[16]

[15] Letters of Lawrence to Verplanck, Jan. 29, April 13, 1826, in Verplanck papers, New-York Historical Society. Storch's original edition of six volumes was published in St. Petersburg (now Leningrad) and was the product of his lectures while serving as tutor for the sons of Alexander I. Say edited a second edition of four volumes (Paris, 1828) and K. H. Rau prepared a German translation of three volumes (Hamburg, 1819–20).

[16] Calhoun was then strongly urging the promoters of his candidacy in New York to demand that the state legislature pass resolutions in favor of a protective tariff and internal improvements. In this way, he informed Wheaton, the hopes of his opponents, the "radicals," would be blasted. Not long afterwards, Calhoun changed his views on these matters, especially the tariff, and became an ardent leader, in Lawrence's words, of the "liberal school of political economy." Lawrence later wrote that since a man like Calhoun, whose honesty of mind was unquestioned, had made such a reversal, people should "regard with indulgence, the changes which inferior minds undergo." (Lawrence, "Introductory Remarks" in Wheaton, *Elements of International Law*, p. xliv.)

After Calhoun's withdrawal from the contest Lawrence and Wheaton supported John Quincy Adams, a change of some consequence, because after his election both were appointed to diplomatic posts. Wheaton went to Copenhagen and Lawrence to London in 1826. He was to aid the minister plenipotentiary, Albert Gallatin, in the delicate negotiations then going on with the British. Lawrence was brought to the attention of President Adams by Charles King, who had also married a daughter of Gracie. King was the publisher of the New York *American*, and later president of Columbia. Lawrence's appointment as secretary of legation was contingent upon the expected resignation of King's brother, John Alsop King.[17] When Gallatin returned in 1827 Lawrence was appointed chargé d'affaires.

While in effect the American minister to Great Britain, Lawrence "examined thoroughly the commercial system of Great Britain" in order to discharge his public duties. He was highly skeptical of those British statesmen like the Tory leader and chancellor of the exchequer, John Charles Herries, who espoused liberalization of foreign trade, but managed to follow in practice the old "restrictive" system. He informed his chief, Secretary of State Henry Clay, on one occasion that he was describing Herries's opinion in matters of political economy as "theoretical" because "we have heretofore seen that his abstract principles have had little influence on his practical *legislation*." He was elated, however, that the recent convert to Ricardo's economics and strong believer in government financial retrenchment, Sir Henry Parnell, was made chairman of the House of Commons Finance Committee, for he was "distinguished for his attainments in political economy . . . on which he has written several essays." [18]

[17] Letter of W. B. Lawrence to John A. King, July 22, 1826, New-York Historical Society collection.

[18] Letters of W. B. Lawrence to Clay, Nov. 12, 22, 1827; Feb. 22, 1828 (copy), in Lawrence papers, Library of Congress.

Lawrence appreciated the value of historical research for the statesman. In preparing for the negotiations for the settlement of the northern boundary between Canada and the United States, and the navigation of the St. Lawrence River, he went to the British Museum in order to study what the Congress of Vienna had done about European rivers.[19]

A task that well accorded with his scholarly propensities, and one to which he devoted considerable time and effort while in England, was that of finding for ex-President James Madison a suitable professor of natural philosophy for the newly founded University of Virginia.[20]

For other reasons, too, this was an exciting time for a young intellectual to be in London. The Benthamite Philosophical Radicals, with the assistance of the rising class of industrialists, financiers, and merchants, were then at the beginning of their onslaught on the aristocratic control in Britain of law, politics, and society. Lawrence was made a member of the Political Economy Club, which Ricardo had helped to found, and which was dominated by the Benthamites. Joseph Hume, one of the most radical of the Benthamites in Parliament, was a particular friend;[21] and

[19] Letter of W. B. Lawrence to J. Bancroft Davis, May 16, 1871, in Davis papers, Library of Congress

[20] To find a suitable candidate, Lawrence visited among other places Oxford and Cambridge. "At Oxford from the preference given classical studies, I hardly expected to accomplish my views, but I found that though the abstract sciences were particularly cultivated at Cambridge, little attention is given to experimental philosophy. There were young men of great promise and extensive mathematical attainments pointed out to me, but in talking with them I found that they would have to learn other than their peculiar Department if chosen to chairs of Natural Philosophy." The candidate Lawrence approved of was not a graduate of an English university, but he had been recommended by William Whewell, "the leading fellow of the principal college [of Cambridge], Trinity." (Letter of Lawrence to Madison, Nov. 29, 1827 [copy], Lawrence papers, Library of Congress.)

[21] In Lawrence's library, two volumes of *Poor Laws, Reports and Extracts from Information Received by H[is] M[ajesty's] Commissioners* (1833–34) carried the inscription: "To W. B. Lawrence, esq., New York, with best respects from Joseph Hume, London, May, 1834." In *Catalogue of the First Part of the Library of the Late William Beach Lawrence*, p. 85.

Lawrence's son recorded that he often shared "the solitary dinner of his friend, Jeremy Bentham," to whose philosophy of "the greatest happiness of the greatest number" he quickly became a convert. Bentham, in a letter to President Jackson in 1830, spoke of his friendship with "Mr. Lawrence . . . and Mr. Wheaton . . . to whom I have been obliged for various important services." Bentham, who expected a good deal of reform to be achieved through replacing the common law by a philosophically oriented "constitutional code," wrote in the same year to Edward Livingston, the author of the Louisiana code, that

By reputation, at any rate, if not personally, Mr. Lawrence . . . can hardly . . . be altogether unknown to you. I have the honour and pleasure of a considerable degree of intimacy with him. He looked eventually to a seat in the House of Representatives; should that prospect be realized, Codification, I dare venture to hope, will receive in him, a powerful support.[22]

Late in 1828 the Adams administration appointed as minister James Barbour of Virginia, and Lawrence was in effect demoted to his old post as secretary of legation. This was so much a disappointment that he resigned. Shortly afterward, while he was in Paris observing LaFayette's efforts to democratize the municipal organization of France, he wrote an unsigned article for the Benthamite *Westminster Review*, in which he noted some deficiencies in American institutions, as well as their great virtues, especially in providing for equality of opportunity.[23] After speaking of the opinions of "profound philosophers, like Mr. Bentham," and noting that "the spirit of codification begins to manifest itself in various parts of the Union," he declared that "nothing short of a complete and *accessible code* founded on an all-comprehensive and philo-

[22] Jeremy Bentham to Andrew Jackson, April 26, 1830; Bentham to Edward Livingston, Feb. 23, 1830 in *The Works of Jeremy Bentham*, ed. John Bowering, 11 vols. (Edinburgh: Tait, 1843), XI, 40, 36.

[23] "Government of the United States of America," *The Westminster Review*, X (January, 1829), 51–71. For Lawrence's authorship see Allibone, *A Critical Dictionary*, p. 1068.

sophical view of the whole field will answer the ends of justice." [24]

In this same article he acknowledged that the big blot in America was slavery; but he expected, he said, that it would gradually disappear. He did feel, however, that the southern slave states should have done more than they had to bring about the gradual amelioration of conditions. "Of the objections to negro slavery many—we wish we could say the whole—of the people of the United States—seem duly sensible." He granted that there were many impediments to abolition, arising from "the rights of the proprietors and the social condition of the slaves"; but nevertheless slavery was

[24] In the post-Civil War years Lawrence lost some of his faith in codification. He came to feel that to impose a perpetual uniformity on the codes and laws of different countries, as Bentham had advocated, might block the progress of civilization. The best procedure would be to follow the "historical method" that had been laid down by Friedrich Carl von Savigny of the University of Berlin, and secure "gradual and progressive reforms" through treaties. His admiration and criticism are contained in the following eloquent tribute:

"It was the absence of a due regard to the modification of laws required by the varying circumstances of different peoples that most detracted from the value of the labors of Jeremy Bentham, whom our Wheaton denominated 'the greatest judicial reformer of modern times.' Having myself had, half a century ago, the good fortune to be inculcated in his doctrines by the great philosopher himself, I can in some degree appreciate the extent to which the reforms in English jurisprudence may be traced to him, though ordinary minds, influenced by his proposition to make a universal code applicable alike to all states, without regard to their peculiar conditions, were wont to treat as visionary his best reasoned suggestions." (W. B. Lawrence, letter to the editor, in *The Albany Law Journal*, Aug. 25, 1877, p. 131.)

Lawrence held that the establishment of an international code should be preceded by conventions among the different states comprising the family of nations. Nevertheless, he urged uniformity in the rules, especially those prescribed for prize tribunals. If the great powers agreed to such rules, the secondary powers would also adopt them. (W. B. Lawrence, letter to D. D. Field, May 14, 1873, in *The Albany Law Journal*, June 14, 1873, p. 379.)

He recalled that while serving as chargé d'affaires in London he had recommended to Secretary of State Henry Clay that the issues between the United States and Fngland be submitted to "savants" instead of, as was done, a "royal or imperial arbitration." He had strongly approved of the "system adopted in Germany for the submission of legal questions to the Universities & particularly the views of Savigny at the time of the establishment of the University of Berlin." (Letter of W. B. Lawrence to Francis Lieber, Oct. 14, 1870, in Lieber papers, Huntington Library.)

a plague spot upon the social condition of the American people. It was no answer for them to retort that the British colonists "are slaveholders too, and that the slaves of the West Indies are less privileged than theirs. Recrimination is not the sort of argument honest men should use. They must get rid of slavery altogether; it dishonors—it degrades them; and they should set about it speedily."

Lawrence had been hoping that he might be appointed to a suitable diplomatic post, but this hope disappeared when Jackson was elected President.[25] He turned, in his next phase, to the practice of law, but was soon also involved in business ventures. His real interest remained in scholarly matters; and this was true even when his legal cases involved his own or his family's private fortunes. An illustration of this is furnished by the kind of presentation he made of the claims of his family for spoliation under Napoleon's decrees against neutral commerce. His elaborate investigation of the rights of belligerents and neutrals in this case supplied materials for his future treatises on international law.[26] Later, a suit over the sale of some of his property involved him in writing a long history

[25] On informing Gallatin of his resignation from the diplomatic service on January 12, 1829, he wrote that "owing to events at home, . . . there is probably an end to my hopes of being useful in that service which I have been ambitious of making my profession." (Letter of W. B. Lawrence to Gallatin, in Gallatin papers, New-York Historical Society.)

Lawrence also had difficulties with the new President on the settlement of his accounts. Ex-President John Quincy Adams complained of the treatment of Lawrence. Jackson, said Adams, had snatched at the letter of the law so as to "give himself the appearance of a reformer and thus get a special act of Congress to remove the senseless obstacle caused by himself." (John Quincy Adams, *Memoirs*, 12 vols., [Philadelphia: Lippincott, 1874–77], VIII, 236.)

[26] Lawrence made his claims under the Treaty of 1831 with France. At the time he issued a letter circular addressed to all would-be claimants "offering my services as agent and counsel to prepare your cases, and attend to your business before the Board of Commissioners at Washington." (A copy of the circular, dated September 21, 1831, is in the Biddle papers, Library of Congress.)

Lawrence's father-in-law, Archibald Gracie, was his largest client, for $127,000. (Letter of W. B. Lawrence to Virgil Maxcy, May 14, 1836, in Galloway, Maxcy, Markoe papers, Library of Congress.)

of the relations of equity to common law in England and the United States.[27]

These were much more detailed than they would have been if they had not become enterprises interesting in themselves to a student. For a period, beginning about 1832, Lawrence had a law partnership with another wealthy, politically ambitious, Columbia graduate who had also been a student of John McVickar. This was Hamilton Fish (A. B. 1827), who belonged to the Federalists and their successor parties and was to become secretary of state under President Grant. The partnership did not last long; but the friendship was permanent. Fish later explained Lawrence's withdrawal. Lawrence, he said,

> had been absent from the Bar for several years, and lost some of the familiarity with the course of the courts, and with the personnel of the Bench and of the Bar which is so desirable for the practitioner of the law. And he found men much his juniors in years and many of them altogether and vastly his inferiors in learning and in ability, who had by continued familiarity with the courts and their habits and their practices, felt at home, and occasionally shied out little impertinences toward him as a sort of intruder. More than once . . . he spoke to me of this . . . and finally assigned it as a reason for withdrawing from the practice and terminating our partnership. For some time after the close of the partnership, he engaged in other pursuits, and frequently entrusted to me the matters in which he was interested requiring professional investigation.[28]

Instead of going on with the law, Lawrence, in the 1830s, was occupied primarily by large business and financial

[27] Lawrence's brief ran to 176 pages. See W. B. Lawrence, *Administration of Equity Jurisprudence. Caveat Filed Feb. 1874 in the Case of Lawrence vs. Staigg in the Supreme Court of Rhode Island* (Boston: privately printed, 1874.) Staigg was the noted artist Richard M. Staigg. The case, which involved the sale of an acre of land in Newport, Rhode Island, went on for twenty years from its inception in 1862. As the Newport *Mercury* put it in 1881, it became "one of the celebrated civil suits of the day from the learning and ingenuity manifested in its conduct."

[28] Hamilton Fish to Wilson, cited in Wilson, "William Beach Lawrence," p. 5.

operations and in pushing Ricardo's economics, especially in the area of currency, banking, and foreign trade. He was also prominent in the controversies over the rechartering of the Second Bank of the United States, the tariff, and internal improvements. His business pursuits comprised not only land speculation in New York City and elsewhere, but also pioneering ventures in insurance and railroads. For example, there was the New York Life Insurance and Trust Company, which was the first life insurance company in New York and the fourth in the United States.[29] It had permission to do a banking business, but was forbidden to issue its own notes, or other evidence of debt for circulation as money.[30]

[29] It was chartered in 1830. Life insurance companies had already been established in Boston, Baltimore, and Philadelphia.

[30] Lawrence and his father were among the original incorporators. Others were such leaders of finance, industry, and public affairs as Verplanck, John Jacob Astor, and the leading investment banker, James Gore King, who, like his brother Charles King and Lawrence, had married a daughter of Archibald Gracie. Serving with Lawrence on the Investment Committee of the Board of Trustees was Isaac Bronson, who had stimulated McVickar to espouse a free banking system.

The New York and Erie Railroad, another venture, was expected to solidify New York's paramount commercial position, a result of the Erie Canal. The incorporating group included most of the prominent figures in the New York Life Insurance and Trust Company. The first president and chief promoter, Eleazar Lord, like Lawrence and Bronson, was a combination of entrepreneur and man of learning.

Lord was originally a minister; after leaving the ministry, he engaged in mercantile enterprises, but kept up his religious interests. He was a pioneer in the Sunday School movement, and helped to form both the American Bible Society and the Home Missionary Society. He was prominent in the organization of the University of the City of New York. In 1821 he obtained a charter for the successful Manhattan Fire Insurance Company. From 1819 to 1824 he was a lobbyist for a protective tariff in Washington, having been selected by "leading merchants [of New York] for this task." (E. H. Mott, *Between the Ocean and the Lakes* [New York: Collins, 1899] pp. 459–60.)

Two years after McVickar published his free banking scheme Lord, in *Principles of Currency and Banking* (1829), urged a similar proposal: the capital of a bank should be invested in "permanent securities," against which bank notes could be issued; and small notes should be abolished. In his revision, *Credit, Currency and Banking* (1834), he eliminated the provision for the abolition of small notes and made a spirited defense of the Second Bank of the United States. During the Civil War Lord presented his scheme as a means of providing a national currency. The banks would

Lawrence's financial fortunes fluctuated violently in this period of promotional ventures. In 1834 his father was forced to dispose of Murray Hill property to cover $50,000 of his son's debts. Lawrence also involved other members of his family in some of his losses.[31] But two years later, matters must have improved; at least, Henry Wheaton, then chargé d'affaires at Berlin, congratulated his friend at that time on approaching—if he had not yet reached—that acme of felicity: becoming a millionaire. He wrote Lawrence: "I rejoice that you, in common with some other valued friends, have participated in the flow of prosperity with which a kind providence has blessed our country." The magnitude of Lawrence's operations at the time can be gauged by his request for a two-year $200,000 loan from the Second Bank of the United States on joint note by himself and his father, secured by bonds and mortgages.

But in 1841 Lawrence's fortunes were low again. His father died insolvent; and notes amounting to $18,500, drawn by the son in favor of Isaac Lawrence and endorsed by the latter, were placed by the Bank of Commerce in the hands of Fish for settlement.[32] So there were ups and downs in his fortunes; but on the whole he was successful. Soon he could be rated as a wealthy man. But whatever his speculative successes or losses, he continued to interest himself in economic theory and in public affairs.

In an address before the New-York Historical Society in

issue inconvertible notes which would be backed 100 percent by federal bonds and be redeemable in these bonds.

[31] For instance, Benjamin McVickar, husband of one of his sisters.

[32] [Scoville], *The Old Merchants of New York City*, pp. 65, 68, 244; Wheaton to Lawrence, June 19, 1836, in *Circuit Court of the United States, Massachusetts District: In Equity. Lawrence vs. Dana* (Boston: privately printed, 1867), p. 473; letters of W. B. Lawrence to Nicholas Biddle, Oct. 14, 1835, Jan. 18, 1836, Biddle papers, Library of Congress; Fish to Lawrence, Dec. 17, 1841 (copy), Fish papers, Library of Congress; *King et al. vs. McVickar*, February, 1846, in *New York Chancery Reports*, VII, ed. Robert Desty (Rochester, N.Y.: Lawyers' Cooperative Publishing Co., 1889), p. 824.

1832 he outlined the legal and sociological foundations of his theory.[33] He began by saying that the elements of American institutions were to be found in the German forests and later in the feudal system, whose very spirit was "national independence and freedom from oppression." The principles of this system were still "interwoven with the laws, which determine the political relations of the citizen, as well as with those which regulate the rights of private property." [34] The lesson to be derived from this was that, if Congress observed the spirit of the Constitution and abstained from imposing or continuing any unnecessary restrictions on the freedom of industry, then, as heretofore, the prevailing discontent would yield to considerations of enlightened patriotism. But the preservation of the powers of the states was also essential for preventing the greater evils of "tyranny and despotism, which would but too probably follow in the train of consolidation."

It was typical that he should have great faith in the diffusion of political economy. This could be, he felt, one of the most effective instruments for achieving sound government policy, and he took advantage of every opportunity on the platform

[33] Under the title: *The Origin and Nature of the Representative and Federative Institutions of the United States of America.* Philip Hone noted (in his *Diary*) that Lawrence not only delivered the address, but "provided the means of getting to and from the lecture [held at Broadway and Chambers Street]; for, in common with eleven other gentlemen, he contracted with Abraham Brower to run a line of stages from Astor Place to Wall Street, the gentlemen agreeing to pay the return fare, for . . . no one ever came up Broadway at eleven o'clock in the morning." Cited by Isaac Lawrence, "Governor William Beach Lawrence," Part 1, *The New-York Genealogical and Biographical Record*, XXVI (April, 1895), 55. It is taken from the original manuscript (now in the collection of the New-York Historical Society). Published versions of the famous diary do not contain it. Lawrence was vice president of the society from 1836 to 1843.

[34] In his unsigned "translator's notice" of the Marquis de Barbé-Marbois, *The History of Louisiana, Particularly of the Cession of That Colony to the United States* (1830) Lawrence had expressed the hope that his translation would attach the American people still more firmly to those institutions which were praised by the "enlightened and distinguished foreigner as making for orderly development, despite the heated political controversies."

Barbé-Marbois had served in the French Embassy in the United States during the American Revolution and had in 1803 conducted the negotiations on behalf of Napoleon of the sale of Louisiana to the United States.

and in the press to stress the possibilities of public education.

When McVickar went abroad in the spring term of 1830 Lawrence conducted the course on political economy at Columbia. His lectures were expositions of Ricardian theory with emphasis on free trade. Later, in December, 1831, he repeated part of the same course at the Mercantile Library Association of the City of New York. The printed version, *Two Lectures on Political Economy* (1832) was dedicated to Gallatin, whom he especially praised for his well-earned international reputation as an authority on money and banking, his able support of a sound currency, and his portrayal of the manifold evils of an irredeemable paper currency. These lectures are a convenient compendium of Lawrence's views. We may look at them at some length.

The principles of political economy, he insisted, rested on a firmer foundation than any branch of moral science. Citing Robert Torrens, he said that "Political Economy is analogous to the mixed mathematics: the data upon which it proceeds are furnished by observation and experience, while the conclusions, to which it leads, are attained by a process of ratiocination self-evident in all its parts." There could be no differences in method. There might be differences in application; but a proposition could not be true in theory and wrong in practice.

He reiterated Ricardo's doctrine that under ordinary circumstances labor as a commodity was an invariable standard of value. The return to capital in any one line of endeavor depended on the yield in other modes of investment in which there were openings. In a stationary state, a "tranquil state of things," wages could not fall below the minimum of subsistence of the laborer and of his infant children incapable of self-support. Since in America capital was increasing more rapidly than labor, wages were greater than mere subsistence.

This implied his view on population, stated in his *Westminster Review* article, that "the immense districts of the

West must be filled before the Malthusian theory is fully developed."

He went on to a modified version of the classical theory of rent. The progress of society resulted in diminishing returns from the soil; and the capitalist suffered with every increase of rent—which was the difference between the produce obtained from the capital first applied to the land and that last applied. However, this tendency was offset for the United States because it was a new country. For old countries like England it would be counteracted by the free importation of foodstuffs and the terrritorial division of labor.

Any interference with the free adjustment of prices was a violation of the first principle. During the recent cold weather, Lawrence said, the public had displayed a general ignorance of sound practice by calling the coal dealers the vilest names for raising prices "so as to regulate them by the probable increased demand and diminished supply of the article." The coal dealers, he continued, were acting in the interest of the poorer classes in particular, since the price rise forced economy of consumption and induced supplies to be brought from distant points.

Turning to the burning question of the tariff, Lawrence first congratulated both national political conventions for defending their views on commercial policy by referring to political economy. Then he presented the familiar case against a protective tariff, but warned against sudden substantial changes on the ground that since human happiness was the end in view, and the acquisition of wealth only a means to its attainment, to "disregard vested interests would be as inconsistent with the principles of Political Economy as with the dictates of justice."

On the question of government aid for internal improvements such as roads and canals, he took a position somewhat different from that of McVickar and Vethake. He granted that if the state of New York had not constructed the Erie Canal it probably would not have been done; but just because it was so successful a pioneering venture, state aid was no longer needed for such enterprise. No such public work should be undertaken unless it would pay for itself; but he doubted that under current conditions there was any enterprise which promised an adequate return that could not be more effectively done by the capital of individuals aided by the facilities which the institution of joint stock companies afforded.

If any public involvement was necessary it should be by the individual state rather than by the general government, because of the greater pressure for purely local benefits, and because of the greater extravagance and carelessness where the responsibility of the agent to the employer was the furthest removed. This argument, he held, was a conclusive objection to public contributions for undertakings which could be carried on by individuals.

Turning to another subject, he spoke of Ricardian economics in connection with "commercial revulsions." After calling attention to the fact that no one conversant with the "transactions of our commercial emporium" could be ignorant of panics and disturbances of credit, especially that of 1825, he noted that these periods of extraordinary excitement in the commercial world frequently originated in very slight causes. Under a specie standard, the equilibrium could be no more than temporarily disturbed. The rise of prices would lead to the export of specie; this would force the banks to contract their circulation to the "natural relation which commodities bear to specie; and trade would then, though after the sacrifice of the fortunes of individuals, resume its former channels."

Concerning usury laws he thought the arguments of all moralists and economists from Calvin to Bentham conclusive.

If the banks were free to raise interest rates, they would have a potent instrument for rectifying the exchanges. The rise would tend to reduce transactions and so lower prices. "The fall of prices leads to increased exports and reduced imports, and "consequently to the return of gold and silver, till the currency is restored to its ordinary state." Furthermore, by raising the price of money the banks could check the "inordinate speculation before it reached a ruinous extent." [35]

Finally, since the principles of political economy demonstrated that the prosperity of one country was closely linked with that of others, their adoption would eliminate the ordinary causes of war, and by "appealing to their self-interest establish in relation to nations what Christianity inculcates with respect to individuals."

In general, Lawrence was presenting the rationale of the Jacksonian position on questions of internal improvements and the tariff then under discussion. On a third current issue, that of the monetary and banking system, Lawrence agreed with the Jacksonians on the desirability of "hard money" as the basis, but differed with them as to the need for a Bank of the United States, especially the existing bank.

It was President Jackson's belief that "Both the constitutionality and the expediency of the law creating the bank are well questioned by a large portion of our fellow citizens." [36] These doubts were soon amplified by the administration into complaints that the bank had played politics and had not fulfilled its fundamental purpose of supplying the country with a sound and uniform currency. Lawrence quickly became a leader in the defense of the bank and the

[35] [W. B. Lawrence], *An Inquiry Into the Causes of the Public Distress* (New York: C. & C. & H. Carvill, 1834), p. 48. The pamphlet was an expanded version of his article, "The Public Distress," *The American Quarterly Review*, June, 1834. For Lawrence's authorship see Allibone, *A Critical Dictionary*, I, 1068.

[36] *First Annual Message*, December, 1829.

need for its recharter before its twenty-year term expired in 1836.

Lawrence waged an intensive campaign through the press in support of the bank as "at present established," for to him the bank and "the constitutional power of the Judiciary" were the most important existing institutions. He resorted not only to the journals and newspapers read by the leaders of dominant opinion but those read by "the 'workingmen,' who comprise a large portion of the middle & lower classes" notably the *Evening Journal.*[37]

[37] Letter from W. B. Lawrence to Nicholas Biddle, Feb. 10, 1831, Biddle papers, Library of Congress.

Lawrence combined this effort with his political ambitions as a zealous supporter of Henry Clay's aspirations for the presidency.

He informed Clay on August 31, 1829, that the opponents of the Jackson administration in New York City should avail themselves of some local question "instead of meeting the whole force of the Jackson party." Such an opportunity, he felt, was provided by the unpopularity in the city of the recent law sponsored by Van Buren while governor. This law made all the banks in the state "in a measure responsible for each other" (the safety fund system of a guaranty of bank notes through contributions of a percentage of capital to an insurance fund). If the tactic of opposing the Jacksonians on local lines showed promise, Lawrence's friends would run him for the state senate. A year later (August 9, 1830) he wrote to Clay that his own group had not been able to overcome the obstacles of the "peculiar grounds [the Anti-Masonic movement] on which the opposition [to the Van Buren Party] in the western part of the state rests as well as some of the views of the 'workingman' who constitutes a considerable part of the anti-Van Buren electors in the city & the other large towns." He said that the Workingmen's Party was favorably disposed to his group, and that these "workingmen" with few exceptions were comprised of "mechanics or persons literally engaged in manual labor" and given to "moderation and good sense."

On October 30, 1830, he wrote to Clay that the "workingmen" comprised two parties. One was carried away by the "extravagances" of Robert Dale Owen and Frances Wright for full free elementary education including the housing and feeding of the children. The other was comprised "principally of the rank & file of the late administration party [of John Quincy Adams] & of a very considerable secession from the Jackson ranks growing out of state politics." With the latter Workingmen's Party, Lawrence and his group, all men of "respectability," had joined to serve as the party's candidates for the legislature. Lawrence complained that the opposition misled people into believing that their Workingmen's Party was the same as that of the partisans of Owen and Wright, although the principles of the two parties were radically different. This might have lost them some votes of the "higher classes of society." After the defeat of his ticket, he took solace in the fact that, in future elections, universal suffrage would

In an anonymous essay in the April, 1831, issue of *The North American Review*, he made his strongest defense of the Second Bank, especially as a most potent instrument for "the increase of the productive resources of the country at large." First he disposed of the constitutional issue in the manner of Alexander Hamilton; but he went beyond Hamilton in saying that since the Supreme Court could determine the constitutionality of the acts of the state legislatures and Congress, and since the court had upheld the constitutionality of the bank, further questioning of its legality threatened to subvert the nation's political system.

A direct government bank was undesirable, not only because, as he had said before, it would issue an excessive amount of notes in periods of financial embarrassment, but also because it entailed the evils of the patronage system. A private national bank, however, like the Second Bank of the United States, through convertibility of its paper into specie and the play of the foreign exchanges and exports of specie, would regulate paper issues so that the paper would not exceed the amount of metallic money that would otherwise have been circulating and thereby prevent its depreciation and loss of value. The bank had, by restraining inordinate issues by state banks, prevented their excessive curtailment which frequently destroyed commercial enterprise. He attributed to ignorance of the principles of banking

---

give control to the "practical mechanics and workingmen," and overcome the defection of their "timid friends" who accepted the fantastic charge that Lawrence and his running mates, who were all men of "property and education," favored "agrarianism" (Nov. 8). On November 29 he informed Clay that he was engaged in openly organizing a "Clay for President" party, but he found that only one of Clay's three main planks could be pushed in New York: that in favor of recharter of the bank. The other two were dangerous. Federal aid for internal improvements, although popular in other states, would not carry in New York, he pointed out, because of "the interest felt in the existing canals belonging to the public and private companies." The tariff might be popular in the western part of the state but not in the city and neighboring counties. (Clay papers, Library of Congress.)

the unpopularity of the bank in the west, where it was forced at times to curtail its operations in order to maintain the metallic standard.

The bank with its prestige and its branches in all parts of the country, Lawrence insisted, not only provided a sound national medium of exchange and eliminated the great fluctuations in the price of bills of exchange,[38] but it lent more cheaply to the government than could individuals and corporations. "In time of war, by lending to the contractors [underwriters] on a pledge of public stock, until there is an opportunity for distributing it among the capitalists of the country," it extended the competition for government loans, and thus raised the price of these securities to the great advantage of the nation.

He suggested as a desirable monetary reform that the country adopt Ricardo's famous ingot plan of requiring redemption of bank notes presented in gross, by bars, at the mint standard and price for coin. Lawrence argued that since convertibility was only a means to an end, namely, the regulation of the quantity of currency, it was unnecessary that the notes should be exchanged for coin in order to be free of fluctuations. The scheme would largely save the

[38] Lawrence called attention to the bank's policy of maintaining foreign balances as a means of eliminating great fluctuations in foreign exchange rates. This was the one practice of the bank that the powerful, able governor of the Bank of England, J. Horsley Palmer, sometime later, approved. Writing to Gallatin on December 12, 1832, he said, "One part of their plan is excellent; viz.: the balances they keep at interest in Europe, in lieu of overloading their vaults with bullion in America; that measure answers in every respect the same purpose, and I confess it is one that I have long wished to see adopted here with French securities. We however are old fashioned people, and it will I apprehend be some time before such a measure can be carried. Indeed, I have sounded the Bank of France, to ascertain whether it would not be possible to propose that intimate correspondence between them and ourselves, which would admit of a direct correction of the exchanges without the transfer of any material amount of bullion: the measure I am convinced is perfectly practicable and safe, but too much timidity exists at present for the consideration of a proposal of that nature." (Letter of Palmer to Gallatin, in Gallatin papers, New-York Historical Society.)

expense of coinage and the wear of specie, while the quantity of specie necessary to be retained unproductively would be greatly reduced.

When Jackson was reelected in 1832 Lawrence saw little hope for the bank. As he informed Gallatin from Washington, "I hear nothing respecting a National Bank. I take it for granted that no possible chance exists for the rechartering of the present institution." [39]

For Lawrence, as for the rest of the country, the tariff question was at this time a center of interest. The Tariff Act of July, 1832, was shortly followed by passage in the South Carolina legislature of an "Ordinance to Nullify certain acts of the United States, purporting to be laws laying duties and imposts on the importation of foreign commodities." But President Jackson was adamant. He proclaimed that "the laws of the United States must be executed. I have no discretionary power on the subject." Lawrence's friend Congressman Gulian C. Verplanck was, with the President's blessing, busily engaged as a major designer of Clay's Compromise Tariff Act of 1833, which would gradually reduce the tariff

[39] Letter of Lawrence to Gallatin, Jan. 5, 1833, in Gallatin papers, New-York Historical Society. At this time the groundwork was being laid for promoting a new central bank but with headquarters in New York (as McVickar later would propose). In the *Annual American Register*, to which it is definitely known that Lawrence contributed the articles on foreign countries, it was asserted in 1833 that the administration of the bank had been excellent, and had not warranted the attacks by the administration; but it had had faults. "Shortly after going into operation its direction fell into the hands of a few speculators, who brought it to the verge of bankruptcy, and it did not escape without the loss of more than a million of dollars, and no small portion of character. In the distribution of capital, dissatisfaction has been caused by the small amount apportioned to the City of New York; and it has been with too much reason asserted that the illiberal policy pursued by the present bank towards that city, originated in a jealousy of the increasing wealth and trade of the commercial metropolis of the United States. At times, too, it had indiscreetly enlarged its discounts, and in order to bring the currency within proper limits, was obliged to bear harshly upon its customers." ("The United States Bank" in *Annual American Register of Public Events for the Year 1831–1832* (Brattleboro, Vt.: Fessenden, 1833), p. 71.

to a revenue one by 1842. From Washington Lawrence informed Gallatin in January, 1833, that

> the people of the North are insufficiently alive to the importance of early action [for tariff reduction]. Nothing is now to be apprehended from nullification in South Carolina, and it is probable that the President's proclamation has prevented the recourse by the state to any measures, requiring the forcible interposition of the government; but should the tariff not be reduced this winter, is there not reason to fear a southern convention in which its discussions will not be limited to the tariff and may embrace a recognition by a respectable assembly of delegates from several states of the right of secession, etc.[40]

The tariff was reduced. But hardly had the issue been settled in 1833 than the monetary issue was again being agitated. There was a panic in 1834 and a more severe one in 1837. The long depression after 1837 led to a Whig victory in the New York State elections. Lawrence, in a letter to his old friend Luther Bradish, the most powerful Whig leader of the New York Assembly, suggested that the state legislature could do much to end the suspension of specie payments and restore prosperity. He substantially qualified his early support of free banking, the elimination of small bank notes, and opposition to state aid for internal improvements. More specifically he supported legislative charters for heavily capitalized banks and aid for the state chartered railroad companies.

The most effective method to restore business confidence and prevent future panics and their calamities, he felt, would be an incorporated Bank of the United States, with headquarters in New York "where under ordinary circumstances, exchanges center." But he doubted that any such bank could be attained at least for several years, because it would have to face a President's veto again, as well as the constitu-

[40] Letter of Lawrence to Gallatin, January 5, 1833, in Gallatin papers, New-York Historical Society.

tional scruples of some southern congressmen and the hostility aroused by the manner in which the Second Bank of the United States had obtained a charter from the legislature of Pennsylvania when its federal charter expired in 1836.

He would not deny that the state legislature was not the most appropriate source for remedies; but it could render considerable help. The recently enacted prohibition of small bank notes should be immediately repealed. This had deprived the banks of means for meeting demands from depositors—the only class of liabilities which could seriously threaten the solvency of such institutions.

As a "free trade advocate," Lawrence supported the successful movement to lift the restraining law of 1818 "so far as respects the receiving of deposits & the discounting of notes [for this was] an unnecessary infringement on natural liberty." He did not, however, think that the measure would have much practical result: most of the other states had no restraining act, but neither did they have much private banking. But he strongly opposed a free banking act the advocacy of which, unfortunately,

> has been recently adopted by small Whig papers. . . . [Such banks] could not possess the ability like chartered companies, of introducing that foreign capital which . . . is absolutely required to restore vigor to this community. . . . Let it be understood that, as has long happened with regard to insurance companies & is practiced as to Banks themselves in Massachusetts, all proper applications for bank charters will be granted, the success of the institutions to depend upon the confidence, with which they can inspire the community, & it seems to me that all reasonable allegations as to monopoly will be removed; while a salutary supervision by the Legislature over the issues of paper, will be preserved. . . . A capital of thirty or forty millions in one Bank would be infinitely more efficient in resuscitating our commerce than twice that amount distributed in numerous institutions. The stock of such a bank . . . would answer for remittance abroad and thus

foreign capital, to the extent of the stock transmitted, would be furnished us.

Furthermore, on the strength of such a capital, it could in periods of temporary commercial embarrassments afford immediate adequate relief on reasonable terms to solvent merchants and institutions by interposing its credit between the borrowers and the European lender. In fact, "had the late Bank of the U.S. been rechartered by New York, instead of Pennsylvania, the recent derangement of the currency might have been averted."

Finally, the chartering of such banks might be used to aid in the construction of New York railroads. It should be made a condition of any new bank that it subscribe five millions to

the capital stock of companies, already chartered for works of internal improvement, and the interest of the State might be identified with that of the corporation, either by one half of the capital's being subscribed in bonds, irredeemable during the continuance of the Charter, or the whole or a portion of the stock, as has been done in similar cases, in some of the South western States, might be paid for in bonds and mortgages for which the state could issue its stock on such terms as from the sale of it the Bank could readily obtain funds in the European market. In the latter case, the difference of one per cent between the interest of the mortgages & of the state stock . . . might be appropriated, either to the general fund or to works of Internal improvement.[41]

Despite Lawrence's disapproval, the Whigs sponsored and enacted the Free Banking Act of 1838.[42] However, his

[41] Letter of Lawrence to Bradish, Nov. 25, 1837, in Bradish papers, New-York Historical Society.

[42] Immediately after the passage of the Free Banking Act, in 1838, Lawrence's father headed a group described as "our most intelligent merchants and capitalists," organized to take advantage of the Act, which promoted the American Exchange Bank. It included such notables as Gulian C. Verplanck and the famous diarist and mayor of New York City, Philip Hone. The bank had an authorized capital of $50,000,000. The promoters contemplated branches, not only in New York but also in other states,

proposals for state aid for internal improvement companies were partially successful. Among the beneficiaries was the New York and Erie Railroad, of whose powerful executive committee (of the Board of Directors) Lawrence was a member. He had in his *Two Lectures on Political Economy* expressed the view that the road would be speedily constructed and without recourse to government aid whether federal or state. But not until 1835, after the election of James Gore King as president of the railroad, were the first contracts let for construction; meanwhile the company had already begun a campaign for substantial aid through a state subscription to the stock or loans—the issuing of state bonds to the company for which the state guaranteed payments of interest and principal if the company should default.[43]

and called on their state and their city to subscribe to the capital stock in 5 percent public debt stock. (American Exchange Bank, *The Articles of Association of the American Exchange Bank* [New York: privately printed, 1838], pp. 23–24.)

The repeal of the prohibition of small bank notes—those under $5.00—was a major issue in the gubernatorial campaign of 1838. The Democratic party supported the prohibition on grounds cogently expressed in resolutions in the Assembly by one of its able leaders, Samuel J. Tilden: "That by filling the lesser channels of circulation with gold and silver, it gives greater stability to the whole monetary system and through it to all kinds of business; that by providing a metallic currency for minor transactions including payments for labor, it affords more protection against forgery and fraud to the working classes." The Whig, William "Small Bill" Seward, won, and the prohibition was quickly repealed. Later Tilden commented that while the prohibition had the support of the British practice and "most economical writers," the public demand for repeal, evidenced by the great Whig victory, made opposition to repeal futile.

[43] The company received the aid of federal army engineers for preliminary surveys in 1832, and a $15,000 appropriation from the state legislature in 1834 to hire engineers to survey the route and determine the cost of construction. Supporters of substantial state aid drew on a variegated list of arguments.

The City of New York argued that the railroad would prevent the diversion to rival port towns of the expanding commerce of the west and thereby "augment enormously the population, wealth and taxable incomes of the commonwealth." Furthermore, the road would be useful in wartime for the expeditious passage of the nation's troops, and at all times for the swift transmission of the mails and consequent diffusion of commercial intelligence. The State Senate Committee on Railroads in its 1836 *Report* urged aid on the ground that few people had adequate capital to finance so great a project.

In 1836 the company was granted a $3,000,000 loan from the state; but the legislation, even after it was liberalized in 1838, required that the company had to raise $100,000 of its own cash before it could receive an equal amount in state bonds. Early in 1839 (February) Lawrence and Lord led the movement to have the state take its choice of two policies: (1) grant the company $3.00 of state stock for every $1.00 advanced by the stockholders, pay the interest on the bonds, and have the right to purchase the road on completion, at cost including interest; or (2) buy out the stockholders, upon "just and equitable" terms.

The legislature, however, refused to take any action. King, having become convinced that such a large enterprise could only be carried on by the state, resigned the presidency in September, 1839; Lawrence, after serving with his successor, Lord, for a few months, left the following January.[44]

For Lawrence the one bright sign in 1840 was the victory of the Whig candidate for the presidency and the defeat of Jackson's chosen successor, Martin Van Buren, for re-election. He quickly announced that this meant the end of Jackson's boasted "experiment" in banking policy. He re-

William H. Seward, the eminent Whig leader in his *Address of the New-York and Erie Railroad Convention, to the People of the State of New-York* (1837) warned the legislators that since "true national wealth consists of the resources and ability of the people to bear taxation, whenever it is required for great objects of public good," government should help "develop these resources and increase that ability by every feasible improvement which can be effected with an expense having a reasonable proportion to the results to be attained."

The company in urging state purchase of at least $3,000,000 of company stock in its *Memorial* (1837) contended that the mere revenue of a railroad was only a small part of the social benefits conferred, for it should be credited also with "the thousands which are saved in avoiding the expense of an old mode of transportation and the millions of property which new markets call into existence."

[44] E. H. Mott, *Between the Ocean and the Lakes*, pp. 42-43, 46-47.

Lord in 1840 obtained further liberalization of the terms. The company defaulted on interest payments in 1842; but the state in 1845 in effect agreed to a donation of the stock to the company. When the road was completed in 1851 the Whig President of the United States, Millard Fillmore, and members of his cabinet, participated in the celebration.

mained, however, a free trader, and not a protectionist Whig; he could hardly recant those "principles of political economy which teach that every nation is benefitted by the prosperity of every other with which it maintains commercial relations." [45]

The death of President Harrison, after but one month in office, and the accession to the presidency of the states' rights Virginian and ex-Democrat, John Tyler, gave the cause of the bank a death blow. Lawrence was one of a large number of former anti-Jackson Democrats who seceded from the Whigs and returned to the Democrats. It was shortly afterward that he reasserted his old Jeffersonian faith in the progress of knowledge. In a public address in 1842 he maintained that the ante-Columbus discoveries of America, like the investigations of modern geology, "open to us an entire new field of exploration, obliging men, as it were, to unlearn much that, as children, we had been taught." [46]

In a celebrated case in which he successfully defended the right of a church corporation to retain an endowment set up in the colonial period although it had changed its religious principles, he held that there was "progress in science and knowledge of all kinds, and that it ought not to be arrested by any arbitrary decision for the purpose of perpetuating old error, as believed in two hundred or three hundred years ago." [47]

[45] [W. B. Lawrence], "Northeastern Boundary," *The New York Review*, VIII (January, 1841), 195, 259. For Lawrence's authorship see Allibone, *A Critical Dictionary*, I, 1068.

[46] W. B. Lawrence, "Anniversary Address, before the New-York Historical Society," November 1. 1842. Ms. in New-York Historical Society collection.

[47] The quotation is from a summary in W. B. Lawrence, "Charitable Endowments—Discussion," in *Transactions of the National Association for the Promotion of Social Sciences, Bristol Meeting, 1869* (London: Longmans, 1870, pp. 146–47. Lawrence's original brief is *The German Reformed Church in the City of New York. In the Court for the Correction of Errors . . . at Rochester, on 2nd, 3rd, and 4th of September, 1845* (New York: privately printed, 1845).

A qualified but significant change from his earlier doctrines was his questioning of the usefulness of a national bank and a public debt. These views he expressed in an unsigned article on Gallatin in the influential party organ, the *Democratic Review*, in 1843.[48] He said that Gallatin had favored paying off the public debt because, under the most favorable conditions, its "tendency is to increase by artificial means the inequality of fortunes, and that if permitted to become an ordinary state of things, the payment of interest, however just, becomes a permanent tax on industry in favor of idleness." He added that Gallatin's success in infusing his views "into the mind of both parties and into the legislatures of the country, was perhaps the most important of . . . [his] many services." [49]

Lawrence now followed Gallatin in supporting the opposition to the resurrection of the bank. Lawrence wrote that in the earlier poverty of the country the "stimulus and aid of the artificial capital" created by the bank was perhaps beneficial, but that insufficient attention had been given to the fatal end of its liability and tendency to abuse. The "great national experiences through which we have passed" helped to clarify the subject.

Somewhat later he became extremely active in politics.

[48] [W. B. Lawrence], "Albert Gallatin," *The United States Magazine, and Democratic Review*, VIII (June, 1843), 641–53. For Lawrence's authorship see Allibone, *A Critical Dictionary*, I, 1068.

[49] The eminent economist and Whig, President Francis Wayland of Brown University, at about the same time, after noting the complete redemption of the federal debt in 1834, said that "no more money went out of the country through this channel. . . . We were the first, and are still the only nation in modern times, which has ever wholly freed itself from debt. This fact tended to raise the spirits of the country, to give the people great confidence in their resources and to incite them to large undertakings." "Debts of the States," *The North American Review*, LV (January, 1844), 111. For Wayland's authorship, see Francis Wayland and H. L. Wayland, *A Memoir of the Life and Labors of Francis Wayland*, 2 vols. (New York: Sheldon, 1868), II, 368.

For a penetrating historical study of the public debt in American economic thought, see Lewis H. Kimmel, *Federal Budget and Fiscal Policy, 1789–1958* (Washington: Brookings Institution, 1959).

In the 1848 New York State elections he prepared newspaper articles on the lives of the Democratic candidates for governor and lieutenant governor, Reuben Hyde Walworth and Charles O'Conor; but they were defeated by the Whig ticket headed by Lawrence's former law partner Hamilton Fish.

Lawrence's political prospects looked more promising in Rhode Island, where he had purchased an estate in 1845.[50] After establishing his permanent residence there in 1850, he was nominated the following year for lieutenant governor along with Philip Allen for governor, on the Democratic ticket. Although Whigs attacked both candidates on the ground of their great wealth, they won the election.[51]

Lawrence supported the secret ballot and the liberalization of voting requirements; he favored the abolition of imprisonment for debt and of the Registry Tax. Supporters claimed that these proposed measures would free the poor debtors and employees from voting as their creditors or employers directed on penalty of imprisonment; opponents claimed that they would destroy "the last remains of our old institutions as they existed under the charter of King Charles." To the charge that the measures, being "agrarian" in nature, would lead to "an equal distribution of property," supporters pointed out that both Lawrence and the governor were very wealthy men.[52]

Lawrence was deeply moved by the plight of the inmates of debtors' prisons. Before proposing a relief bill in the Senate,

[50] Lawrence bought a sixty-nine acre estate in Newport for $12,000, which his friends expected would be a loss, but which on his death in 1881 realized for his heirs almost $1,000,000. (Isaac Lawrence, "Governor William Beach Lawrence," Part 2, *The New York Genealogical and Biographical Record,* XXVI [July, 1895], 149. For a description of his estate see J. G. W[ilson], "Ochre Point, the home of an American Jurist," *The Newport Historical Magazine,* III [July, 1882], 33–55.)

[51] Charles Carroll, *Rhode Island: Three Centuries of Democracy,* 4 vols. (New York: Lewis Historical Publishing Co., 1932), I, 578.

[52] The Newport *Advertiser,* Nov. 20, 1851; March 31, 1852.

he investigated the debtors' ward in the Providence prison and country jail. He found that the six prisoners had been incarcerated from one week to four months, and that five of them owed from one to three dollars and the sixth no more than five dollars.[53]

In urging the state legislature to abolish imprisonment for debt, he pointed out that such a penalty was no deterrent of imprudent speculation. "Those individual enterprises which have resulted in elavating our state and nation to the highest condition of prosperity . . . would probably have failed to obtain the sanction of any Conservative Board, but fortunately, none of those eminent citizens whose success was that of the State, allowed themselves to be arrested in their career by any apprehension that the mishaps to which all human undertakings are exposed might bring them within the purview of the imprisonment laws. The American character is too sanguine to fear possible evils, and the remote danger of imprisonment, as a consequence of failure, has never, it is believed, prevented a single transaction of magnitude; but while every advantage which wealth can command, is readily conceded, to the successful merchant or manufacturer, humanity forbids that in addition to the ills of poverty, his less fortunate, though not less worthy and intelligent competitor, should be consigned to an ignominious punishment." [54]

Lawrence was equally zealous in pushing state aid for education, especially the common schools, as one of the most effective means of economic and social improvement, including the prevention of drunkenness. To this end, he labored to restore the school fund to the condition in which he held the state constitution had originally placed it. He

[53] Letter of W. B. Lawrence to Thomas W. Dorr, June 30, 1851, in Dorr correspondence, Brown University Library.

[54] W. B. Lawrence and Seth N. Macy, "Report of the Select Committee [of the Senate] on the Bill to Abolish Imprisonment for Debt," The Newport *Weekly Advertiser*, Nov. 26, 1851. Abolition of imprisonment for debt was not achieved in Rhode Island until 1870.

had such a strong belief in the efficacy of education that he later asked, "Is it not infinitely more important that money should now be expended in educating different classes, the results of which would benefit future generations, than that it should accumulate at compound interest for our grand-children?" This proposition, he claimed, was based on the converse of the doctrine that his "old friend and political schoolmaster," Thomas Jefferson, used to inculcate. If, as Jefferson taught, no generation had a right to contract a debt that could not be paid within that generation; that is, every generation is to pay for itself, "is there any reason why any bequest should be left to it from a preceding generation?" [55]

Lawrence ran into political difficulties by his forthright opposition to a proposed prohibition bill, as a "most barbarous sumptuary enactment diametrically opposed to the cardinal principles on which our party is constituted." [56]

His economic arguments accorded with his free trade principles, but some of them were of an extreme sort. For a public body to supply medicinal and sacramental liquor, he informed the state senate, was "obnoxious to every principle of political economy." Whatever might have been the "usages of barbarous times or in remote antiquity," the Pasha of Egypt was the only prominent case today of a prince as the sole merchant, manufacturer, and agriculturalist. The bill also violated the first principles of common honesty and "the bill of rights" which provides that "property shall not be taken for public uses without just compensation" and thus required full indemnification to those injured.[57] The following year Allen was reelected; but the prohibition candidate cut so deeply into Lawrence's vote that he was defeated.

[55] W. B. Lawrence, "Charitable Endowments—Discussion," *Transactions, National Association for the Promotion of Social Sciences*, p. 147.

[56] Letter of W. B. Lawrence to Thomas W. Dorr, June 6, 1852, in Dorr correspondence, Brown University Library.

[57] Lawrence, *Maine Law* (Newport, R.I.: Atkinson, 1852). There were at least two printings of the speech in Providence.

However, he did not cease to have an active interest in politics; he held a number of party offices, local and national, and was supported by a leading party organ, the Newport *Advertiser*. He helped to nominate a dark horse, Franklin Pierce of New Hampshire, for the presidency at the Democratic National Convention in 1852; but he would have preferred a westerner, Lewis Cass or Stephen A. Douglas, for president, and for vice president Thomas W. Dorr, who had suffered imprisonment for leading an armed revolt in order to bring Rhode Island's political arrangements abreast of other states, especially the broadening of the franchise beyond the freehold limitation that went back to Roger Williams's day. Finding his own party unwilling to recognize even in principle the doctrine of universal suffrage, and especially the need for all to participate in altering the organic law or constitution, he complained to Dorr in 1853 that his democracy so little accorded with that of a large proportion of those who were nominally Democrats that he was tempted to abjure politics.[58]

He remained active, but shifted from his old views on slavery. In supporting the Democratic party's presidential nominee, James Buchanan, in 1856, against the new Republican party, he bitterly denounced the demand of the "black Republicans" for a prohibition of slavery in the territories. He took his stand on the doctrine that Congress must not interfere with the right of the territories, as well as the states, to decide for themselves whether to have slavery or not.[59]

He painted a dismal picture of the future that faced the North, and especially the great manufacturing state of Rhode Island, if the South ceased cotton production, as he held it would do if slaves were presently freed. He went on to warn that Northerners, when criticizing the institution of slavery,

[58] Letter of W. B. Lawrence to Dorr, Oct. 4, 1853, in Dorr correspondence, Brown University Library.

[59] "Remarks of Hon. W. B. Lawrence in the Democratic State Convention," The Newport *Advertiser*, July 2, 1856.

should remember the barbarities of the legal system toward the destitute free laborers. "At the South, the cruelty of the master, if restrained by no principle, is controlled by those considerations of self interest, which every man has to protect his own property. There is no check on the rapacity or avarice of a creditor." [60]

The Democratic victory raised Lawrence's hopes for national service. Hamilton Fish wrote a friend that "politicians, hopeful and patriotic gentlemen, who are willing to serve the public, either in diplomatic positions or at home, are congregating here [in Washington]. Beach Lawrence has taken a house here for the winter and hopes to succeed Mr. [George Mifflin] Dallas [as minister to England].[61] Dallas, however, was a Democrat in good standing and continued at his post.[62]

In the presidential campaign of 1860 Lawrence was particularly active as the Rhode Island member of the Democratic National Committee. To avoid the effect of the split in the party, which he described as "the great conservative party," Lawrence helped to set up in Rhode Island a "Union National Democratic Electoral Ticket," which would vote for the national candidate who "might the most fully concentrate the conservative vote" and be a "rebuke to sectionalism and radicalism," represented by Abraham Lincoln.[63]

Although after the outbreak of the Civil War Lawrence supported the Union, and although one of his sons, General Albert Gallatin Lawrence, was wounded while leading the

[60] "Address of the Hon. Wm. B. Lawrence, before the Newport Democratic Union Club at Acquidneck Hall on Thursday Evening, October 16th, 1856," The Newport *Advertiser*, Nov. 3, 1856. Also printed as a pamphlet (Newport, R.I.: Atkinson, 1856).

[61] Letter of Fish to D. D. Barnard, Jan. 8, 1857, in Fish papers, Library of Congress.

[62] The Newport *Advertiser* on November 26, 1856, had expressed the hope that the American minister would resign, since under the American system of rotation of office, four years in office was sufficient honor especially for the cabinet officers and diplomats.

[63] The Newport *Advertiser*, Oct, 3, 10, 1861

successful assault on Fort Fisher, there continued for a time to be criticisms that his famous editions of Wheaton's classic, *Elements of International Law*, contained sentiments favorable to secession.[64]

But after peace had come Lawrence's eminent services as an international lawyer were recalled,[65] and his reputation in this field continued to be a high one. He added to it in notable cases—for instance, when he served successfully as attorney for British claimants before the British and American Mixed Commissions set up under the Treaty of Washington of 1871.[66] In explaining his willingness to take these cases,

[64] The book was responsible for a lengthy and far-reaching dispute between Lawrence and Richard Henry Dana, famous author of *Two Years Before the Mast*, who was commissioned by Wheaton's heir in 1864 to prepare a new edition. When Dana's edition appeared two years later, Lawrence brought suit for plagiarism of his notes in the previous editions.

In its decision as rendered in 1869 and summarized by Dana's biographer, the court held that "while the work of Mr. Dana contained much material both valuable and original, yet he had in preparing it so far followed in the footsteps of Mr. Lawrence that he must be declared to have infringed upon his rights. The case was then referred to a Master to report upon the extent of the infringement; but the demand of Mr. Lawrence that the sale of the edition should be stopped by an injunction pending the examination by a Master was denied." The Master reported twelve years later just before both parties died that there were fourteen instances where Dana's notes "infringed the rights of the complainant." (Extracts from the Master's Report in Charles Francis Adams, Jr., *Richard Henry Dana* [Boston: Houghton, Mifflin, 1891], II, 395.)

[65] Lawrence had once complained that despite his international reputation he "had on more than one occasion been passed over in the conferring of college or university honors for some country attorney whose name was never heard beyond the sound of his village bell" (Adams, *Richard Henry Dana*, II, 293–94), but in 1869 Brown University awarded him an LL.D. "for eminent services as a publicist" (letter from Alexis Caswell to W. B. Lawrence, Sept. 7, 1869, in Brown University Library collection); and the Regents of the University of the State of New York gave him a D.C.L. in 1873. He lectured on international law at Columbian (now George Washington) University in 1872–73, and Boston University Law School, in 1873–74.

[66] This treaty provided arbitral machinery for the settlement of claims between the United States and Great Britain arising from the Civil War. Fish, then secretary of state, seriously considered proposing Lawrence as the American member of the arbitration tribunal, but his being a Democrat proved a bar. (Allan Nevins, *Hamilton Fish* [New York: Dodd, Mead, 1936], p. 511.)

In the most significant case, *The Circassian*, Lawrence received a fee of $40,000 in gold.

Lawrence said that he wanted to reassert the traditional principles of international law. These principles, he insisted as an old Ricardian, were primarily concerned with the protection of the freedom of commerce, upon which industry essentially depended.

He retained to the last one major tenet of his old Jeffersonian creed: namely, a fear of executive power. On the eve of the presidential campaign of 1880 he warned the nation that the enormous power of the presidency signalized the monarchical principle in our constitution. It was the cause of the notorious scandals that had especially characterized President Grant's administrations. These were small pickings compared to the future "*bonanza* of bankers' syndicates, of railroad monopolies, steamship subsidies and the great future oceanic canal." The President's veto power was especially potent. Before President Andrew Johnson's time, Lawrence pointed out, the veto had been overridden only once. That was in 1856, when President Pierce on constitutional grounds refused to sign several bills for appropriations for making navigable some interior rivers. The solution Lawrence advocated was to follow the Swiss model of entrusting the executive power to a federal council of seven members.[67]

To the end, Lawrence remained a scholar. He passed away in New York City on March 26, 1881, while at work on an address on Albert Gallatin for delivery before the New-York Historical Society.[68]

Lawrence considered himself rightly a publicist in the most comprehensive meaning of that term; and actually he was a

[67] W. B. Lawrence, "The Monarchical Principle in Our Constitution," *The North American Review*, CXXXI (November, 1880), 401–2, 407, 409.

[68] One of Lawrence's few adverse comments in his notes for the address was that Gallatin had not been a good enough Ricardian in his early days to have appreciated that the best speculations were in New York rather than Virginia and western land. "Life, Character, and Public Services of Albert Gallatin," ms. in New-York Historical Society collection.)

recognized, although self-constituted, arbiter in matters of public policy—local, state, national, and international. He kept alive the tradition of the man of affairs who was also a scholar. In this as in so much else he resembled his master, Ricardo. He contributed greatly to the popularization of Ricardo's economics in the United States, although to a somewhat lesser degree than McCulloch did in England. And he also showed how the Ricardian scheme could be adapted to American conditions. The modifications were sometimes such that it seems doubtful whether Ricardo would have recognized the modified system as his own.

Lawrence called himself an advocate of laissez-faire; but his views on such matters as the national debt and government support of internal improvements indicated that laissez-faire was a very complex philosophy; as he interpreted it, it did not mean that the economy was simply to be left alone. It meant that private initiative was to be fostered. But he ended, as he began, a Benthamite—a philosophical radical—and a Ricardian disciple. If these English doctrines could be adapted to the conditions prevailing in an expanding, speculative economy he meant to make such an adaptation. And more than any other individual he made the imported philosophy seem universal.

FRANCIS LIEBER

FRANCIS LIEBER: GERMAN SCHOLAR IN AMERICA

In 1904 there was established at Columbia University in the Faculty of Political Science the Lieber Professorship of History and Political Philosophy.[1] This was somewhat belated recognition for one of the nineteenth century's most impressive academic figures.

Lieber's exile from his native Germany began in 1826. His boyhood had been varied, his youth stormy. After serving with Blücher and being wounded at Waterloo he had entered a gymnasium in Berlin, going from there to the University of Berlin where the interests awoke which were considered treasonable at that time and place. Europe, it will be remembered, came under the hegemony of Metternich and Czar Alexander after the Congress of Vienna; and the German student movements were involved in agitation for a more genuine unity than existed under the Metternich-controlled confederacy of princes. No republic, it was felt, would achieve this. The desire was then, as it was again a century later, after the humiliations of Versailles, for a strong leader. Lieber, in a way, was an early martyr to the nationalist cause, not so very long before his time, but long enough so that he became a marked young man. His tribulations involved

[1] William Archibald Dunning (A. B. Columbia, 1881; Ph.D. 1885) occupied the chair from its establishment until his death in 1922; in 1929 it was revived under another name—Political Philosophy and Sociology—and given to Professor Robert Morrison MacIver.

something like persecution. He was forbidden the institutions of higher learning; his effects were searched; he was even imprisoned more than once. This treatment created understandable mortification in one who had soldiered for his country. He finally escaped and went to England.

He was then twenty-six. His education had been about what might be imagined. His service in the army; a trip to Greece; a year in Rome as tutor to the children of the historian and diplomat Barthold Georg Niebuhr; interrupted attempts to study at Berlin, Jena,[2] Halle, and Dresden—all these left him with more sense of frustration than of accomplishment. He had begun by hoping, as boys will, to emulate the personification of his ambitions, Linnaeus, the great classifier. (On many occasions later in life he betrayed the frustrated social organizer within the professor's clothes. He thought he might command armies successfully, or manage plantations; and his astonishing suitability for the presidencies of the College of South Carolina[3] and Columbia seemed to him so obvious that its neglect by others could hardly be explained except as oversight.) Yet there he was in England, a young man unable to find satisfaction for his ambitions and employment for his abilities. Even his living was precarious. All he could find to do was a little tutoring in German, a little writing for German magazines. He made one bold try for place. This was for nothing less than the professorship of German at the proposed University of London, which, however, remained in the planning stage. It then appeared that in far-off Boston he might have an opportunity. A gymnasium and swimming school needed oversight—German oversight. Lieber jumped at the chance.

[2] Lieber is supposed to have received the degree of Doctor of Philosophy at Jena in 1820. M. Halsey Thomas, the curator of the Columbiana collection in the Columbia University Libraries, sent a letter to the University of Jena on April 4, 1938, to verify this, but no reply was received. Harvard made him Doctor of Laws in 1850.

[3] Lieber served as acting president during the year 1849.

It was not so strange in 1826 as it would have been a century later for one with scholarly ambitions to begin as a teacher of gymnastics. So far as Lieber was concerned, he felt no inferiority on this account. The revolutionary student societies in Prussia had grown out of the gymnastic societies of Dr. Friedrich Ludwig Jahn. The building of bodies was even then linked with spiritual growth, and mass exercise had a mystical relationship to a united Germany. These intoxicating associations of youth were strange to the authorities of that day. The movement was forced to take a course which later involved just such costly punishments as Lieber had to undergo. The Germans learned gradually to use these latent emotional forces; but not much understanding of them was to develop in England or America. America, however, was just then tasting everything with foreign prestige; New England, especially, was looking abroad for the materials and standards of her culture. It was some such imitative impulse as this which inspired the school in Boston. Lieber's predecessor there had been Charles Follen, also an exile with much the same background; he had gone on to the teaching of gymnastics along with German languages and civil law at Harvard, as well as ethics and ecclesiastical history at the Divinity School. This varied list of subjects reveals something not only about the abilities of German exiles but also about the state of higher learning in the United States at that time. Yet this very backwardness was what encouraged the young physical education instructor to hope for advancement in the academic occupations which had been closed to him in England.

The gymnasium offered neither a satisfactory career nor good living. If he had hopes of founding, in emulation of Jahn, something like a youth movement in New England, he was soon disillusioned. The Bostonians took their exercise in moderation; they also preferred it individual and competitive, like their businesses. But the young instructor's confidence in his own abilities was not shaken; nor had he ever any doubts of their universality. This was never better illustrated than in the curious transition from athletics to scholarship which he now proceeded to effect. The occasion was the translating and rewriting of a popular German encyclopedia. He promoted this enterprise with characteristic energy, first laboring to convince Henry C. Carey, the leading publisher in the country,[4] of its possibilities, then turning to the immense task of securing American collaborators, translating hundreds of articles himself, and seeing the thirteen volumes of the *Encyclopædia Americana* (1829–33) through the press. It became clear after two volumes were out that the scheme would be successful; and this was Lieber's first bulwark against fate.

The encyclopaedia served his purposes well. It taught him how to get along with all types of people, including his influential publishers. He wrote Carey that "I have no disposition to quarrel. When I was a young dog, I had my full share of duels when people unintentionally wanted to ill treat me, or purposely attacked my nation, as for instance in France, but for the rest people always used to wonder that I was so ready to make up a disagreement." [5]

Furthermore, it taught him to use his adopted language fluently and brought him into contact with many outstanding American professional people who would be of use in furthering his career. His published letters [6] tell how he evolved continuing contacts through correspondence as well as

[4] Carey was to become the foremost protectionist economist. His firm at this time was known as Carey, Lea & Carey.

[5] From an undated memorandum of Henry to Mathew Carey, in the William L. Clements Library of the University of Michigan; printed in David Kaser, *Messrs. Carey and Lea of Philadelphia* (Philadelphia: Univ. Pennsylvania Press, 1957), p. 136.

[6] Thomas S. Perry, *The Life and Letters of Francis Lieber* (Boston: Osgood, 1882), pp. 79–96.

through visits. Such men as Joseph Story, James Kent, George S. Hillard, William Longfellow, Charles Sumner, and Robert C. Winthrop were included in his list. It was, indeed, eight years before there came to him the thing he longed for most —a settled job into which he could throw himself and make a career. In the meantime, he resorted to many expedients. In addition to his work on the encyclopedia, for which he himself prepared articles on subjects ranging from cooking to Kant, he wrote articles for German and French periodicals, translated books on prison reform, and published a curious travel book called *Letters to a Gentleman in Germany* (1834), and his reminiscences of Barthold Georg Niebuhr (1835). He lectured, too, at the Athenaeum and the Society for Useful Knowledge. On the whole, although this was for him a time of constant uncertainty and considerable money shortage (he had married in September, 1829, Matilda Oppenheimer with whom he had become acquainted during his stay in England and who had followed him to Boston), he was adding to his knowledge of America, widening if not deepening his knowledge of legal literature, of economics, and of politics, and increasing his contacts with men of affairs. He also traveled a good deal. New York, Philadelphia, and Washington became familiar. In New York he became acquainted with James Kent, in Philadelphia with Nicholas Biddle, in Washington with Daniel Webster, Henry Clay, and others. Among them Biddle proved the most useful. He not only secured for Lieber a commission to prepare a scheme for the organization of Girard College, a task which Lieber characteristically turned into a magnum opus of some two hundred pages,[7] but he also helped Lieber to make the contact with South Carolina College which resulted in the coveted position of permanence.

[7] *A Constitution and Plan for Girard College for Orphans* (Philadelphia: Carey, Lea & Blanchard, 1834).

At this time, in spite of what might have seemed somewhat bizarre beginnings—the fighting in Greece, the arrests in Germany, the swimming school—Lieber was developing an impregnable respectability. Not only the character of his acquaintanceships but also the kind of opinions he professed fostered for him this sort of reputation. On slavery, for instance, his early views were eminently fashionable. In the abstract the institution was vicious; it was against the spirit of the times. But concretely it actually existed; and the real question was what should be done about a system embedded in the South's economy. Emancipation was the foolish solution of violent and impractical persons. They did not realize that freedom would lead to social equality and even to intermarriage, consequences which would conflict with the congenital dislike of whites for blacks. This might be prejudice, but it was founded on human nature. Above all, the consideration to be kept in mind was the purity of the superior race in civilization. History, Lieber felt strongly, has shown that wherever whites appear they become masters, because they assemble all the good qualities which are scattered among the other races—intelligence, sociability, activity, instinct for property, and elevation of mind. This was, however, not a bar to solution. It simply indicated that exportation to Africa or a remote section of our own continent would be necessary.

This led to the statement of another respectable thesis. In the slavery matter, as in other matters, Congress could do nothing; these issues belonged to the state legislatures, "those true foundations of our liberty without which it would not have been possible even to preserve her appearance." Lieber was learning rapidly the secret of federalism. This might be supposed to have predisposed him to favor Jackson, the ultrademocrat, but there was a hint of disorder, of slovenly manners in the Jacksonian regime. These were distasteful. The ground Lieber occupied in this matter was the highest possible: continual change, he said, undermined society even to its basic principles of morality and the pursuit of knowledge. It prevented the "firm adherence to right and law" from rooting as it should.[8] This was a convenient vantage point from which to flatter New England conservatism and at the same time to disparage the institutions of revolutionary France. Fortunately, Lieber said, people here can live under law rather than under contract. The trouble with a governmental system avowedly contractual was that one party inevitably resorted to force, overthrew the other, and instituted a system of absolutism—and this was worse in a democracy than in a monarchy since a monarchy could at least guarantee stability which, to use a term of his own invention, a "democratic absolutism" could not.

Only the adumbration that education is the cure for social ills was lacking. Lieber added it. His interest in penology was rapidly developing into a bid for professional recognition in the field. It was in an essay pursuing this interest that intemperance was put forward as the most active cause and education the most effective preventive of crime, thus ministering simultaneously to two favorite American prejudices.[9] This likemindedness with New England was effective. When Gallatin in 1830 invited a group of savants to discuss the establishment of a university on the European model, Lieber was asked to represent the German point of view. This, he hoped, might lead to something, but a few lectures on history ended his connection. The best chance for service seemed for a time to be in government, but for once Lieber's opinions were wrong: Andrew Jackson was in power. It was his mistake, for this purpose, to have acquired such knowledge as he

[8] Lieber, *Letters to a Gentleman in Germany* (Philadelphia: Carey, Lea, & Blanchard, 1834), pp. 288–301.

[9] Lieber, *Remarks on the Relation between Education and Crime* (Philadelphia: privately printed, 1838).

had of the American background from Timothy Pitkin's history books,[10] and to have set up as his ideal statesmen the Whig leaders, Webster and Clay. The friendships he had sought, too, had been among the die-hard Federalists or the anti-Jackson Democrats who became Whigs. They were the mighty names of his time, the ultra respectable members of the community; furthermore, they understood and sympathized with his faintly nostalgic interest in a united Germany. Of all those who influenced his ambitions two jurists counted most. One was the Federalist James Kent, twice Professor of Law in Columbia College and former Chancellor of New York; the other was Joseph Story, Harvard professor, bank president, and associate justice of the United States Supreme Court. In adopting these particular intellectual godfathers Lieber seemed to be going counter to dominant contemporary sentiment. Although that was a bar to political advancement, it did no harm to Lieber's academic career.

There was, however, another difficulty. Lieber's interests were widely scattered. He had acquired, in working on the encyclopedia, a little knowledge in many fields. It was not like him to be superficial; he was a serious digger, always irritated by loose ends, unsolved riddles, uncultivated fence corners. But the academic world required, at that time, such a spread of interests that an active teacher scarcely ever found time or energy to carry on any outside activity, or indeed, to make much progress in advancing knowledge. Lieber wanted to be ready for anything in the way of a job and so felt forced to maintain a number of interests that he might otherwise have dropped, for his contacts with Story and Kent had centered his attention on the law. He had been more or less immersed in politics from his boyhood and had created

[10] These were *A Political and Civil History of the United States* (New Haven: Howe, Durrel & Peck, 1828), and *A Statistical View of the Commerce of the United States* (New York: J. Eastern, 1817). Pitkin was an aggressive Federalist.

political contacts in America at every opportunity. These, combined with his unusual ability to use several languages, determined the most congenial field to which he might devote himself. He was, indeed, about to begin the study of law when the offer came from South Carolina College. He accepted at once.

The catholicity of Lieber's effort to specialize in many things was perhaps justified; his appointment was as Professor of History and Political Economy.[11] He did not expect to be particularly happy at Columbia. Although it was the capital of the state, it was a small town in the back country of South Carolina, and was singularly lacking in the romantic appurtenances of the storied South. The houses were diversely ugly in design and not too solid, the streets were sandy, the countryside burnt in summer and drab in winter. But it seemed to offer a refuge where he might get deep into his books and have that assurance of the future without which scholarship develops so reluctantly. He expected also that the title—Professor of History and Political Economy—would be but a slight limitation to his activities. On the whole, therefore, in spite of some bitterness at "exile" in the South and regret for contacts which he could no longer maintain, he hoped for the best. He knew also that his growing family would now have a home, his children friends, and his wife a settled center for her activities. On these important matters, at least, his mind, after years of disburbance, was at last tranquil.

The college was being reorganized. Thomas Cooper, the fiery economist who had been president, had been got rid of as gracefully as possible. He had offended the prevailing

[11] At a salary of $2,500. A house was provided. (Letter of Lieber to Samuel B. Ruggles, May 19, 1842, published in C. S. Phinney, *Francis Lieber's Influence on American Thought* (Philadelphia: International Printing Co., 1918), p. 65.

religious prejudices—even in that most unlikely of places, a textbook on political economy—he had spoken of the clergy as unexcelled as a "money-seeking, grasping set of men" and as obtaining money under false pretenses.[12] Almost at once the trustees were dismayed to discover that there were those among the clergy who believed Lieber to be a bird of the same feather. About all that could be adduced in substantiation was his acceptance, in the plan he had recently devised for Girard College, of the proviso in the cantankerous old gentleman's will barring ecclesiastics from any part in the enterprise. This was pretty thin; as a matter of fact Lieber had said in the same document that religion was the only safe foundation for morals and that there could be no true education without religious instruction; besides that, he was a member in good standing of the Episcopal Church. The religious attack was fantastic; no one was ever more solidly based on established orthodoxy in everything; it would have outraged the whole design to have neglected the church. The real difficulty was that he was an outsider—not only was he of European origin, but he had also to meet the mixed resentment and respect with which learned northerners were received in the South.

His inaugural address, as well as his dignified demeanor and the respectability of his family, soon revealed, however, the absurdity of such attacks. But they hurt; and he felt then and later the confinement of his essentially unintellectual surroundings. This, though, loomed no larger in his mind than the compromises he had to make on such issues as slavery. Here he avoided public statements, except once, in 1835, when he denied that he was an abolitionist, though he was candid enough in exchanges with his northern correspondents. These were years of heightened sensitivity in the South on a number

[12] Thomas Cooper, *Lectures on the Elements of Political Economy* (1826; 2d. ed., Columbia, S.C.: M'Morris and Wilson, 1831), pp. 331, 344. For a scholarly study of the issue, see Dumas Malone, *The Public Life of Thomas Cooper* (New Haven: Yale Univ. Press, 1926), pp. 337–67.

of related issues. Slavery was only one; another was free trade as against protection; still another was states' rights with its accompanying doctrine of nullification. He needed to use great care. It came hard, for, although he had great respect for authority, and infinite patience in seeking preferment, he had also the intellectual arrogance so often associated with those traits. What made the situation so maddening as the years passed was the necessity for truckling to obvious inferiors. Although he found no real relief from this humiliation, he tried his best to find it in hard work and sometimes seemed to have succeeded. It needed only a reminder from the North or from abroad to tap the springs of lamentation, however, and his letters, almost from the first, were filled with regrets and with a new seeking for something more worthy.

Luckily, although he was in difficulties over slavery and over nullification, he could bear down hard on free trade; the South believed in this with a strength unequaled in any other region. Lieber was glad to be able on this issue to pull out all the organ stops.[13]

He was a good debater; and on this issue he pointed out that originally American protectionists had argued that high tariffs were essential to provide employment for "American or 'National' capital." It was contended that "the American

[13] Writing to Senator Calhoun for government documents in 1847, in connection with his "Newspaper Lectures" in which "it is my endeavor . . . to teach the students how to read the papers," he said: "I suppose I hardly need add that in my Newspaper Lectures I am constantly mindful that I am paid by the *State* and have no right to use my chair for propagandism of specific and personal views, although I am aware that a professor is no abstract being, no empty bottle, and that what he considers sacred truth he may not only, but is bound to teach; so, for instance, Free Trade with me. It is for the trustees to see that they appoint the right man as to vital points. I stand, in this respect, upon the same footing, I think, with our professor of Christian Evidence. He must not use his chair to preach sectarian views, but he cannot float in the clouds of indifferentism, above protestantism and Catholicism." (Lieber to Calhoun, Dec. 29, 1847, in "Correspondence of John C. Calhoun," ed. J. Franklin Jameson, in *Annual Report of the American Historical Association, for the Year 1899*, [Washington: 1900], II, 1155–56.)

producer is obliged to work with capital which bears higher interest than in Europe," therefore the much cheaper European products should not be allowed to compete with domestic products. As this argument became increasingly less popular, the protectionists, Lieber pointed out, speedily shifted to the view that protection was for the benefit of labor. Without a high tariff, they now argued, the import of cheaper foreign goods would reduce domestic production and thus force American wages down to the European standard. Lieber pointedly noted that the protectionists did not draw the logical conclusion and in consequence demand the prohibition of immigration.[14]

Free trade to Lieber was merely one aspect of that increase of facility of exchange that characterized civilization. As he wrote in *Some Truths Worth Remembering* (1849), "Rapid circulation promotes civilization, and as civilization advances, it requires circulation increased in extent and rapidity. Man removes natural obstacles by roads, canals, navigation and he creates greater ones by protective tariffs."

He was a busy teacher, too. Almost at once he began a regimen under which most men would have broken within a few months. He rose at dawn and worked far into the night; sometimes he wrote steadily for twelve or more hours, but his health stood up. An abounding physical power stayed with him throughout life; it helps to account for his conviction that he possessed abilities which ought to be put to better use. Several hours of each day had to be spent in the classroom and pretty fruitlessly spent, for although southern youth had varied interests in that day, Lieber's cosmic and abstract views of political principles and historical developments can scarcely have been among them. His touch was heavy, his exploration of remote occurrences minute. The

[14] Lieber, "Free Trade and Other Things, "*De Bow's Review*, XV (July, 1853), 63.

lecture periods his young men endured must have seemed interminable. Even those who had a professional interest in creditable examinations could hardly have felt that this material had tangible value to small-town lawyers. However, they accepted it. Small children and college students are alike in their nonprotesting adaptation to environment. The young gentlemen of South Carolina College doubtless thought that it had always been this way in colleges and that some benefits beyond their comprehension were accruing in their minds.

So far as Lieber's educational ideas were concerned, he believed in, or at least supported publicly, the established curriculum. That he was in a way pioneering by teaching rudimentary social studies modified in no respect his belief in the classics as pedagogical material. He protested on one occasion [15] against a proposal to abolish at South Carolina the teaching of evidences of Christianity; the Bible, he said, revealed the great creative forces of modern culture; most importantly, it showed the superior moral value of individual responsibility. In his inaugural address he spoke of history as "practical morals" and pointed out its importance to the sons of republicans who in future must guide the nation. This was his justification for some very long, dull lecture hours. Thomas Cooper, who violently dissented from accepted doctrine, must have been more entertaining. But solicitous parents could sleep better at night knowing how Lieber felt. Although the old-fashioned doctrine that change must be opposed was untenable, he was strongly against such radical overturns as the French Revolution; nations had much better develop gradually. It was perhaps reassuring too that the new professor, although he regarded ambition as one of man's

[15] "The Necessity of Religious Instruction in Colleges," written in 1850, published in his *Miscellaneous Writings*, ed. Daniel Coit Gilman, 2 vols. (Philadelphia: Lippincott, 1881), II, 525–30

noblest attributes, thought that young people should be taught not to abuse it; moderation was better gained by self-discipline than by law.[16]

In political economy Lieber taught from J. B. Say's textbook. Its doctrine was orthodox and congenial. He considered political economy a valuable subject matter: it emancipated minds from accidental and pernicious ideas; it showed how ideal was "the natural, simple and uninterrupted state of things in which man is allowed to apply his means as best he thinks." The bucolic conservatism of his students probably approved all this. Probably, also, they found extracurricular excitements to compensate for classroom somnolence. College students always have.

Lieber's scholarly work, during his South Carolina residence, ranged from translating a dictionary of Latin synonyms to writing a monograph on the blind deaf-mute, Laura Bridgman. In spite of this universality, it was in this period that he gradually narrowed his spread and concentrated on law and politics. Of his writings in this field it can still be said, as Chancellor Kent remarked of the first of his works, "[Lieber,] you are so sound and conservative . . . You are . . . a very safe writer." [17] The work which provoked this comment was *Legal and Political Hermeneutics; or Principles of Interpretation and Construction in Law and Politics* (1839), which had originally appeared in two issues of Charles Sumner's *American Jurist*. It was dedicated to Kent. These auspices indicate its content: the law makes its own way in accordance with the principle of historical development.

The *Hermeneutics* was a slight effort compared with *The Manual of Political Ethics*, whose two volumes came out in

[16] Lieber, "On History and Political Economy, as Necessary Branches of Superior Education in Free States" (1835), republished in his *Miscellaneous Writings*, I, 179–203.

[17] Lieber, "Diary," Aug. 12, 1841, in Perry, *Life and Letters*, p. 155.

1838 and 1839. Chapter XIII of that work began with a passage which defined, perhaps as well as any, Lieber's conception of public law and of its importance: "The civilization of the ancient Greeks and Romans was in many respects higher than that of the moderns; in others, the latter would have the advantage. . . . That subject in which we most . . . surpass them, is public law, or that branch of law which defines the relation of the individual to the state." Beginning thus, he found the opening he needed to state his characteristic doctrine:

> The . . . political science of the ancients does not occupy itself with the rights of the individual. . . . The ancients start with the state, and deduce every relation of the individual to it from this first position; the moderns acknowledge that the state . . . is but a means to obtain certain objects both for the individual, and society collectively. . . . The ancients have not that which the moderns understand by *jus naturale*, that is, the law which flows from the individual rights of man as man. . . . Indeed, what are all modern constitutions but fundamental laws, by which the supreme power is to be restricted to proper limits, and the individual rights of the citizen to be secured?

This was the level of academic political science at the mid-century. Lieber merely stated what all the best people would have agreed to. What began with the Magna Carta as a victory of subjects over irresponsible despots had gradually been transformed into a defense of property. Lieber's phrase, "democratic absolutism," opened a road to the writers who were concerned lest the lowly, through the state, should encroach on the well-to-do. His rationale led to his purely speculative excursion into the anthropology of property—an excursion, let it be said, which the majority framers of the Constitution, though they preceded him in viewing that document as keeping "the supreme power within proper limits," would not have bothered to take, for it was a long and circuitous journey.

Lieber's conception of freedom always had a strong economic reference, but included more than a mere defense of property. As he wrote in *Some Truths Worth Remembering* (1849), "Freedom, which is security of untrammelled action, is one of the first requisites of general and healthy wealth. With our race, commerce has almost always prospered or fallen with religious liberty (because, in Europe, religious liberty has, generally, been the highest test of liberty)."

To be sure, at times, Lieber's analysis of property was so involved as to lead John McVickar to describe it as "too German." [18]

"Man yearns," said Lieber, taking the liberties with human nature which were then customary, "to see his individuality represented and reflected in the effects of his exertions—in property." There grew out of this the necessity for protecting these rights; and these extended, it must be understood, to the exclusive mastery of the object, even to its abuse, as in the instance of foolishly spent funds.[19] Anything less than this full protection would so endanger the steady and moderate pursuit of gain as to engender idleness, immorality, and "unfitness for substantial liberty." Then, taking a wide swing into imaginary history, he ventured the thesis that property existed before society and the state; these merely confirm primordial claims. He went so far as to contradict, on this point, the accepted doctrine that the earth was originally held in common. If it had been, it might have been inferred that government preceded property and created it by a division which it therefore might rescind. He in this way

[18] [McVickar], review of Lieber's *Essays on Property and Labour, as Connected with Natural Law and the Constitution of Society*, in *The New York Review*, X (January, 1842), 237. For McVickar's authorship of the review see letter of Lieber to Alonzo Potter, Nov. 10, 1842, in the Historical Society of Pennsylvania collection.

[19] Lieber, *Essays on Property and Labour as Connected with Natural Law and the Constitution of Society* (New York: Harper, 1841), p. 183; Lieber, "Diary," Aug. 18, 1837, in Perry, *Life and Letters*, p. 120.

succeeded in surpassing all other defenders of property. No one could better a defense which began with universality. In the *Political Ethics* a great deal was made of this basic theme, and many variations grew out of it. The original and fundamental nature of property created also the defense for unrestricted exchange, accumulation, and bequest; these, indeed, had become the sign of man's superiority over brutes, and of Western man's superiority over Asiatic man.

Feeling for property was not exactly an instinct, in Lieber's view; it was rather a higher sense which all men bent on civilization possessed. It was, therefore, a predisposition, a capacity; and men who did not have it were doomed to savagery. Similarly, the monogamic family was a characteristic of civilization, intimately related to property, since its division of labor gave rise to exchange. When the matter was put in this way it could be seen that both property and the state arose historically from the patriarchal family—the state from the authority of the paterfamilias and property from the division enforced by him. This might have been thought to have come dangerously close to acknowledging some right inhering in the state to redivide; but no, said Lieber; the state made no rights; it merely protected original ones. Meddling of the state in private affairs ought to be avoided—it was not only unjust but burdensome and dangerous. Thus: "Individual industry, private combination and associations, which are conscious that they depend upon themselves alone, are possessed of a vigor, keenness and detailed industry, which cannot be expected of the action of the state." Exchange ought rarely to be interfered with and "never to promote, as it is called, the interests of the many." The state must neither disturb individuals in these rights nor allow others to do so "as the trades unions have of late done."

Lieber was a decent citizen, a kindly man, and an approved teacher. His expressed opinions concerning unions are the more significant because of this, just as were Lord Brougham's. The economic reasoning was curiously similar, though Lieber was inclined to thunder a bit and Brougham was always suave. The economics consisted in arguing that labor combinations interrupted "the free course of supply and demand," thus causing unnatural prices and forcing shutdowns. Even when unions succeeded in raising wages, capital tended to migrate toward cheaper non-union regions, and so the union workers became unemployed. The thundering consisted in pretty severe talk about morality. Unions were, said Lieber, most oppressive and unrighteous aristocracies, knowing no interest or code but their own. Such "aristocratic monopolies" not only promoted expense and immorality among the members by strikes, but also weaned them from their families, "and crimes, as is exhibited by statistical tables," increased lamentably along with trades unions. In fact, such "mobs," such laborite protests, constitute opposition "to the majesty of the law and render property insecure."

But if labor combinations were unlawful, added Lieber, so were combinations of employers to lower wages or prevent their rise. In fact, they were even more reprehensible, for the employers would more easily combine and could hold out longer than the wage earners.[20] Interestingly he complained that the critics of trade unions did not equally and clearly enough criticize employers combinations.

When a legalist, however, begins to write about the "majesty of the law," it is easy to infer that judicial supremacy will soon appear. *The Manual of Political Ethics* without hesitation developed the theme in that style. The judiciary was man's great bulwark against "democratic absolutism,"

[20] Lieber wrote on a slip of paper opposite page 344 in his copy of J. B. Say's *Treatise on Political Economy* (American edition of 1834), that "combinations of masters [are] as criminal, or more so than combinations of workmen." This volume is now in The Johns Hopkins University Library.

that constant threat to individual rights. "The people, the majority, are subject to sudden impulses, to passion, fear, panic, revenge, love of power, pride, error, fanaticism." So long as the judiciary stands guard, having the final word, none of these democratic traits can affect more responsible citizens. This view widened out into a theory of the state as a historical growth, evolving under the restraining influence of the judiciary. The law, in this theory, was the common law, "a body of rules of action grown up spontaneously and independently of direct legislative or executive action," and the judges were its conservators. The judiciary emerged as a kind of superinstitution, out of the processes of social evolution; America's place in the scale of nations was securely at the top by reason of her having contributed to civilization the independent judiciary.

At the risk of being thought to exaggerate, this brief account of Lieber's great effort may appropriately close by cataloguing a few of the views he expressed on matters which still seem important. The risk exists because of a certain perfection of consistency which few scholars succeed in maintaining, but which Lieber's persistence and vast capacity for work sustained to the end. Education, for instance, was important; the young should be taught that it was a privilege to obey laws and that it was a "high prerogative" of men to acknowledge superiors and inferiors. It was necessary that "a sacred regard for property in all its manifestations, be early instilled in their souls." So also should patriotism be inculcated. As for manhood suffrage, it was gravely to be doubted whether this had a foundation in natural right. The vote ought to have as prerequisite a certain amount of education and a steady employment. And, with pointed reference to America and the South: "No civilized nation in which . . . there are vast classes, ignorant, rude, and poor, excluded from the common stream of civilization, can endure universal suffrage." In this connection, too, it seemed clear that women ought to be excluded from suffrage. They had a different nature; they should not be in politics. Certain kinds of literature dwelt on the possibility of equality between the sexes; these were of a "loathsome immorality, pitiful and superficial reasoning and gross ignorance."

Story, at least, had no doubts concerning *The Manual of Political Ethics*. After going through it carefully he wrote that it was "one of the best theoretical treatises, on the true nature and objects of government." [21] Praise could come from no higher source. Lieber felt in view of this that the public might have bought more copies than it showed evidence of doing. Still, posterity would be influenced by the book. On the whole he was content.

Naturally, he had hopes that such a work would bring opportunities which had been unaccountably delayed. In this he was disappointed; as yet his "exile" was less than half over. He went on writing. In 1841 another book was published, *Essays on Property and Labour as Connected with Natural Law and the Constitution of Society*. There was not much that was new in these *Essays* [22] about economic

[21] Joseph Story to Lieber, Aug. 15, 1837, in *Life and Letters of Joseph Story*, ed. W. W. Story (Boston: Little and Brown, 1851), p. 278.

[22] At the end of the introduction in his copy of the book (now in Johns Hopkins University Library) Lieber inserted an illuminating lengthy note of its origin, "Genesis of the Duodecimo," dated 1842. In the course of his discussion he explained that he had long thought about and written letters to friends on the valid foundations of property. He had finally decided to publish a volume on property, because of the tremendous interest aroused by the publication of Orestes Brownson's famous essay of 1840, "The Laboring Classes."

Lieber wrote, "In 1841, I read the pamphlet of the Rev. Mr. Brownson, which strives to demolish individual inheritance, and was received by a large part of our Northern community with such an avidity that at least from 30 to 40,000 copies were disseminated." Then he added a parenthetical comment supporting the view of some scholars that Brownson's essay was a campaign document in support of the Democratic presidential candidate which backfired, and not a document expressing the aspirations of wage earners. According to Lieber's note, "There can be no doubt but that this very pamphlet which also attacked the U. S. Bank and was designed at least by the disseminators as an aid to the Democratic party in the election matters. They began with the familiar outline of reference. Private property and monogamic marriage are the two fundamentals of the social structure; out of these all the mechanisms of civilization have evolved. Some of the particular mechanisms, Lieber was finding, however, needed justification of another kind. At one point, for instance, when he found himself discussing property as a universally acknowledged right, he felt it necessary to aim a blow at some men who, forgetting the continuity of mankind and society, have reasoned from arbitrary, abstract principles instead of from experience as manifested by prevailing institutions which are the outcome of the "feelings and irresistible impulses" of man. Another variation from his own method appeared when he came to discuss the then-rising land question. How to dispose not only of the Mexican lands in California but also of much Indian land was part of the whole problem of subduing the west. Occupancy must be justified by use. Lieber cited facts: these Mexican lands were rich, they possessed useful outlets to the Pacific, which would contribute to that first of all civilization's requisites, the exchange of produce; but instead of furnishing a home for millions of people as they should, they were peopled thinly by savages. The Indians ought to be dispossessed because "they do not use the land as it was destined to be used, for the support of mankind." Only a few, he said, could be maintained by hunting.

This book, midway in Lieber's career, is most interesting to the student of American thought for its development of his

struggle for a president of the U. S. caused many people in the North either to take alarm or to make them believe that these were the ultimate views to which 'Democratic' notions lead. It thus aided, I believe, effectively in many cases, the cause of Genl. Harrison." Lieber immediately after the parenthetical note added, "Brownson, as all writers, who attack individual property, wholly or in part, e.g. individual inheritance, start from the universally adopted view that originally all things belong to all, and that property is a creature of the law for real or supposed convenience. I now thought it was high time to give my whole view of the origin and essence of property."

views on economics. These by now were beginning to be rounded out. It was disclosed that an understanding of property as well as of wages required a previous analysis of value as used in political economy—exchangeable value.[23] Any increase in the supply of goods depreciated value, desirableness. Property, in fact, had value only with reference to its owner; and if this was kept in mind, it was "far easier to see the justice of exclusive property, even in land." Nothing could pay for produce except produce—which must be created by labor and capital, itself stored up labor. Even in the case of money exchange the axiom held, since the money was obtained by giving a product for it.[24] Therefore, the more saved from consumption, the more accumulated and used reproductively, "in other words, the more wealthy people there are in a community, the better for all."

But if Lieber stressed accumulation—savings—for economic growth and national prosperity, he was quite aware also that the rise of the American standard of living was due to more than capital. The United States, he contended,

[23] "Value is everything that is useful or desirable for more than one, and for which those that do not possess it are willing, because they desire it, to part with other values called equivalents, that is, things which are as much desired by the possessor of the value of which we first spoke" (*Essays on Property and Labour*, p. 42). Lieber stated, in *Some Truths Worth Remembering* (1849) that there was no such thing as inherent value. "Value requires a thing desired and a person desiring. Value is a relation." Gold had no inherent value to a starving man as such. In short, value referred to things desired and for which we were ready to part with other things we possess. Thus "national wealth is nothing but a term for the aggregate wealth of individuals."

[24] A clearer statement of this proposition, generally referred to as "Say's Law," was given in *Some Truths Worth Remembering:* "Products alone can create a demand for products. Not hunger, not cold, create a demand for bread or raiment, but products which may be given in exchange for them. If money be given for them, this money must first be obtained for products."

Lieber explicitly rejected the view of Say, as well as of the British classical economists, that land was distinct from capital. He criticized especially Say's conception of land as a "natural agent," on the ground that a natural agent was a principle, while land was a thing. Therefore land could no more than a hog be a natural agent, although natural agents were at work in both, just as they were in a clock.

despite the fact that it had less capital than Europe had "far more consumption and more comfort." This happy state of affairs he attributed to two factors: (1) Having no army, the country had less taxes; (2) "The quicker industry" of the nation meant "returning quicker profits." [25]

The trend of the argument is by now clear, perhaps, to the reader. Let us follow a little further the better to appreciate the design. Not only, said Lieber, was the employer interested in his accumulations, but so were other producers. If he consumed all his production, he would have nothing left to exchange for the products of others. Above all, those without capital would be without means of livelihood. This, it will be seen, is the point made so clearly in *The Manual of Political Ethics*, but here its implications were more extensively developed. Wages were no more an invention than was property; they were the outcome of a natural and necessary state of things, and interference with them by unions or even by governments violated the great economic principle that in "the free exchange of mankind" all things —labor, talent, capital, learning—obtained the price they were "considered worth." Wages, in consequence, could be increased only by industry, thrift, saving, improvement in political morality, the consistent fulfillment of contracts, and by the prevention of idleness, riots, and other civil disturbances. Workmen ought to be told that restrictions on the accumulation and transfer of property hurt them more than others, that legislative acts limiting large fortunes were vicious. Riches were incompatible with liberty in Rome when democratic absolutism prevailed, and the wealthy fostered corruption to prevent seizure of their fortunes. Under our "noble constitutional liberty" no danger of this sort existed. No one would seriously assert that the richest men—the Astors or the Girards—were politically the most influential.

[25] Lieber's insertion opposite p. 204 of his copy of Say's *Treatise*.

Lieber was deeply interested in promoting workers' education. In 1842 he wrote to Sumner and to Samuel B. Ruggles[26] that the great businessmen, like the textile magnates Nathan Appleton and Abbott Lawrence, should subsidize publication of a series of cheap, well-directed "tracts for the people" on such subjects as "Government, Obedience to the Laws, Property, Labor, Social (Political) Economy, Trades Unions, etc." At least five hundred thousand copies ought to be distributed, he felt, and then the series should be made into a textbook for the higher common schools. "Those who attack many important institutions at their very foundations, are busy to do it frequently with plausible arguments. It behooves the others to be active too."[27]

In some respects, Lieber's most suggestive work in political economy was his continuous plea, for over a decade, that the general government undertake periodically—every three or four years—a comprehensive statistical survey of the nation's economic and social resources in order to give the people a "clearer insight into the state of our public affairs." This would provide, he contended, the basis for practical, sound legislation and aid the effective operation of business. The Census of Manufactures of 1820 had been so grossly inaccurate that Congress had limited the Census of 1830 to a mere enumeration of the population. Lieber began his drive for an expanded census as early as 1834, and intensified his efforts as the time approached for the Census of 1840.

In 1836 he submitted a comprehensive seventeen-page proposal to the Senate through Calhoun, and with the endorsement of Calhoun and Webster.[28]

[26] Ruggles was prominent in Whig politics, as well as in the advancement of higher learning and internal improvements.

[27] Lieber to Sumner, January, 1842, in Perry, *Life and Letters*, p. 167; Lieber to Ruggles, Sept. 14, 1842, in Phinney, *Francis Lieber's Influence on American Thought*, pp. 31–32.

[28] *Memorial of Francis Lieber, Proposing to Publish A Work on the Statistics of the United States*, 24th Cong., 1st sess., Senate Doc. no. 314.

Lieber's opening statements affirmed the faith in empirical inquiry which was sweeping the western world, following the success of the "bourgeois" revolution of 1830 in France and the radical reform of the British House of Commons in 1834, and which found expression in the establishment of national statistical societies in the United States, in Great Britain, and on the continent, in the 1830s.

With an eloquence that he seldom equaled, Lieber wrote:

It may be considered as one of the characteristic traits of our times, that, with regard to many branches of importance to the well-being of society, a careful collection of detailed facts, and the endeavor to arrive at general results by a comprehensive view and judicious combination of them, have been substituted for mere theorizing. Not only the strictly scientific portion of that great family of civilized nations, which part of Europe and America now constitute, has acknowledged the great importance to the legislator, and every one else who occupies himself with the welfare of his species, of statistical inquiries, when made on a large scale and used with proper caution, but several governments have shown how much they value accurate statistics, by ordering them to be collected and properly digested.

It is possible to quibble over what today may seem limited notions of the value of statistical inquiry, but Lieber had caught its spirit when he wrote:

Statistics consist, in a great degree, in the collection and classification of a number of isolated facts, which thus isolated have little value for human experience and lead not infrequently to views entirely erroneous. If they are patiently and faithfully collected, judiciously arranged and applied, and wisely digested, they lead to a more positive knowledge of the real state of things . . . than any other mode of inquiry. They often exhibit errors, though cherished for centuries, in their real light, unveil evil never suspected before, or show their roots where they were never expected to be found, thus enabling us to choose the most or the only efficient means of counteracting them. They are, therefore, of the greatest use to the legislator and to every one whose duty it is to frame general measures for his community, in whatever branch.

The detailed outline was all-embracing. It provided for the determination of the "national wealth," for the standard of comfort of the different classes, including the prices and amounts of the various items that comprise what today is called the family budget, not only of manual laborers but also of professional people.[29]

The census could not be undertaken as a venture in private enterprise. First, it was much too costly; second, it required a certain amount of government authority to obtain the necessary materials. The country could well afford such surveys, especially since the national treasury was overflowing with a surplus, which was an evil. Congress took no action; but Lieber continued to agitate for his project through articles and letters in newspapers.[30]

As the taking of the census of 1850 approached, Lieber again pushed his proposals for an extensive statistical survey. He wrote to influential friends in and out of Congress in 1847 of the necessity that Congress do "something *judicious* to prepare in time for as good a census as we can have." He

[29] The titles of the divisions were: I. The Country; II. The Inhabitants; III. Nature and Man in Relation to Each Other; Industry, and Commerce Flowing from It; IV. Intercourse and Communication; V. Standard of Comfort; VI. Charity; VII. Moral and Intellectual Culture; VIII. Political State; IX. Army; X. Navy; XI. Pensions; XII. Medical Statistics; XIII. Miscellaneous; XIV. Results, in tables or otherwise, drawn from combinations of the preceding.

[30] In June, 1838, the House of Representatives passed a resolution for the establishment of a joint committee to consider the collection of data in agriculture, commerce, and manufacturing, in connection with the 1840 Census. The Senate refused to concur, but on December 4 President Martin Van Buren urged the need of such a survey in his annual message to Congress:

"In recommending to Congress the adoption of the necessary provisions at this session for taking the next census or enumeration of the inhabitants of the United States, the suggestion presents itself whether the scope of the measure might not be usefully extended by causing it to embrace authentic statistical returns of the great interests specially intrusted to or necessarily affected by the legislation of Congress." The response of Congress was hardly satisfactory. It ordered federal marshals to "collect and return in statistical tables all such information relating to mines, agriculture, commerce, manufactures and which will exhibit a full view of the pursuits, industry, education and resources of the country."

suggested that Congress should appoint a three-man committee including himself to propose a plan for connecting "the census and a sort of statistical Board . . . with the Smithsonian Institution." He frankly noted that among the difficulties in achieving a satisfactory national board was "our Federative character and the absence of gend'armes, etc, etc." [31]

Although Lieber's services were never utilized in the area, he was helpful in the enactment of the measures that were achieved.[32] His strong sense of nationalism was a stimulus.[33]

Now came years which were at once difficult and exciting for America and for the world. The conflict between North

[31] Letters of Lieber to Ruggles, May 2 and Oct. 3, 1847, in Lieber papers, Library of Congress.

The Southern Literary Messenger in April, 1836, after pointing out that Lieber used the term "statistics" in its "truest and most expanded acceptation, as a view of the actual state of the country," went on to say that, should his scheme be adopted, America would be taking the most important step ever yet taken in aid of the most important of sciences.

Lieber's predecessor, Thomas Cooper, had sketched in his *Lectures on the Elements of Political Economy* (1826) a basically similar but less elaborated scheme. He wrote that "it is of great importance to the people . . . in particular the governing powers of any country, to be fully aware of the facts, that indicate truly, the state of improvement or deterioration in all the details that make up the sum of national prosperity. When these facts are left to conjecture, the people are kept in the dark." There ought to be one or more low priced annual volumes "to serve as a perpetual book of facts to reason from, as to the real state of the nation and the means of its improvement." He asked, at the end, whether "a statistical board or a permanent committee" would not be a considerable improvement on the present method of conducting the census.

[32] In 1849, at the suggestion of members of the American Statistical Association, Congress established a Census Board composed of the secretary of state, the attorney general, and the postmaster general, which would prepare and print the forms and schedules for enumerating the inhabitants and collecting data on mines, agriculture, commerce, manufactures, education, etc. (Meyer H. Fishbein, "Early Statistical Operations of the Federal Government," *National Archives Accessions*, June, 1958, p. 19.)

[33] A popular argument against comprehensive surveys by the federal government was that only the states, and not the general government, could deal with such matters as manufacturing and agricultural industry, the health habits and morals of the people, crime, pauperism, education, religious institutions, and special taxation. ("Russell's *Principles of Statistical Inquiry*," *The New York Review*, IV, [April, 1839], 498.)

and South was approaching the crisis of civil war; the conquest of the west and of Mexico went on; Europe was progressing toward the abortive revolutions of 1848; industrialists were fumbling with new techniques of manufacture, transport, and communication which would make necessary some revision of the static theories of economics and politics which Lieber and his contemporaries were propagating.

It would not be true to say that Lieber was untroubled by change. He was a scholar, an observer, and, as he himself said, "a publicist." He saw much that was going on and was deeply disturbed by most of it. By temperament, perhaps, or by identification with the past through study of it, he was relieved of doubt, at least on many issues. He stood uncompromisingly for the old ways, the settled principles, wherever that was possible. But there were issues not easily disposed of in this way. There were conflicts.

He did not resign until 1855, when, after many disappointments, he came to feel that his career was more failure than success. The years went on, therefore, as before, divided between classroom and study and with vacation visits to the north. His three boys were growing up. Once he had a serious spell of illness described as brain fever from which he recovered slowly. He was aging; weight oppressed him—one playful letter to a friend spoke of the writer as a "fat fogey." His place in the life of the south was scarcely more secure—he felt almost as much an alien as ever. It was impossible for him to settle into the country-town regime; he was too much the citizen of the world. This, rather than any inability to accommodate himself, was the source of his unhappiness. His friends in the north developed some little suspicion of one so long stationed in a slave state. He made the most of what anti-secession sentiment there was and was apt to discover it in unexpected places. But after all he was in an obscure retreat far from "the moving and literary world." He felt the slight when scholars of eminence overlooked him as Bancroft did on one conspicuous occasion, and as he inferred had been done when he was not invited to the semi-centennial meeting of the Historical Society. "Such things prove very strongly," he said, "how a man is lost here." [34] There were times when the classroom oppressed his spirit. Here was a man who felt himself born to be a leader in great causes, a man strong and intelligent, who was frittering away his good years in a country college in the south. He walked impatiently about the South Carolina countryside flinging his energy to the dry winds from the sand hills. Or, sitting at his table, he wrote, "Scholarship in my case is but a morganatic marriage . . . I was made for a different sphere, for action through masses." [35]

The approach of the revolution in Europe with all its possibilities of fulfilling old Germanic ambitions filled him with restless distaste for the lethargy and obesity of the middle-aged scholar. For the moment, military action, leadership on the battle field were what his nature craved. He revived an old admiration for Cromwell. He took to dating his letters according to battles; he was pleased to be made an official visitor to West Point. If it had not been, he said, that the Mexican war was unrighteous, he would certainly have applied for a commission. All the unease came to nothing. He had always to come to earth—and it hurt. His one overt act was to hurry to Prussia in 1848 only to find that the revolution had petered out and that there was nothing he could do.

It was the French revolution of 1848 which first reexcited his nationalist ambitions for Germany; his enthusiasm led him to reason that a series of wars was imminent out of which a unification movement would emerge. There is nothing to

[34] Lieber to Ruggles, Christmas Eve, 1854, in L. W. Sears, "The Human Side of Francis Lieber," *The South Atlantic Quarterly*, January, 1928, p. 51.
[35] Lieber to G. S. Hillard, Dec. 29, 1849, in Perry, *Life and Letters*, p. 226.

show that he read or heard of *The Communist Manifesto*, but he did begin to use the term communist as another and more picturesque derogation of those disorderly manifestations of common people always so disturbing to him. Following the pattern he had previously set, he indicated that in his view communism was merely another phase of that "democratic absolutism" against which he had given so many warnings. In Europe at the moment the "red republicans" had a role to play; but the nationalist movement would reestablish order. He thought back to his own sufferings in the cause; and his gorge rose once again at the "crowd of princes" which stood in the way of German destiny.

Something of a crisis had to be faced in the winter of 1849–50 when the question of the extension of slavery into the territories came up so prominently in Congress. We have seen how delicate was the situation of a foreigner who came to South Carolina by way of New England. Hitherto slavery could plausibly be treated by a historian in the south as a "deciduous institution"—one "which always falls at a certain time, as the first teeth are absorbed and give way to the second." [36] But now southern leaders were arriving at the thesis that slavery was a blessing and were working it into their religion. Not to extend it to the territories would be a taking of property without compensation. Mrs. D. J. McCord, Lieber's friend,[37] through the columns of *The Southern Quarterly Review*, denounced abolitionists along with protectionists and reformers as communists. The de facto white slavery of England and the north was a curse. Starvation and deprivation of what little property he might acquire were the lot of the northern freeman; and the wretchedness of the English wage slaves made them fit material for communism. Besides, only slaves could produce cotton, and if the cotton

[36] Lieber to W. C. Preston, Jan. 18, 1850, in Perry, *Life and Letters*, p. 238.
[37] Lieber wrote a preface for her able standard translation of Frederic Bastiat's *Sophisms of the Protective Policy* (New York: Putnam, 1848).

crop failed, the north and England would find themselves ruined.

The slave, the argument ran on, was inferior and not only would he be unhappy with the liberty which the abolitionists threatened to thrust upon him, but he would be destroyed—a result which the example of the Indians showed all too clearly to be the destiny of inferior races. Just as women accepted a legal position inferior to that of man in return for protection, so the Negro accepted his status to avoid extinction. Thus, by the standard of the greatest good for the greatest number, there was no system of government in all history which equaled the beneficence of the slave system. She concluded that "Mr. Jefferson's great humbug flourish of free and equal has made trouble enough, and it is full time that its mischievous influence should end." [38]

Lieber, on the same principles of economics, property, and historical development, ventured to oppose the extension of slavery. According to the drafts of some letters to Calhoun, who was then fighting Clay's compromise measure, Lieber contended that slavery "annihilates the two first elements of all progress and civilization . . . property and marriage as legal institutions . . . as much as the vilest communism." [39] Slavery did not exist by the law of nature. It was merely a municipal institution and thus existed only when positive law was laid down to that effect. Therefore, forbidding slavery in the territories was no deprivation of property. Finally, slavery was against the times, and the worst revolutionists and promoters order, whereas wisdom taught that everything must eventually of disorder were those who blindly adhered to the existing change or go down in violent death. The institution had outlined its necessity. At the same time the North should not interfere with slavery in the slave states, and those who opposed

[38] L[ouisa] S[usanah] M[cCord], "Carey on the Slave Trade," *The Southern Quarterly Review*, XXV (January, 1854), 167.

[39] The drafts are in Perry, *Life and Letters*, p. 230.

the Fugitive Slave Law and maintained that there was a higher law than the Constitution, were fanatical and seditious.

The South accepted the compromise. Lieber could write, finally, that secession was dying and could take a hand in organizing a Union Party in South Carolina. At a meeting for this purpose he argued against secession, but in such a way as not to involve slavery or states' rights. The Union had been a boon, he said, to all the states. No such idea as secession could be found in history, "the common law of mankind." If the idea were logically pushed, then the states might, contrary to the Constitution, establish monarchies. To assume that the Constitution tacitly acknowledged the right of secession was ridiculous, for that would assume the founders to have instilled a principle of self-destruction into the very instrument which constituted the government. It would be like the provision in the first democratic constitution of France providing that, if the government acted against the laws, every citizen had the duty to take up arms against it. This was "Jacobinical democracy tempered by revolution." Furthermore, those who insisted on a right of secession on the ground of contract must admit the correlative right of the Union to expel states. Were they prepared for this? There was also the further—and the strongest—objection that war would result and the North be victorious.[40] The party he looked for, he said, was one with a platform of "free trade" or "exchange as God wills it"; with "rational views on slavery," which meant the exclusion of fanatical abolitionists and eulogists of slavery; and with "progress in a conservative spirit—a spirit which acknowledges society to be a continuum." [41]

[40] Lieber, "An Address on Secession," written and delivered in 1851; published in his *Miscellaneous Writings*, II, 125–36.

[41] Lieber to Hillard, Feb. 25, 1847, in Perry, *Life and Letters*, pp. 208–9. The trouble with Whigs, incidentally, according to Lieber, was that they were "demented on protection," not perceiving that protection would soon come to its logical end. (Letter dated Feb. 10, 1847, in University of South Carolina Library.)

In this atmosphere of alarms and renewed hopes, of public fears and private agitations, Lieber went on into the decade of the fifties. Outwardly he was a prematurely aging scholar, correct, severe, and respectable, attending to his duties with regularity and thoroughness; inwardly he was in the throes of a last revolt against what seemed to him a cruel and repressive fate. For compensation there was his book: by now he was writing *On Civil Liberty and Self-Government*, which appeared in 1853.

Civil Liberty was Lieber's richest book. Into it as into a vat of precious liquor he poured the distillation of his aspirations, his knowledge, and his theories of history. Its theme was grand, one which had been dealt with by many distinguished predecessors. This was the area in which he felt himself most at home—on the high levels of assumption and dictum with occasional authoritative excursions into the lower country of practice. There was no meaning in the great word "liberty" outside government. That was clear. Civil liberty—that is, liberty in government—was something worked for, something at the end of a long evolution. It could be assumed—at any rate it was assumed—that the furthest development was to be found right here at home.

> We belong [said Lieber in a characteristic passage] to the Anglican race, which carries Anglican principles and liberty over the globe, because wherever it moves, liberal institutions and a common law full of manly rights and instinct with the principle of an expansive life, accompany it. We belong to that race whose obvious task it is, among other proud and sacred tasks, to rear and spread civil liberty over vast regions in every part of the earth. . . . We belong to that nation whose great lot it is to be placed, with the full inheritance of freedom, on the freshest soil in the noblest site between Europe and Asia.

Lieber's main purpose in writing *On Civil Liberty and Self-Government* was an ambitious one. This was to provide his adopted land with a codification of its evolved understandings;

he succeeded well in presenting the Whig view. His structure of theory built itself up from the basic conception of liberty, using as materials the familiar building blocks of representative government, and, as the cement holding all together, the prevalent law. As the structure rose the cement became thicker and thicker, the blocks less conspicuous, and there emerged at the top a kind of fancy Victorian tower in which sat a robed judiciary guarding the familiar gods of liberty for the fortunate sharers in freedom.

Lieber, for all the unkindness of time to his conclusions, and even to his apparatus, was neither simple nor superficial. He said clearly enough that "We cannot hope for liberty in a pervading negation, but must find it in comprehensive action. All that is good or great is creative and positive." To be sure, in this same passage he did enlarge on the fortunate fact that the "negation which is necessary to check and restrain is found in the self-government of many and vigorous institutions. . . ." Still, there was the recognition that checks were not enough; and not even our constitution-makers had always understood that. It was this feeling which brought the book to its unique climax—at Chapter XXV—in a discussion of "The Institution."

Just here Lieber conveniently summarized what had gone before:

It has been shown that civil liberty, as we understand and cherish it, consists in a large amount of individual rights, checks of power and guarantees of self-government. We have more or less fully indicated that self-government, in the sense in which we take it, and in connection with liberty, consists in the independence of the whole political society, in a national representative government and local self-government, which implies that even general laws and impulses are carried out and realized, as far as possible, by citizens who, in receiving an office, be it by election or appointment, essentially remain citizens, and do not become members of a hierarchy of placemen. We have seen that self-government, in general, requires that there be an organism to elaborate and ascertain public opinion, and that, when known, it shall pass into law, and, plainly, rule the rulers; that government interfere as an exception, and not as the rule; and that, on the other hand, self-government neither means self-absolutism, nor absence of rule, but that on the contrary, liberty requires a true government. . . . In other spheres it may be true that license is exaggerated liberty, but in politics there can be nothing more unlike liberty than anarchy.

Up to this point it had not been explained how the system of civil liberty was to be realized. "Liberty," Lieber said, "cannot flourish, nor can freedom become a permanent business of actual life, without a permanent love and a habit of liberty. How is the one to be engendered, and the other to be acquired?" Not, he was sure, through any mathematical formula; not through flattery;[42] not through enthusiasm, which is transitory; not even, as many think, through education.[43] How then? "There is no other means than a vast system of institutions, whose number supports the whole, as the many pillars support the rotunda of our capitol."

This was shrewd appraisal. It may well be that in the long run Lieber's reputation as a political theorist will rest heavily on this acute analysis of our characteristics. He had penetrated our habitual flight from consistency, our reliance on muddling through, our feeling of individual self-sufficiency, our resentment against authority, our satisfaction with accustomed ways—in a word, the whole genius of English and American public behavior.

[42] This was aimed at "Gallican Liberty" at which he had directed shots before: "Each one of us may be declared a sovereign, as every Frenchman was designated in a solemn circular, by the provisional government; or the people may be called almighty . . . as in the midst of loathsome political obscenity they were termed by the dictatorial government when they were expected and led to vote for a new emperor, and thus by an act of omnipotence extinguish every vestige of their power. . . . Self-immolation, even where it is an actual and not a theoretical act of free agency, is not life."

[43] "Prussia is one of the best educated of countries, but liberty has not yet found a dwelling place there."

His definition of institution ran through some seven chapters. It was not an idea which could be encompassed in a few words; his best attempt, perhaps, was as follows:

A system or body of usages, laws, or regulations of extensive and recurring operation, containing within itself an organism by which it effects its own independent action, continuance, and generally its own further development. Its object is to generate, effect, regulate or sanction a succession of acts, transactions or productions of a peculiar kind or class. The idea of an institution implies a degree of self-government. Laws act through human agents, and these are, in the case of institutions, their officers or members.

He had grasped the truth, so often overlooked, that there is more government than is performed by government; that, indeed, our self-government extends to government itself. He was inclined to overpraise the virtues of this system. There were moments of caution as when he remarked that it was "like the press. Modern liberty or civilization cannot dispense with it, yet it may be used as its keenest enemy"; but on the whole he was fulsome.

Institutional self-government trains the mind and nourishes the character for a dependence on law and a habit of liberty, as well as for a law-abiding acknowledgment of authority. It educates for freedom. It cultivates civil dignity in all the partakers, and teaches to respect the rights of others. It has thus a gentlemanly character. It brings home palpable liberty to all, and gives a consciousness of freedom, rights and corresponding obligations such as no other system does. It is the only self-government which is a real government *of* self, as well as *by* self, and indeed is the only real self-government, of which all other governments assuming the name of self-government are but semblances.

Here were evidently two unreconciled attitudes: the rather overbearing moralist bent on discipline, opposing organization for labor, careless of Indian and Mexican rights, firm in insistence on judicial rule, oblivious, in some instances, of the guarantees of the Bill of Rights, believing in an intellectual aristocracy; and, in contrast, the writer who perceived, he said, the evolutionary nature of our groups, the salutary arrogance of individualism among enterprisers, the weakness of all authority except self-discipline. The only tenable explanation would seem to consist in a determined ignoring of lower classes. Self-government appears pretty clearly not to be thought of as extending much below the upper middle class. Experience both in New England, where the artisans were well behaved, and in South Carolina, where the slaves did not count, might have contributed to this. Perhaps it is sufficient, without attempting a reconciliation which, at this distance, must necessarily be conjectural, to record the genuine intellectual achievement of this discussion of institutions.

Another observer, more than half a century later, would depend largely on an institutional explanation of our culture. This, of course, would be Thorstein Veblen, whose followers would even speak of their school of economics as the Institutional School. Thus Lieber, in an important instance, anticipated one of our most significant later theorists. Perhaps he was too prone to treat rather new institutions as if they had a long past. To him it seemed that "antiquity is prima facie evidence in favor of an institution." But there was considerable validity in his warning "that many persons believe nowadays so little in this truth that not only does antiquity of itself appear to them as proof of deficiency, but they turn their face from the whole Past, as something to be shunned, thus forgetting the continuity of society, progress and civilization."

But it must also be said that his test of a government was its double ability to prosper and to last.

To last long—to last with liberty and with wealth, is the great problem to be solved by the modern state. Our destinies differ from that of brief and brilliant Greece. Let us derive all the benefit from Grecian culture and civilization—from that chosen nation, whose intellectuality and aesthetics, with Christian morality, Roman legality and Teutonic individuality and independence, form the main elements of the great phenomenon we designate by the term modern civilization, without adopting her evils and errors, even as we adopt her sculpture without that religion whose very errors contributed to produce it.

As he read history, he was immensely impressed by the staying power of England and the United States.

Eastern despotism is exposed to the danger of seraglio conspiracies, as much so as the centralized governments of the European continent showed their insecurity in the year 1848. They tottered and many broke to pieces, although there was, with very few exceptions, no ardent struggle, and nothing that approached to a civil war. To an observer at a distance, it almost appeared as if those governments could be shaken by the loud huzzaing of a crowd. . . . During all that time of angry turmoil, England and the United States stood firm. . . . No fact seems to be so striking in the revolution of England as this, that all her institutions of an organic character, her jury, her common law, her representative legislature, her local self-government, her justice of the peace, her sheriff, her coroner—all survived domestic war and despotism, and, having done so, served as the basis of an enlarged liberty.

Lieber's institutionalism was therefore founded on a kind of historical necessity. He may have felt it to be a rather low order of organization, but since it was amorphous, close to the ground, it survived when other systems broke up. He made this defense of it; but he did not neglect the other half of his formula—the prosperity half. His counsel was to well-born youths, to the educated, to the enterprising. Do not, he said, in effect, acquiesce in any one-man dictatorship. It will not last. And, after all, you can work this institutional system to your own sufficient good.

In the early forties Lieber had begun a correspondence with certain of the trustees of Columbia College which in review assumes the character of a campaign for an appointment. With Ruggles, at least, this contact was steadily maintained. The institution at this time could definitely be said to have possibilities, if only because it existed in the city which by now was clearly destined for metropolitan grandeur.[44] As early as 1842 William Kent,[45] knowing something of Lieber's desire to be quit of the south and all its strange and distasteful customs, had told him of funds given for a professorship of German. It was a disappointment to discover that the salary was only half of what he got at South Carolina College. But he also heard of the likelihood that the Rev. John McVickar would be given the vacant presidency and he had for a time some hope of succeeding in that case to McVickar's chair, which he understood was that of political economy, history, and moral philosophy. It is somewhat amusing, but also somewhat affecting, to read this correspondence. It was often foresighted but sometimes clumsily so—as when, having heard erroneously that to be appointed at Columbia it was necessary to be a graduate, he elaborated in a letter to Ruggles on the advantage of choosing a foreigner. Or as when he facetiously commented to Ruggles that, aside from being a foreigner, he himself might make a good president.[46]

Lieber still hoped that, although McVickar had not been made president, part of his professorship might be cut off and combined with German. There was some talk of it; but one of those economy waves which interfere so often with academic plans intervened. Instead, to Lieber's disgust, the economist Johann Ludwig Tellkampf, of Union College, was appointed

[44] Boston was still pretty definitely the intellectual hub, of course. Philadelphia's pretensions were sustained with fewer enthusiasms than they had been two decades earlier when the house of Carey had published the encyclopedia. On the other hand, that sad day had not yet arrived when a William Dean Howells would think it advantageous to move from Boston to New York in the interest of his budding career. *Harper's* was beginning to face up to *The Atlantic Monthly* with spirit; but Boston could not yet be said to have declined in arrogance.

[45] Son of James Kent.

[46] Lieber to Ruggles, May 19, 1842, in Phinney, *Francis Lieber's Influence on American Thought,* p. 65.

to the German professorship.[47] Tellkampf, however, having found better prospects in Prussia, resigned four years later. Ruggles then wrote Lieber that he might obtain an adequate income in New York by taking the professorship and starting a German newspaper. "Politically speaking," the newspaper "would be of enormous importance in this early stage of German colonization to give its infant mind the proper bias and direction" especially in enlisting, or at least modifying, "the torrent of democratic sentiment that this stream of German population is hourly rolling into our country." Lieber replied that a German newspaper under his editorship would not succeed, because the only subscribers would be the German merchants. The mass of German immigrants, he said, had "Jacobinical ideas," and felt that he was not one of them in politics. "They are democrats" of the Bancroft type who believe in the principle of the unrestricted will of the majority of people. Two years later, in 1849, he wrote Ruggles that he would like to buy into the New York *Journal of Commerce*, and become an editor of it.[48]

Possibilities at Columbia again improved for Lieber with the installation of Charles King as president in 1849. In King an American institution had for the first time chosen a head whose interests were definitely not theological and classical but rather historical and commercial.[49] In his inaugural speech

[47] Governor William H. Seward, after receiving a letter from President Eliphalet Nott of Union College, wrote Ruggles that Tellkampf was a "profound scholar. . . . For his own sake and for Dr. Nott's, I should rejoice if he should be found worthy of the appointment." (Letter of April 9, 1843, in Seward papers, Library of Congress.) Tellkampf was an expatriate with interests like Lieber's, but with more success here—he had collaborated with the Reverend Alonzo Potter in the writing of his text *Political Economy*—and he had later achieved considerable prestige in Prussia both as a university professor and as a government official.

[48] Letter of Ruggles to Lieber, April 18, 1847, in Lieber papers, Huntington Library; letters of Lieber to Ruggles, May 2, 1847, and March, 1849, in Lieber papers, Library of Congress.

[49] McVickar, at King's inauguration, hailed his accession "on the peculiar score of being a public and business man, opening thereby a new sphere of popular influence, and creating a new bond of sympathy between the col-

he outlined a project for a school of commerce. It was premature; college was still mostly for preachers. Future businessmen, even professional men, for the most part, considered the arts college to be a waste of time. There was a ferment at work, however, and dissatisfaction abroad. President King wrote to Lieber in 1854 asking suggestions for a course of university studies to cover both graduate and extension teaching. For a time the matter was dropped; but it was clear that some sort of educational reform impended.

In that same year the presidency at South Carolina again became vacant. Lieber had genuine hope this time that he might be chosen. He had, or so he thought, a considerable following among editors, politicians, trustees, clergymen, and students. In January, 1855, he wrote to his friend, G. S. Hillard: [50]

I shall not move a finger, or a toe either, to obtain the presidency. Since then it has come to pass that every *up-country* paper, nearly, has nominated me with a heartiness and zeal of which I had no idea. . . . No low-country paper has yet come out for me. I wish you to keep this between ourselves, but it is significant. The low country is the real seat of our anti-national fever and furor. Whether Doctor [James H.] Thornwell will really go away, or whether the trustees will not dislike this popular movement in my favor, and consider it a trespass on their domain, or whether secretly this rush will not be viewed by many trustees as a latent hostility toward hyper-Calvinism, I cannot say. . . . How delightful this spontaneous movement for me—without party, sect or section to back me—would be, were it where I felt psychologically at home. Even as it is I cannot help considering it a welcome incident in my life. It proves to me, besides, that I could be, under proper circumstances, a man of the people, in the sense in which Luther was one, if the sparrow can be compared to the eagle.[51]

---

lege and the needs and wants of our great commercial metropolis." (Address of John McVickar, in *Addresses at the Inauguration of Mr. Charles King* [New York: Columbia College, 1849], p. 10.)

[50] Prominent in Massachusetts politics and in Harvard affairs.

[51] Lieber to Hillard, Jan. 21, 1855, in Perry, *Life and Letters*, pp. 277–78.

He overestimated the strength of his candidacy. The succeeding president was not elected for nearly a year. Meanwhile the suspense was considerable. During the summer he went north, but not this time to Boston: "I never find anybody," he wrote rather sadly to Hillard.[52] His diary shows how he occupied himself on this trip:

July 4—Leave Columbia, with Matilda and Norman, and go to Philadelphia. See Doctor Kirkbride, and have a long talk with him about the reform of our asylum.

July 9—Leave Philadelphia for Danville. Visit my Quaker friend Wood at the Chulasky Iron Works. To Pittston, on the left bank of the Susquehanna, through the Wyoming Valley. Lovely. Lovely. From Wilkesbarre to Rupert—an exquisite sail or glide; charming scenery! Strange contrast with the eternal swearing of the boatmen. God's wonderful blessing and man's dirty curses! Here lived Dr. Joseph Priestley. It is the Susquehanna of Coleridge's and Southey's youthful dreams.

July 16—. . . To Pottsville. I love this scenery, with its grand trees. On the top of Locust Mountain, I found two tulip trees. Return to Philadelphia. Overwhelmingly hot; still I worked hard from eight to two o'clock.

July 20—Trübner of London breakfasts with me. What a peculiarly fine type a German bookseller is,—intelligent, well read, and largely informed in bibliography, a good adviser, and proud to belong to the literary commonwealth, honoring the author and disdaining to be a mere book manufacturer. Trübner is one of the happiest realizations of this type. I asked him if he had observed, what has often struck me, that a German becomes much better looking in America, more manly and intellectual. He answered that a German artist in London had made the same remark with regard to the Germans in England. I spoke of the common class.

July 21—In Bordentown, to join Mrs. Lieber, Hamilton, and Norman.

July 30—Again in Philadelphia. Made the acquaintance of [S. Austin] Allibone, writer of the *Critical Dictionary of English Literature*. He has an excellent library for it. He rises early,

[52] Lieber to Hillard, June 30, 1855, in *ibid.*, p. 281.

writes until ten o'clock, from ten to one is at his counting house, and writes again until late in the evening. He is a merchant, and does a large business. How curious and interesting. He spoke to me always as one of his "teachers"; has studied my *Political Ethics* and my "Pardoning Paper" attracted him much. He was present at the convention where it was first read.[53]

In September Lieber was back teaching his classes. On December 1 he wrote to Hillard:

I continue my letter. Next Tuesday the president of this college will be elected. There is a majority of trustees in my favor, and the people outside want me. All the alumni insist on my election; but it is very possible indeed that your friend remains a simple professor, because the outgoing president—a regular hard-shell Calvinist, who meanly hates me simply because I am not a bitter Calvinist—has urged another professor, who has been here a year only, as a good president. This professor is a Presbyterian. No one thinks that he stands the least chance; but the movement is made to induce the trustees to say "Since neither of these two will work well under the other, we had better take a third, indifferent person." It is a low election manoeuvre, and may succeed. So be it! [54]

From this it will be seen that the expatriate was no match for the natives when it came to college politics. He was so enraged at his failure to be elected that he resigned. The whole thing, he wrote Ruggles, came about because the slavery issue would soon bring war, in which case he preferred to be with his friends in the north.[55]

He wrote also to Allibone:

I have resigned my professorship at this college. You do not sufficiently know me to be convinced that no irritation at not being elected has been the motive. My reasons are, not that I have been passed over, although a large number of trustees voted for me, and for several ballotings I stood at the head; but because a

[53] Lieber, "Diary," in *ibid.*, pp. 281-82.

[54] Lieber to Hillard, Dec. 1, 1855, in Perry, *Life and Letters*, p. 285.

[55] Lieber to Ruggles, Jan. 20, 1856, in Sears, "The Human Side of Francis Lieber," pp. 52-53.

professor unknown to the trustees and utterly incapable of ruling this institution, has been elected, and because the college will go to ruin. I am too old to play the college constable for another man. When I see you I shall tell you all about it. Bitter Calvinism—simply bitter because I do not visit the Presbyterian but the Episcopalian church—and my "Union" letter, and villanously hinted suspicion of abolitionism, carried the day. [J. L.] Petigru of Charleston fought strenuously for me. All this is strictly confidential.

I am, then, a mason out of work. Professors here are obliged to give a year's notice of resignation. Next December I shall be a "promenading" workman. For this purpose, I am desirous that my resignation be known all over the Union. It is here in the papers, and will soon make a noise.[56]

Columbia College, by the spring of 1857, was at last ready to put into operation a plan for expansion which would mean an increase of staff. Lieber was aware of this; but his many disappointments at Harvard and Columbia had made him wary. Still, it did seem that something of use to him might at last be taking shape. A trustees' committee of Columbia, set up to determine ways of improving the college, had sent Lieber in 1856 a questionnaire of 123 items. This awakened hope which was strengthened by his visits to friendly trustees. At any rate Lieber sent in his suggestions with some confidence.

The result of all the investigation and suggestion was greater specialization and the doubling of the college faculty by splitting the old chairs in 1857. McVickar's comprehensive chair was finally divided into three. McVickar was left with the Evidences of Christianity. Charles Murray Nairne (M. A., St. Andrews), student of the eminent Scottish philosopher, Sir William Hamilton, and editor of a popular edition of Paley's *Evidences of Christianity*, was given the chair of moral and political philosophy, and of literature.[57] Lieber, thanks to

[56] Lieber to Allibone, Dec. 13, 1855, in Perry, *Life and Letters*, pp. 285–86.

[57] Nairne followed the tradition of complaining that "we have too much law already. I want not law but manliness. I want not statutes but virtue." But he was dubious about letting morals rest on utilitarian considerations.

the support of President King, S. B. Ruggles, and Ruggles's son-in-law, George Templeton Strong, was appointed to the chair of history and political economy at a salary of $3,000 plus $1,000 for house rent. He sold his slaves and left the south forever.[58]

The long ordeal was over. Would the rest of his life be merely respectable and serene? The man of fifty-seven, after a lifetime of work, of discipline, of frustrated hopes, had reached the most constant of his objectives. But there were difficulties yet to come. The constant striving for a place in which to satisfy his manifold ambitions had become too much a habit to be given up. Also, the Columbia professorship involved no reduction of his teaching burden. Life would still be difficult.

Even the title of his new professorship was unsatisfactory. Apparently either "Political Economy" lacked the dignity he sought or its connotation was wrong for the picture he had of his future activities. He actually wrote to Hamilton Fish asking that the title be revised. He said that he had not as yet written to European friends in high political office, because it would gratify him to tell them that he had been made professor of "the greatest branches in the greatest city of the greatest Union—that of History and Political Science." [59] It

---

As he explained in an oration before the literary societies of Lafayette College, *The Morals and Manners of the Class Room* (1858):

"Honesty, they tell us, is the best policy—and this is doubtless just, but he who on that ground alone, acts fairly, would as lief be dishonest, if knavery were the best policy. Such a man is, after all, a mere huckster—his aim is not virtue, but profit; and so is every man who would make virtue an affair of exchange—a simple barter of duty for happiness. Happiness is good, and greatly to be desired; but personal worth is a nobler end than happiness. . . . The merchant or broker does not cease to be a man, when he transfers himself from Fifth Avenue to Wall Street; nor can the supposed necessities of business justify any departure from the candor and fairness, the liberality and rectitude, for which he claims credit as a gentleman or a scholar."

[58] E. L. Green, *A History of the University of South Carolina* (Columbia, S.C.: The State Co., 1916), p. 61

[59] Lieber to Fish, May 20, 1857, in Perry, *Life and Letters*, p. 295.

made little difference to the trustees and the request was granted. But he expanded the economics offering from McVickar's twenty or so lectures in the last semester of the senior year to two hours a week throughout the year.[60]

His bow to political economy in his inaugural address was sufficiently impressive. It was, he said, a valuable study because its concerns formed the basis of national life and, indeed, of civilization. Exchange was fundamental; its necessity showed that natural theology, instead of being abandoned, should be further developed. In another sense political economy was useful, as could be shown by reference to the conduct of suffering workers in England during the recent depression. They had resorted to no violence because "they knew full well that a factory cannot be kept working unless the master can work to a profit." Had they been uninstructed they would have rioted as laborers did in the Middle Ages; but political economy had provided a tempering knowledge "regarding the relations of wealth, of capital and labor, which in spite of the absurdities of communism has penetrated in some degree all layers of society."

In speaking of the teaching of history he took his reference from *On Civil Liberty*—it was the history teacher's highest duty to foster in the young an "institutional spirit" which an earnest study of history showed to be of inestimable value. But the references to all these matters were only preliminary, really, to a dithyramb on the significance of political science. People were suffering, he said, from "the afterpain of Rousseauism, which itself was nothing but democratic absolutism." Political science could dispel such fancies, but it must not be confused, as was done by many, with various Utopias, which

[60] Lieber continued to use Say as the textbook in political economy and in history, like Vethake, he used Georg Weber's *Outlines of Universal History*. Lieber insisted that political economy could not be taught earlier than the senior year. (Lieber, "Suggestions for President King as a Basis of Discussion on the Distribution of Instruction" [1857], in Columbia University Libraries collection.)

were all communistic. The advocates of these wild schemes, instead of studying the historic genesis of institutions and understanding that civilization is accumulative, wanted to introduce new governments based on some fanatical theory. They generally attacked marriage and religion. This criticism of not understanding history applied also to August Comte who, although he acknowledged property and monogamy, offset these by his "apotheosis of absolutism" and "an incredible amount of inane vagaries," which came close to the idea of universal organization.

There was objection to the use in political science of the Benthamite theory of utility or expediency, because it allowed communists like Rousseau and Proudhon to argue that society could undo its own doing, and thus destroy the property it also created.[61]

In this connection, also, the increasing use of the term "sociology" as a neater description of the field of political philosophy was to be deplored. It implied a dangerous centralization. It was natural, perhaps, for "Gallicans," but it was socialism. Mere knowledge was not the ultimate aim of the student of political science. As was mere erudition to real knowledge so was knowing to doing and being. Action and character stood above science.

The new professor touched in passing on a few contemporary issues. We loyally adhere, he said, in speaking of secession,

[61] Lieber himself, like any thinker, frequently resorted to argument from expediency in controverted issues where justification was difficult on the previous ground of principle.

His criticisms of utilitarianism generally had reference to his attempt, like that of the Reverend John McVickar, to dissociate political economy from Benthamite "materialism." He explained in *Some Truths Worth Remembering:* "Political economy is associated by many persons with utilitarianism, that is, the system which seeks for the *ultimum bonum* in the merely physical welfare of man. This is no truer than confounding religion with certain religious errors, or with fanaticism, hypocrisy or priestcraft. Political economy simply endeavors to ascertain the laws of production and consumption—the principles of exchange. Exchange is an exclusive characteristic of man, and a basis of his highest interests and aspirations. So long as man's soul is united to his body, so long is political economy of importance."

to the conception of government as a federal union, but we should face the risk involved in it: "Confederacies are exposed to the danger of sejunction as unitary governments are exposed to absorbing powers." On the tariff he acknowledged that while economists might disagree over protection and free trade, that question touched only "a small portion of the bulk of truth taught by political economy." In reality greater agreement prevailed among economists than among any other group of scientists except, perhaps, mathematicians. He referred to slavery in passing as a "deciduous institution." [62]

Within a few months of Lieber's coming the trustees passed a statute requiring every professor to teach fifteen hours a week or three hours a day. He protested, saying that at South Carolina he had been required to teach only eight hours a week.[63] So far as the burden of the work went, he had gained nothing by his move.

He had, however, gained immensely in prestige. For sixteen active years he was to function as a recognized authority, a distinguished leader in New York. He was at last free of the south—or was he free? He no longer need be silent on slavery; he might denounce "sejunction"; but there was still the tariff matter, growing even more ticklish. Furthermore, he had left a son in the south who, when a choice had to be made, would fight for South Carolina against the Union. Since his other sons would join the Northern side—and one of them was to be wounded—his family would represent in itself the division of a nation. There was plenty of unhappiness in this alone. It did not happen suddenly. His son's disaffection was known to him for years; and he fought it with those poor weapons a father can find to combat heresy in the young, knowing from the

[62] Lieber, "History and Political Science Necessary Studies in Free Countries" (1858), reprinted in his *Miscellaneous Writings*, I, 350, 351, 358, 366; "The Ancient and the Modern Teacher of Politics" (1859), reprinted in *ibid.*, p. 383.

[63] Lieber to the trustees, August, 1857, in L. R. Harley, *Francis Lieber* (New York: Columbia Univ. Press, 1899), p. 195.

first how hopeless the endeavor was and sensing that it must end in tragedy.

He continued to maintain relations of a sort with southerners; although it was by now clear to him that civil war was nearly inevitable. To James J. Hammond, senator from South Carolina, for instance, he sent a copy of his inaugural address and in a long letter solicited aid in getting an academic post for his son. He also asked congressional support for the purchase of a German library and for a polar expedition proposed by the New York Geographic Society.[64] But southerners at last understood his hostility to their principles. In 1860, answering a letter from his son, he said that when public duty should compel him to state publicly in New York his convictions concerning free trade he would "be attacked in the North as violently, perhaps not as abusively, as I am at the moment in your portion of the country." [65] He strongly urged influential friends to denounce slavery. He had wanted Ruggles to say at the Protestant Episcopal Convention at Richmond in 1859 that slavery was godless, the greatest evil in modern history, which must be ejected, and that while unity and peace were desirable they were not the highest good.[66]

Privately he had denounced slavery to the extent of substantially qualifying his political theory and his economic principles. Thus he wrote his German friend Councillor Mittermaier, agreeing with him that democratic absolutism, the tyranny of the masses, was the worst form of absolutism, but saying that at present the minority, the slaveholding aristocracy, tyrannized over America.[67] On another occasion the question of reopening the slave trade provoked a denunciation of its unrighteousness and the sacrifice it involved of justice to

[64] Lieber to Hammond, Jan. 15, Feb. 2, and April 5, 1859, in Phinney, *Francis Lieber's Influence on American Thought*, pp. 71, 73, 75.

[65] Lieber to Oscar Lieber, autumn of 1860, in Perry, *Life and Letters*, p. 314.

[66] Lieber to Ruggles, Friday morning [1859], in Sears, "The Human Side of Francis Lieber," p. 56.

[67] Lieber to Karl J. A. Mittermaier, in Perry, *Life and Letters*, p. 296.

profit: "We economists have, thank God, been enabled to show the utter viciousness and erroneousness [of Mandeville's theory that private vice is a public benefit]," he wrote a former South Carolina student. Still, supposedly moral people continued to speak and act on the principle of private vice, public virtue, so that a reopening of the slave trade was justified on the ground that it was profitable for the slave trader and cotton producer.[68] This was suspiciously close to reversal. The firing of the first gun at Sumter was justification enough for the break with the South and all its notions. But it brought personal tragedy. His eldest and dearest son joined the South Carolina volunteers in much the same spirit in which Francis Lieber had joined the revolutionists in Germany in '48. Now the old man from his house in 38th Street had to see his son sacrificed to a cause which seemed utterly repugnant. Something of his affection can be understood from a birthday letter written to the boy in 1856:

This very moment, my own Oscar, I despatched a letter to you, and hardly had it gone than I remembered that I had not mentioned your birthday. . . . If I knew a sterling book for you, I should send it. But what is more important, my son, let us solemnly resolve to remain closely attached friends to our deaths. I am writing this with solemn feelings, and not without sadness. I know that on great things which agitate our times, and will do so far more than now, you think differently from what I do. It has not been granted to me, as to many others, to be in every respect of the same opinions with my first-born. I do not complain of this. You cannot have the experience or the knowledge of history which I have in my advanced years. You are living in the midst of a community with which you are essentially united by circumstances. Your youth has been so different from mine that I cannot expect you should feel and think as I do on every point, however sad it may sometimes make me that it is not so. I will never doubt your integrity and sincerity. You will never, I am

[68] Lieber to Wade Hampton, Sept. 5, 1858, in Perry, *Life and Letters*, pp. 302–3.

convinced, doubt that, as I commenced life in the cause of justice and liberty, I shall end it as truthfully and conscientiously. Let us, my son, then, love one another, and hope for the time when the light of truth will no longer be obscured to our sight, but will shine clear and pure into the souls of the blessed, and we shall know where we have erred. May God protect you. Good-bye, dear boy.[69]

Still, there were two sons loyal to the Union; and when war came the old martial feelings roused themselves again. In spirited verse the suppressed warrior celebrated the beginning of this war as he had celebrated others. He wrote Sumner for a commission for one of his younger sons,[70] and reminded Fish, now a member of the union defense committee of his state and a commissioner of the federal government for the relief of prisoners, of his own availability for any useful service.[71] He became legal adviser to Secretary of War Stanton. His most serious contribution to the War Department was its famous General Orders No. 100. *Instructions for the Government of Armies of the United States in the Field.* There was another, *Guerrilla Parties Considered with Reference to the Laws and Usages of War,* which was also used as a reference by generals in the field. He became archivist for the War Department. He also helped to organize the Loyal Publication

[69] Lieber to Oscar Lieber, Sept. 5, 1856, in Perry, *Life and Letters,* p. 289. There was a sad epilogue. Among Lieber's letters one to Samuel Tyler, January 14, 1867, had the following passage: "If ever you go to Richmond, go to the churchyard, where you will find my hope expressed on the tombstone of my son Oscar. He fell on the Southern side, and his two brothers went to Richmond to place the tombstone on the grave. They have fought and bled on the National side. You see, the Civil War has knocked rudely at my door." (*Ibid.,* p. 368.)

[70] This son, Hamilton, lost his left arm at Fort Donelson in 1862. Lieber mentioned this in a letter to Attorney General Bates, April 8: "You may have observed that General Halleck has nominated him aid on his staff, with the rank of captain, for distinguished services in the capture of Fort Donelson, in which he was twice wounded. . . . His bravery is very highly spoken of." (Perry, *Life and Letters,* p. 327.) Hamilton's feat was balm in Gilead for an old man's spirit which had suffered so many hurts.

[71] Letter of Lieber to Fish, Jan. 11 and April 24, 1861, in Fish papers, Library of Congress.

Society. The level of his discourse of this time must be judged, of course, by the circumstances. Nothing else had ever excited Lieber as the Civil War did. The division in his own family, his long exile among secessionists, the old impulses to action suppressed during a long sedentary career, the compromises of which his life had been so full—the mixed impulses rising out of all these causes found a sudden focus.

With heightened emphases, Lieber increased the output of his writing, passionately supporting the Union cause, pillorying every move of the rebels. The action of the seceding states proved to him, he said, that providence had wisely imposed tasks on mankind to keep them out of mischief. Every time they had leisure they made fools of themselves. Their so-called right of revolution was silly. As a jurist, not a sentimentalist, he could distinguish between colonies revolting against a distant mother country and rebellion in the bowels of a country itself. The law allowed no formulated distinction between them, but the difference was nevertheless essential, and every thinking and feeling man had known it in all ages.[72] Those who spoke in favor of the South should get short shrift. When a newspaper cited a passage from his *Political Ethics* on "the unmanly state of things when a people lose the energy of enduring an opposition" Lieber replied that he had written this in South Carolina which suffered no opposition on any question involving states' rights. "And now to apply my remarks to those who are in favor of *Rebels!*" Certain Democratic members of Congress also cited the *Civil Liberty* in opposing conscription. Lieber answered that conscription was constitutional because it would be ridiculous to say "that the Constitution prohibits this nation from doing that which Nature commands every creature to do . . . to defend its own skin." [73] In *Civil Liberty*, he had maintained that the President

[72] Letter of Lieber to Fish, Jan. 11, 1861, in Fish papers, Library of Congress.

[73] Lieber to Martin R. Thayer, Jan. 2 and Feb. 1, 1864, in Perry, *Life and Letters*, pp. 337, 338.

should not have the right to suspend the writ of habeas corpus, but now he wrote that this right of the President was essential in time of necessity, and that if he did not have it, he must arrogate it.[74]

There could however be little question that, as a Columbia trustee put it: "Lieber upholds the nation and cares little for state rights in comparison." [75] Through the Loyal Publication Society he sought the support of all classes for the Union cause. The Constitution was not a compact, and candid opponents of the national government could not assert that there was "ever a tendency toward *centralization* . . . in Congress." He quickly granted that there had been a "tendency of a portion of the people toward democratic absolutism at the time when General Jackson was called the tribune of the people, and high-handed measures were asked at his hands by the so-called states-rights men.[76] But he forgot to mention that the states-rights and secession issue had arisen then as opposition to the "tariff of abominations." Even if the doctrine of state sovereignty was valid, said Lieber, then we as a sovereign had the right to conquer other sovereigns to assert our claims.[77] "We must have back the South, or else those who will not reunite with us must leave the country; we must have the country at any price." [78] States' rights and slavery must both be abolished. The one denies humanity; the other, all that is national, by frightening the timid with the false specter of centralization.[79] He thought that the success of the Union cause demanded Lincoln's withdrawal from candidacy

[74] Lieber to Charles Sumner, Jan. 8, 1863, in Perry, *Life and Letters*, p. 330.

[75] Entry of June 8, 1865 in *The Diary of George Templeton Strong*, ed. Allan Nevins and Milton Halsey Thomas, 4 vols. (New York: Macmillan, 1952), IV, 7.

[76] Lieber, "Amendments of the Constitution" (1865); republished in *Miscellaneous Writings*, II, 164.

[77] Lieber, *The Arguments of Secessionists* (New York: Loyal Publication Society, 1863), p. 5.

[78] Lieber, *No Party Now but All for Our Country* (New York: Loyal Publication Society, 1863), p. 3.

[79] *Final Report and Address of the President* (New York: Loyal Publication Society, 1866), p. 11.

for a second term, and that General Ulysses S. Grant ought to to be chosen instead. When Lincoln was nominated, however, Lieber supported him and appealed to the German vote to oppose the Democratic candidate, General McClellan, who, he said, was backed by opponents of immigration and by Southern sympathizers who believed that capital had an inherent right to own labor everywhere as in the South.[80]

He likewise appealed to the farmers; but at least one of his arguments had been given a different emphasis before. In 1856, when Sumner, denouncing the cities as hotbeds of proslavery sentiment, proclaimed that the country was of God, Lieber wrote Ruggles that Sumner's error had been exposed by Robert Vaughan's book, *The Age of Great Cities* (1843). Civilization essentially started with cities and "the cities always remain the lungs and brains of civilization. The country's great business is to keep them from rising to fever heat." [81] Now, referring to the same book Lieber said that a numerous and independent yeomanry was essential for orderly government and for the coherence and permanency of the country because "the tranquility of the farmer must counteract the restless and reckless portions of city populations." A yeomanry could not exist where there are large estates because they use slave labor and the small farm cannot. In England the law of primogeniture created an acknowledged aristocracy with some redeeming qualities. Here the owners of large estates had no traditions, were subject to no public opinion, and hoped to sell their estates at large profits.[82]

Lieber found sufficient reasons in his historical method for supporting the Thirteenth Amendment emancipating all

[80] Lieber to General Halleck, Sept. 1, 1864, in Perry, *Life and Letters*, p. 350; Lieber, *Lincoln or McClellan? Appeal to the Germans in America* (New York: Loyal Publication Society, 1864), p. 3.

[81] Lieber to Ruggles, Oct. 23, 1856, in Sears, "The Human Side of Francis Lieber," pp. 54-55.

[82] Lieber, *Slavery, Plantations, and the Yeomanry* (New York: Loyal Publication Society, 1863), p. 6.

slaves. "We live in a time of necessary and searching reform," he said, because things have changed and must be readjusted. All laws must change in the course of time, for life changes in obedience to reality. The framers of the Constitution were like all human beings "finite and imperfect." [83]

At this time he made an interesting suggestion to the Treasury, in a letter to the New York *Times*. The government might provide bonds of small denomination and with an attractive rate of interest ($50 Treasury notes with 7.30 percent interest) for army men, especially lieutenants and captains. Speaking as a "reflecting economist who knows the incalculable benefit of saving for both the individual and society," he urged that these would be a welcome accumulation for the soldiers at the end of the war. Millions would be saved from dissipation. "Any business man and economist will see at once the excellent moral as well as economical effect it would have if the savings of which we have spoken were thus to be reinvested." [84]

Lieber's growing prestige and his public activities gave him a certain satisfaction, but there were complications. The cost of living rose during the war years and after, and salaries were temporarily cut. His fortunes under the new president, the Reverend Frederick A. P. Barnard, suffered a decline

[83] Lieber, "Amendments of the Constitution," pp. 138, 144.

[84] F[rancis] L[ieber], "The Treasury, a Good Army Savings Bank," The New York *Times*, Sept. 14, 1861, p. 4.

Lieber as early as 1842 was attempting to bring his scheme of army savings banks to the attention of the War Office. He wrote to the Reverend Alonzo Potter, as "one intimately acquainted with the Secretary of War," that "One of the greatest institutions of modern times are the Savings Banks. . . . These . . . may work in two different ways; they may collect and concentrate sums so trifling that separately they cannot be used productively, but collectively may amount to most valuable capitals for national reproduction; as when the little earnings of the servant girls and day-laborers are saved from useless or actually mischievous expenditure. Or the savings banks may prevent large capitals, already collected, from being trifled away into nothing, as in the case of army and navy payments." (Letter of Nov. 10, 1842, in the Historical Society of Pennsylvania collection.)

partly because of budgetary problems, but also partly because he was not a success as an undergraduate teacher. There were also tempermental differences between himself and the president. He did not object to the adverse comments of the president, in his inaugural address in October, 1864, on recent biological theories; Lieber, too, held Darwinism in horror. The theory of natural selection denied, he felt, the beneficent guiding hand of God in the progress of civilization. Darwinism was an unintelligible, "wayward and repulsive dogmatism" and a flimsy and "visionary materialism." [85] But he dissented violently—indeed, his German blood boiled—when Barnard asked how it happened "that most of the theological schools of Germany have been, during a great part of this century if they are not still, schools of irreligion." Now Lieber had a certain position, and he wrote Fish that only respect for order had kept him from public contradiction. Infidelity, he said indignantly, had begun with Hobbes in England, had then passed to France, and from there had been imported into Germany. It was a fact, he said, that most of the orthodox books on religion of his time came out of the German universities. Barnard's statement about German philosophy, however, served to put Lieber on guard.[86]

The president was faced at this time with a drain of funds for the expansion of the recently opened School of Mines; and some of the clerical trustees were complaining that the college could not afford to pay $4,000 a year for Lieber's four hours a week of teaching. Supporting Lieber, however, were such renowned trustees as Fish, King, and Ruggles.

On June 5, 1865, President Barnard in his first *Annual Report* to the trustees made an adverse declaration:

[85] Lieber to Martin R. Thayer, March 26, 1871, in Perry, *Life and Letters*, p. 409.

[86] Letter of Lieber to Fish, Oct. 7, 1870, in Fish papers, Library of Congress. Barnard's statement is in *Proceedings at the Inauguration of Frederick A. P. Barnard* (New York: Hurd and Houghton, 1865), p. 61.

All the subjects embraced in the two departments of Philosophy and English, and of History and Political Science, might be better put into the hands of a single instructor, with a tutor to assist him, than be disposed as at present. It is quite doubtful . . . whether Modern History, in the proper sense of the word, ought to occupy any considerable space in the teaching of our Colleges. The subject is so vast, and practically so exhaustless, that the little which can be taught in the few hours of class instruction (if that is *all* the learner ever knows) amounts to but a small remove from absolute ignorance. There are certain large outlines that can be sketched boldly out; but this being done, the instructor will much more profitably employ himself in furnishing the student with something of the bibliography of history—in giving him, in short, a guide for his private reading—than in attempting any detail of the growth and decline of particular empires.

. . . In an institution having the character of a proper university where the student is presumed to have been already educated, in the technical sense of that word, and prepared to bring the energies of a matured and disciplined intellect, to bear upon any subject to which he addresses himself, the teacher of Political Economy may find enough, and more than enough, in that single subject, to require the close and constant application of all his powers. But in an undergraduate course in America—in our College especially in which the teaching embraces at the utmost but about twenty elementary lectures, distributed over a surface of nine months—it is impossible that an able teacher can find in this subject adequate employment, or that he can render such service to his pupils as to make it judicious or economical to confine him to this single branch of instruction.

The trustees soon afterwards abolished Lieber's college chair, and transferred history and political economy to the professor of moral and intellectual philosophy and English literature, Nairne.

Lieber, however, was taken care of by being given a chair of constitutional history and public law in the School of Law. Ample funds from general fees were available to meet his salary. After the battle was over, he discovered that he preferred being exclusively attached to the School of Law. He was now midway in his Columbia College years. Since the war's beginning he had grown in reputation until by now he had the widest prestige of anyone in the country in matters having to do with public law and especially with military law. He was consulted by Sumner, by Secretary of War Edwin M. Stanton, by General Halleck, and by others who were more directly responsible for the conduct of affairs. In March of 1865 he wrote to Sumner: "How often I have said 'let us beat the enemy and the logic will soon enough follow.' . . . We want the restoration of the country minus slavery." He unhesitatingly supported Sumner on Reconstruction and he hoped that President Johnson's impeachment would be successful. His policy of moderation made him, Lieber said, an abettor of rebels. Jefferson Davis was really guilty of "the most infernal treason" but he would be found not guilty, because time had been lost in bringing him to trial. If this happened, he said, "we shall stand then completely beaten."[87] The President's impeachment was justified also because he attacked Congress and refused to accept the Tenure of Office Act by which Congress tried to force him to retain Lincoln's cabinet members. He was guilty of the highest treason in removing Stanton in order to test the constitutionality of the act. In this connection Lieber even denied that the Supreme Court could judge in a general manner the constitutionality of acts. It was not a body with a super-veto, to revise and pass on laws of Congress. This was a heresy of the same character as states' rights. If the court had that power it became a fourth estate and assumed the role of the Almighty. Said Lieber of this: "I have never seen the angelic wings penetrating the gown."

The Supreme Court could decide on the constitutionality of acts of Congress incidentally only, in case of conflicts of law—that was, in given, practical, bona fide cases in which

[87] Lieber to Sumner, March 29, 1865; to Halleck, May 19, 1866, in Perry, *Life and Letters*, pp. 356, 363.

the Constitution was presumed to conflict with an act. Thus an individual dispossessed by an unlawful tax could bring his case to the courts for decision as to the constitutionality of the law. But the President was sworn to obey the law, and the law was passed in due constitutional form; therefore he could not trump up a case to bring the issue before the court. This breaking of the law in order to test its constitutionality was "rank rebellion" for which in other countries he would go to the scaffold. As to Johnson's defense of himself on the ground of freedom of speech, Lieber asked, "Freedom of Speech! Is it really meant that a chief magistrate can make a beast of himself, can talk at random, can do all sorts of things with impunity because the law does not punish the same acts in a private individual?" [88]

When Grant was safely installed, some of Lieber's friends, headed by Ruggles, addressed a letter to him stating that Lieber had rendered valiant service for his country in the war and that he was preeminently qualified to "serve our country abroad in a representative capacity or in *international arbitrations*. . . . He would yield to the call . . . of the President if assigned to any duty in harmony with his antecedents and his proper capacities for serving the country." [89] Fish, who had become secretary of state, finally got him in 1870 the post of umpire of the United States and Mexican Claims Commission set up under the treaty of 1868 between the two countries for the settlement of claims arising from the Mexican War. From this time on he led a sort of semiofficial life.

The outbreak of the Franco-Prussian War in 1870 was for Lieber a joyous event. He proudly anticipated that William I of Prussia would become emperor of a united Germany.[90] He blamed the war entirely on France. The French people, he

[88] Lieber to Sumner, April 14 and 24, 1867, in Perry, *Life and Letters*, pp. 371–72, 385, 387.

[89] Copy in letter to Fish, April 23, 1869, in Fish papers, Library of Congress.

[90] Lieber to J. K. Bluntschli, Aug. 21, 1870, in Perry, *Life and Letters*, p. 398.

said, are "just like our rebels in conceitedness, pride, cruelty and arrogance." [91] Americans were incorrigible in their belief that this was a struggle between the cultured Latin race and the brutal Teutonic race and this infuriated Lieber. "Latin race," he insisted, was a misnomer. The German element preponderated in the most densely populated and industrious area of France and from this area came a greater proportion of genius, whether of pen or of sword, than from any other part of "this proud and, unfortunately, presuming country." [92]

He was very much puzzled when the French people oversubscribed many times the indemnity loan to pay the victorious Germans. After placing the question in the "psychological position" of economics, he confessed that although he had been professor of political economy for many years he could not find the clue. Patriotism? "Nothing like that in such a case." [93]

Lieber still held his professorship in the Law School. He thought his position as umpire on the Mexican Claims Commission would end in 1872, and he intended then to give up both government and teaching posts and make a modestly triumphal return to Europe, a return which he hoped might be enhanced by a diplomatic post. So, early in 1871, he sent in his resignation to the law committee. Late in the year, however, he wrote his Columbia trustee friends that his position as umpire might continue until 1873 and that his numerous students were urging him to continue his courses. He wanted them to keep open his resignation until 1873; and they assented to his wishes, setting the date of resignation as of August, 1873.[94]

Lieber's economic views hardly changed; but in the case of

[91] Lieber to J. C. Bancroft Davis, Aug. 27, 1870, in Phinney, *Francis Lieber's Influence on American Thought*, p. 79.

[92] Lieber, "The Latin Race" (1871), republished in *Miscellaneous Writings*, II, 310.

[93] Letter of Lieber to Fish, June 29, 1871, in Fish papers, Library of Congress.

[94] Lieber to Bluntschli, Feb. 19, 1872, in Perry, *Life and Letters*, p. 421; Lieber to Ruggles, Oct. 6 and 8, 1871, in Sears, "The Human Side of Francis Lieber," pp. 60–61; letter of Lieber to Fish, Dec. 4, 1871, in Fish papers, Library of Congress; Columbia University, Minutes of the Trustees, June 3, 1872.

one important tenet, circumstances soon made him a heretic and he did not flinch. In the pre-Civil War period, as a free trader, he had moved with dominant sentiment. During and after the Civil War protectionism became dominant and was a central plank of the victorious party, which was his own, the Republican party. But just as he had been a free-trade Whig, so now he was a free-trade Republican, and joined vigorously, as he did in all things that enlisted his sentiments, in denouncing the protectionists as violators of the basic principles of social ethics and political economy. In an age when industry became dominant and the captain of industry a central figure in the life of the nation, it took no little courage to engage in combat as he did in his often reprinted *Notes on Fallacies Peculiar to American Protectionists* (1869).

In the *Notes*, Lieber expressed sympathy with the view that government might under some circumstances directly encourage production:

> The sacredness of the rights of production, exchange, and consumption does not exclude the right or the duty, as the case may be, of government to take the initiative in cases of production. A government is the agent of a community, and among other things, it ought to do everything which is desirable for the community —if peaceable and not infringing natural rights—and which the individuals cannot do (e.g., defending the country or measuring a degree), or ought not to do (e.g., punish crimes), or will not do (e.g., establish public schools for the poor and poorest). Prussia acted correctly when in the special treaty of 1815, between herself and Spain, she stipulated the delivery of a certain number of merino rams, and established shepherd schools where young men might obtain free of expense, the knowledge of raising merinos. Prussian wool, generally called in the market Saxon wool, forms now one of the important branches of production in that country. This, however, is very different from forcing the Prussian people to use such a species of domestic wool.

Lieber helped to organize the powerful American Free Trade League, and urged his law school students to join the cause. Under his stimulus, for example, Henry Demarest Lloyd started as a zealous protagonist of free trade; then he went on to become one of the outstanding social reformers of the country.[95]

Another Columbia student and admirer of Lieber was Oscar S. Straus, who became an eminent businessman and philanthropist, the country's minister and ambassador to Turkey under Presidents Cleveland, McKinley, and Taft; secretary of commerce and labor under President Theodore Roosevelt; and the candidate for governor of New York on the Progressive ticket in 1912.[96]

Lieber was, perhaps fortunately, not destined to live to see the triumph of protectionism.

He died on October 2, 1872. Five years after his death, through the aid of his old benefactor, Ruggles, and the support of President Barnard, another German-trained economist, Richmond Mayo-Smith, was brought to Columbia to invigorate the study of economics. Mayo-Smith started a movement to broaden the scope of economics to include that institutionalism which Lieber had earlier described, a movement that culminated in the formation of the American Economic Association, in 1885, by a group of German-trained economists.

Lieber's fame rests largely on his contribution to political theory; but no less an authority than Amasa Walker spoke of his interest in political economy, "a science to which he devoted a great part of his life and in which he felt a deep and increasing interest to the end of his days." He was, Walker said, an able publicist, concerned with "important economic questions . . . agitating the public mind." [97]

At the time of Lieber's death, Strong had written percep-

[95] Frank Freidel, *Francis Lieber* (Baton Rouge, La.: Louisiana State Univ. Press, 1947), p. 368.

[96] Oscar S. Straus, *Under Four Administrations* (Boston: Houghton Mifflin, 1922), pp. 30–31.

[97] Letter of Amasa Walker to Daniel C. Gilman, March 28, 1873, in Johns Hopkins University Library.

tively: "With all his foibles of egotism and vanity, he was a learned, thoughtful and valuable man, whom it would be hard to replace. His familiarity with the details of modern history was wonderful, and so was his grasp of the laws that underlie them. But for conceit and inability to conceal it, he would have been great. Everyone has some good story to tell about his weaknesses, and but comparatively few will remember his strength, his erudition, and his earnest patriotism as a naturalized American." [98]

[98] *The Diary of George Templeton Strong*, IV, 441.

APPENDIX I

THE REVEREND JOHN McVICKAR ON BILLS OF EXCHANGE[1]

As the foregoing observations may fall into the hands of some not fully conversant with the subject of Bills of Exchange, it has been thought expedient to add to them the following exposition of their nature and operations.

A Bill of Exchange is a written order drawn by one person upon a distant correspondent, in favour of a third party, by means of which reciprocal and equal debts are settled without the necessity of remitting specie. Thus A of New-York is creditor to B of London £1000, for cotton shipped per order, and C of New-York, debtor to D of London £1000 for goods sent out. Now, both these debts may be discharged by the operation of a single bill. A draws for this sum upon B and sells his bill to C, who remits it in payment to his creditor D, who finally receives the amount when due from B. A simple transfer of debt has settled all their claims. Of the four parties who thus exist to a bill, A is termed the *Drawer*, B the *Drawee*, C the *Remitter*, and D the *Payee*. He who negotiates a bill in its course becomes also its *Endorser;* the possessor of a bill is termed the *Holder;* he who presents it, the *Presenter;* and the Drawee, or other person accepting it, the *Acceptor*. If the parties to the bill be resident in the same country it is termed a *Home* or *Inland Bill;* if not, a *Foreign* Bill of Exchange; of both, the principles are the same, but the latter is more complex, by involving the consideration of a different coin and standard, the bill being bought in the coin of one country, and paid in that of another. Thus, a bill on England is bought here

[1] This essay first appeared as an appendix to McVickar's *Considerations upon the Expediency of Abolishing Damages on Protested Bills of Exchange and the Effect of Establishing a Reciprocal Exchange with Europe* (1829).

in silver, and paid there in gold. This it is which gives to the subject of Exchange its only complexity.

What thus settles the accounts of individuals requires only extension to liquidate those of cities and nations. So far as debts are reciprocal and equal, they are liquidated by an exchange of debtor and creditor claims between the merchants of the same city or country; if a balance remain after such exchange, it must be paid either by a remission of coin or bullion, or by a transfer of funds lying in some third place, or by a new shipment of goods or produce. Of these three modes, payment in coin is the one last resorted to, as being attended in general with the heaviest cost, and gone into only when it becomes necessary to alter the value of money itself.

Price of Bills. The value of these drafts depends like that of any thing else in market, upon the supply compared with the demand. A competition among the buyers will cause their price to rise; among sellers, will cause it to fall; or if the demand and offer be equal, the price will be at par, *i. e.* money will be worth as much in the one place as in the other; this constitutes the *par* or equal value, to which the price of bills is ordinarily referred.

Like all other prices, that of bills has its limits of oscillation, beyond which it cannot go, without creating a reaction, which immediately brings it back. Their *maximum* is thus found. Bills are a substitute for the remitting of coin, or a shipment of corresponding value; he who buys a bill, therefore, will not pay for it a premium which goes beyond the actual cost which attends that operation for which it is a substitute. If the price of bills come up to this limit, it is a matter of indifference to the remitter, whether he buy a bill, or provide funds by a shipment. If their price rise above this limit, it is no longer a matter of indifference; he will ship and not buy; and as the same state of things will make the drawing of bills a money-making operation, bills will be drawn against shipments, or upon credit, and thus the sellers in the market increased at the very moment that the buyers are diminished: thus will the price of bills be brought down. The *minimum* of bills is determined by the reverse of this operation. The owner of funds abroad will continue to draw only so long as it is the most profitable disposal of them; to him, as to the remitter, the bill is but a substitute for a circuitous transaction; he may command his funds by ordering a remittance in bullion or goods, and this he will do so soon as bills fall so low as to make the remittance the more profitable transaction; thus, the sellers of bills will be diminished in the market, while the low price of bills becoming a bounty on importation, the demand for them will be proportionately increased, and their price rise accordingly. The range in the price of bills is therefore thus limited: the cost of their production is the expense of sending money or commodities abroad; this is their *maximum:* while the greatest sacrifice the seller will submit to is the expense of bringing them home; this is their *minimum.* Between these extremes their market price is continually fluctuating. But, neither are their extremes permanent; they have a greater latitude during war, for instance, than in time of peace; whatever, in short, adds to the cost or risk of actual transportation widens proportionably the range in the price of bills; thus, during the late war with England, bills on France rose 10 per cent., and on England still higher, owing to the joint operation of war and a depreciated currency.

Par of Exchange.—A bill of exchange is bought in the money of one city or country, and paid for in that of another; it is therefore based upon the calculation of the intrinsic value of the two currencies. If they be the same, as in the case of all domestic bills, the par of exchange is obvious; so many dollars in the one place are exchanged for an equal number in the other: thus, bills are at par between New-York and Boston, when a draft of $1000 here, will command $1000 there, with allowance, if need be, for interest. But if the currency be different, as in the case of foreign bills, a new calculation is necessarily introduced; the one must be valued in terms of the other. If both be gold, or both silver, this calculation is comparatively simple; the par between such countries consists in the exchange of an equal quantity of the precious metal contained in their respective coins: thus, between this country and France, the real par of exchange is fr. 5 30–100 for the dollar—i. e. there is an equal amount of pure silver in both. Between such countries, therefore, there subsists a natural and consequently a permanent par, towards which the market price is constantly tending; but when one country uses gold, and the other silver in its payments, so that the bill is to be estimated in one of the precious metals, and paid in the other, as is the case between this country and England, a further and nicer calculation becomes requisite; the price of gold in the market becomes a new element in the price of the bill, and the real par consists in the purchase of so much gold in the foreign market as would there exchange for the amount of silver here paid for it. Now, this proportion between silver and gold is constantly varying; it is no doubt permanently regulated by the comparative cost of their production; but as this allows a wide range, and requires a long period of time until demand can regulate supply, their comparative value in the market may in fact be taken as an uncertain and varying element in the price of bills: the result is, that between such countries there can be no permanent natural par; a commercial par there is, in which equal values are given, but it is true only for a short period of time; it fluctuates with every change in either of the precious metals: hence the variation that gradually arises between the legal and real par of exchange between such countries as attempt to fix it by law, while using different standards.

Course of Exchange.—The course of exchange differs from the par of exchange just as the market price of an article differs from its natural price—the one is variable, the other fixed. The par of exchange is a calculation of real values: while the course of exchange often confounds what is real with what is merely nominal, and thus leads to both prejudice and error. Thus, the quotation may show exchange to be against a country, when in reality it is at par, or even perhaps in its favour. What inference, for example, can be drawn from the statement that exchange with London is 10½ above par; that such a premium must be paid for bills? Surely, none other than that our exchanges with England are so much against us, and that consequently we are carrying on a losing trade. To avoid erroneous conclusions in this matter, it is necessary to distinguish between the *Real*, *Nominal*, and *Computed* course of exchange.

1. *The Real Course of Exchange* depends on the comparative demand and supply of bills; or, in other words, upon the comparative exports and imports of the country, and can never continue to exceed, as already shown, the expense and risk of remitting specie, which expense may be estimated, in the case of England, including interest, at about 1 or 1½ per cent. To arrive at the knowledge of this real course of exchange is all important to the merchant, since it marks the proportion which subsists between the exports and imports of the country, and constitutes

the criterion of their comparative profit; it is, in short, the commercial balance which ascertains, by its rise or fall, into which scale commercial capital should be thrown. When this is at par, commercial operations are governed simply by a reference to prices, but so soon as it inclines to either side, it becomes a new determining cause; with every rise, it adds a corresponding profit to exportation, the premium on the bills drawn being equivalent to a bounty on the shipment made; with every fall, the profit of the shipper is lessened, and a corresponding bounty given to the importer. Thus it is, that the real course of exchange governs commerce, it equalizes imports with exports, and liquidates debts with foreign nations; but it is as difficult as it is important at all times to distinguish its real from its nominal variations.

2. *The Nominal Course of Exchange.*—This arises from a difference in the intrinsic value of the respective currencies, in one of which the bill is estimated, and in the other paid. To the variation in the price of bills from this cause there is no certain limit, since there is none to the depreciation to which a national currency may be reduced. Thus, it fell against France during the period of her Assignats, to 3 and 400 per cent.; the same took place against this country, when a bill was liable to be paid in depreciated continental money.

The causes which may give rise to an inferior currency, and thus originate a nominal exchange against a country, are as follows:

1. The comparative natural cheapness in them of the precious metals.—In mining countries, and those which lie near to them, gold and silver are cheaper, i. e. cost less to obtain them than they do in countries more remote; their difference of value is the cost of transportation. Thus, Spain has a nominal exchange against her in Europe of near 3 per cent.; Rio Janeiro has an unfavourable exchange with London of about 5 per cent.; and New-York, which is a great entrepôt of the bullion trade with Europe, of from 1 to 2 per cent. In all these cases, the cause is the same, and the exchange but nominal. Thus silver is worth less in Mexico than in London, simply because it costs less: if it cost 5 per cent. to get it to London, $100 in London is consequently equivalent to $105 in Mexico, and the 5 per cent. premium paid there for a bill on London, is consequently but the par value of that bill, supposing it immediately paid in London. Hence, it would ap-

pear, 1. That those countries which furnish, or forward the precious metals, must have an apparent unfavourable exchange with those that receive them; 2. That the amount of such premium is the expense and risk of remitting them; and 3. That such exchange is altogether nominal, and has no effect on the real exchanges of the country.

2. The cheapening of the currency of a country, by degradation of the coin, will immediately produce a nominal exchange against it. This must necessarily be the case, for the foreigner estimates the coin only as gold or silver bullion. If this, therefore, be adulterated 25 per cent., he will add an equal amount to his demand. In earlier times, this was a common resource of the governments of Europe, when oppressed by debt; of latter years, it has been abandoned, from a conviction of its inexpediency as well as its injustice: a modern instance, however, may be found in the government of Turkey, against which country exchange rose 100 per cent. immediately upon the reduction of the piastre to one half its former value.

3. Another cause of depreciation in the currency of commercial countries arises from the overissues of bank or paper money; the moment this takes place, in any one city or country, exchange rises against it, and that for the same reason as already stated in the case of adulteration, viz: that the money of that country has become of less value. The proof of this is the fact that it will exchange for a less amount than before of any commodity in market; in other words, all prices have risen. The result of this state of things is obvious: exports thereby are checked, imports find a bounty in the new prices, and bills consequently are few and high; and while this state of things continues, the course of exchange will be against the country to the amount of the depreciation. If the paper be redeemable, this unfavourable exchange is soon corrected; coin is demanded for paper, shipped to a better market, and bills drawn against it; the interest of the banks hastens the operation of the cure; while coin is shipped, they curtail their discounts. The result is evident; money rises in value, prices fall, orders are lessened, and foreign funds cease to be in demand; in other words, exchange ceases to be unfavourable. If, on the contrary, the paper be irredeemable, as it became in England by the Suspension Act, in 1797, such unfavourable exchange becomes permanent, limited only by the amount of the

surplus; thus it varied during that period, (1797 to 1817,) from 5 up to 30 per cent. against England, according as the fears or prudence of the bank directors led them to set limits to their issues, or in other words, to their unlimited power of degrading the currency.

The same result was evident in our own country during the suspension of cash payments in 1814 and 1815. Boston, which alone of all our cities maintained its metallic currency, had the exchanges universally in its favour; it was against New-York, 10 per cent.; against other cities, 20, and even as high as forty per cent., according as the bills upon them were to be paid in a currency more or less depreciated. This, however, in all these cases, from whatever cause arising, was but a nominal exchange; thus, at that very time, New-York was carrying on with Boston a most profitable trade, and England deriving from the very commerce thus apparently ruinous, the means of maintaining her largest armaments, and the most expensive contest to which she had ever been called. The real evils of such a currency are felt at home, in fluctuations of wealth, uncertainty of contracts, and, above all, in the reaction produced by a return to a natural and permanent medium of exchange. However depreciated money may be, the individual, in any transaction, is no loser, provided he sell the proceeds of his bill in currency of the same value in which he bought it. In short, the true doctrine on this subject would seem to be that the money of a country is but a *measure of value*, the only essential requisite of which is that it be invariable; whether long or short, of paper or of gold, makes no difference, provided it never changes.

4. The last source of nominal exchange is found in a false mint estimate of the comparative value of the precious metals; hence, in countries using a double standard, it is almost invariably found to subsist. Thus, England uses a gold standard, we both a silver and gold one; and as these two metals bear no permanent or necessary proportion to each other, it has so happened that their market value has wandered far away from the legal value our government put upon them in the establishment of its mint; hence has resulted, in our commercial intercourse with England, a nominal exchange against us, which has been the source of much ignorant prejudice. By an act of Congress, 31st July, 1789, the pound sterling, or the unit of British money, was declared equiva-

lent to \$4 44, or the dollar to 4*s*. 6*d*. sterling, an estimate which was subsequently confirmed by the act of April 2, 1792, establishing a mint, and declaring that one ounce of pure gold should be estimated to be worth 15 ounces of pure silver, and should thereafter pass, and be received at that rate. This estimate, at that time nearly accurate, has now ceased to be so; the pound sterling may now be estimated at about \$4 80–100, or the dollar at 4*s*. 2*d*. sterling; an ounce of pure gold is now worth, on an average, at least 15½ ounces of silver; it has been recently fixed at that by the French mint, and the mint and market price of gold in Paris, now seldom vary more than ¼ to ½ per cent. In our market, on the contrary, the premium upon gold is from 5 to 7 or 8 per cent. and consequently that premium will be given for bills which are, in Europe, to be paid in gold. But this is evidently altogether nominal, a mere form of calculation or expression; we over-estimate silver in comparison with gold; the consequence is, the gold leaves us, the silver remains behind; but when we come to exchange our silver against foreign gold, we must pay the market price.

In the recent regulations of her mint, Great Britain has over-estimated still more than we have done the value of silver, making 14½ ounces silver equivalent to one ounce of pure gold; but this she has done for the express purpose of retaining her silver coinage within the kingdom; while by making it a legal tender only for sums below 40 shillings, she has prevented this over-valuation from having any effect upon the course of foreign exchanges.

Computed Exchange.—The computed exchange, or the quotation of exchange, expresses, according to circumstances, either the sum or the difference of the *real* and *nominal* exchange; if both these be favourable to a country, or both unfavourable, the quotation gives their sum; if one be favourable, and the other unfavourable, the quotation gives their difference. For example, supposing the nominal exchange against New-York with London, arising from her over-estimate of silver, say 7 per cent.; from her greater contiguity to mining countries, say 2 per cent.; and from an overflowing paper currency, say 1 per cent., amounting altogether to 10 per cent. Now, under these circumstances, the real exchange may still be either favourable or unfavourable; if it be one per cent. in our favour, the quotation will be 9 per cent. premium; if as much against us, the computed exchange will then give 11 per cent. premium for bills.

But it would be far better that this mode of expressing the course of exchange, which is almost exclusively confined to English bills, should be entirely done away, and the common language of exchange adopted, viz: estimating the dollar at so many shillings and pence sterling. The existing practice is founded on the false calculation of our legal par, and thus tends to perpetuate both prejudice and error on the subject.

The universal language of exchange in Europe is to estimate the unit money of one country in the coin of another; thus, the computed exchange of London with Paris, is fr. 25 20–100, with Amsterdam, is 36 sch. 8 d. Flem. i. e. the pound sterling is worth so many francs and centimes, or shillings and pence; thus, too, our exchange with Havre is expressed, fr. 5 30–100, and applied to London, would give from 4s. 2d. to 4s. 3d. the dollar, as the commercial par between the two countries.

In this computation, the nation whose unit is taken, is said, in the language of exchange, to give the *certain* for the *uncertain*. Thus, London gives to Paris, Amsterdam, and most other places, the certain for the uncertain, i. e. she gives the pound sterling for a certain estimated number of *francs, stivers,* &c. but with Spain she gives the uncertain, i. e. so many pence sterling, say 35d. for the Spanish dollar of exchange. The United States, in her foreign exchanges, generally gives the unit; with some, however, she values the foreign coin, as in the case of the East India rupee, &c.

Favourable and Unfavourable Exchange.—In concluding these observations on the nature of exchange, it is important to apply them to the removal of common prejudices. The terms *favourable* and *unfavourable* are used to express particular states of the exchange market, with the belief in the minds of most men, that they truly indicate what the terms import, i. e. something profitable or unprofitable to the country. But it may well be doubted, whether this be any thing more than the prejudice of language; the terms were adopted in compliance with a theory now universally abandoned, viz. that the profits of commerce were to be measured by the balance of gold and silver which it caused to be imported; and as high exchange led to their export, and low exchange to their importation, the terms *high* and *low* were naturally converted into *favourable* and *unfavourable*. Now, against the truth of this theory and this language, it may be urged that our own country, both before and since the Revolution, has constantly had against it an unfavourable course of exchange, and yet that its growth in wealth has been unprecedentedly rapid. But to examine this matter more nearly, so far as exchange is *nominal*, no real result, favourable or unfavourable, can possibly arise from it; and, even when *real*, it is by no means clear which party enjoys the benefit of the premium. If both the buyer and seller of the bill be American citizens, the price is obviously a matter of indifference to the country; it is a simple transfer of profit from A to B, and there can be no reason why the interests of the country should be identified with the remitter of the bill rather than with the drawer of it. If, again, the bill be remitted on foreign account, its high price is evidently favourable to the country, since the premium is then paid by the foreigner and pocketed by the American merchant; and as this case is at least as frequent as the reverse, it follows that the premium of bills, however high, is in a national point of view no actual loss.

Up to that point at which specie begins to be shipped, it is therefore perfectly harmless; it is simply the barometer of commerce which indicates the comparative state of imports and exports; if it pass this point, it is indeed an evil, not however in itself, but simply by the derangement it introduces into the money market. Such derangement results not, however, from the loss of specie, which is generally trifling in amount, but from the necessity such shipments impose on the banks to curtail their ordinary discounts; hence follow stagnation in business, loss of credit, general fall of prices, and consequent ruin to such as are unable to bear up under the sudden change. These are, indeed, real evils; but they are evils, not of high exchange, but of over trading and imprudent banking; or if referred to exchange at all, they are fairly attributable to either extreme of it. The low price of bills is the original encouragement to those heavy importations, of which the high price of bills and consequent shipment of coin, is both the result, the punishment, and the cure.

APPENDIX II

EUROPEAN LETTERS OF WILLIAM BEACH LAWRENCE TO PRESIDENT BUCHANAN

On beginning a two-year tour of Europe in 1858, Lawrence accepted President Buchanan's invitation "to communicate . . . any intelligence . . . that I may deem important to the interest of the United States." [1]

The most interesting of Lawrence's letters to the President were those dealing with the current phase of the struggle for the unification of Italy. Two of these, which are in the Buchanan collection of the Historical Society of Pennsylvania, are here reprinted. Included at the beginning of each is the summary which was prepared in the President's office and placed on the back of the letter. These letters are of importance, not only for a complete understanding of Lawrence, but also for the light they cast on the revival of deep interest in and concern for European events by the American government.

W. B. Lawrence
Dresden. Sept. 23, 1859.

Disclaims all connection with the movement urging his appointment to the Turin mission in the event of Mr. Daniel being releived [sic].

Believes Turin will be the Capital of a first rate power & the resort of all the intelligent of Europe. The opinions of the Continent respecting the U.S. are mainly derived from England & it is only through the access afforded by diplomatic representation that these false impressions can be corrected.

[1] Lawrence to Buchanan, November, 1858. Letter in The Historical Society of Pennsylvania collection.

Cites Hon. Chas. Sumner's case, whilst in Turin last winter, as an example—the eyes of Statesmen & Savants in Italy being on him as the recognized exponent of American Sentiment.

The U.S. may do good to the cause of free institutions by giving Italy a full diplomatic mission.[2]

Dresden, September 23, 1859

Private

To the President of the United States

Dear Sir:

When I addressed you from Milan, on the eve of my departure from Italy, it was with the expectation that, as I was quitting the country, where the European drama was being enacted, I should have no further apology for continuing my communication. Nor, should I now feel justified in intruding on your notice, were it not for intelligence, which has reached me from America, that some of my old friends in New York had brought my name to your attention, in reference to the Turin Mission.

However kindly intended the intervention referred to, after what occurred with regard to another application, coming more appropriately from my own State, and the frank declaration made by me, on my departure for Europe, of a desire to make available those studies, to which a large portion of my life has been devoted, my own self respect would seem to require a disclaimer of all connection with any proceedings, which could afford you the slightest embarrassment on my account.

Indeed, it was from an apprehension that the object of my letters from Italy might be mistaken, that I omitted, while endeavoring to do justice to Mr. Daniel's intelligence and personal courtesies, all reference to the earnest wish repeatedly expressed by him to be relieved from his Mission. He assured me that he had several times, in consequence of the State of his health, for which the climate of Turin was particularly injurious, applied to the State Department to be recalled. He added that he was surprized that no competent Democrat could be found to take his place. Similar declarations made, as I have reason to know, to other Americans, constituted, it is presumed, the foundation

[2] Notation and summary made by the President's secretary.

for the statements in the petition recently presented to you, and a copy of which I have just received. And I may here be permitted to remark that, however much I may have deprecated the use of my name in such a form, (aware that should any proper occasion arise, you would need no suggestion from any quarter,) I could not but be gratified, in recognising, among those who had subscribed the paper, many valued friends, with whom I had formerly been connected in the politics of New York or more recently in the National Council of the Democracy.

While disclaiming all intrusion of personal pretensions, I cannot but express my deep conviction, founded on a close observation of the actual state of things in Italy, of the importance of the Mission in question. The fortunes of Victor Emanuel have revived after the blow, which they received at Villafranca, and the most recent intelligence justifies the belief that Turin is to be the Capital of a Kingdom whose population, (including with Lombardy the Dutchies & the Legations,) will be at once equal to that of Prussia, and which from its superior soil, admirable climate & commercial facilities, is destined, even if Venetia & Naples are not added to it, to become one of the primary powers of Europe. And from the fact that the agricultural labour and many other branches of industry are, in the Sardinian States, almost exclusively carried on by females, the development of the resources of the country are comparatively little affected by the withdrawal of the men to keep up the great armies, which the proximity of Austria in Venetia will still render necessary.

To say nothing of the increase of international commerce and the sympathy which a great navigating people, without the military marine of England or France, must have with us,—in the adaptation of existing institutions to a greatly enlarged territory, there will be abundant opportunity of making such friendly suggestions, as may, as far as the difference of circumstances permits, tend to assimilate the constitutional system of the freest government of continental Europe with those to which we look as the most effectual means to secure the happiness of mankind. I remember, during my visit to Wheatland,[3] on an interesting

[3] Wheatland was Buchanan's home in Lancaster, Pennsylvania; the front porch served as the platform in his successful campaign for the Presidency in 1856.

occasion, to have heard you remark that very much might be done in England by an American Minister, who, not confining his intercourse to the Members of the government, should maintain hospitable relations with the members of Parliament and with those who exercise an influence over the public opinion of the country. What was said as to England is applicable to Turin. Even before the late war the movements of 1848 had attracted the celebrities of all Italy, and as the capital of a country, absorbing Florence & Milan, it will hereafter be the favorite resort of the intelligent of all Europe, who are attracted to the classic land. Unfortunately for us, the opinions of the continent on the social condition & political institutions of the United States are mainly derived from England, and, in general, it is only through the access afforded by diplomatic representation that their false impressions can be corrected. In Turin last winter the Senatorial rank of Charles Sumner made him, in the eyes of the Statesmen & Savants of Italy, the recognized exponent of American Sentiment.

At a time, when her great Ally [France] is pursuing a dubious course, the United States may do real good to the cause of free institutions, by extending to Italy that moral support, which a full diplomatic representation would afford, and on whomever your choice may fall, (in the event of the State of his health compelling Mr. Daniels's return,) it is fervently hoped that the peculiar condition & circumstances of that most interesting region will receive special consideration.

In writing from Milan, after the battle of Magenta but before that of Solferino, it could scarcely have been credited that Louis Napoleon, instead of lending himself to the cause of Italian independence, had been taking advantage of the condition of that country, for the purpose of effecting his own objects with regard to Austria. Both his wars, it is now manifest, were undertaken to conquer a position among the Sovereigns of Europe, and when the chance occurred of securing the desired ascendency, at Villafranca as in the Crimean war, the wishes & interests of Allies were no longer regarded. But, though the course of France could not have been predicted, facts have, I believe, fully confirmed the impressions, which I attempted to impart, founded on personal observations, of the unanimity of sentiment that existed in every part of the Peninsula, in regard to Italian unity. The feeling of being citizens of a great country & belonging to a State, which may render itself independent of foreign sway had, I was even then satisfied, overcome all sectional considerations. However, Modena & Parma have, without reluctance, yielded up the rank of capitals of independent States & become with Milan provincial towns.

There is also one other point, connected with Italy, to which I would allude. When writing as to Naples, I referred to the fact, which then existed, that the King was sustained by 10,000 Swiss. In case of a revolt they alone could have been confidently relied on. By the events of the last few months, not only have the regiments in service been disbanded, but the severest enactments have been made by the Federal legislature of Switzerland to prevent the evasion by voluntary enlistments of the provisions of the new Constitution of the Confederation against military "capitulations." The new King of the two Sicilies can, therefore, have no guaranty against being subjected, on the first suitable occasion, to the fate of his brother sovereigns of Tuscany & Modena.

A movement has been commenced in Germany, for which a popular Convention was held last week at Frankfort, to inculcate the same sentiments of national unity, which have been so successfully fostered in Italy. If carried out Prussia would, probably, gain from it the same advantages as Sardinia is now deriving from the other movement. Northern Germany proposes, of course, getting rid of Austria, whose non-Germanic possessions, containing a population of 27,000,000 to 13,000,000 in her German provinces, are so likely, as in the recent war, to involve the other States in matters foreign to their interests. I have not been long enough in this country to trust myself to give any opinion as to results, but, as far as my observations, in Prussia as well as here, have extended, I have not conceived that the proposed measure enlisted public sentiment. The journals of Dresden, though from the Austrian feeling of this government their views are to be received with great caution, consider the Frankfurt Convention an abortion.

In conclusion, permit me to congratulate you on the success, which has attended your administration of our foreign affairs. The adjustment of all difficulties with the States of our continent, following the recognition by England of the great principles of the immunity of the flag, & which your predecessors ever failed effectually to obtain, will present a bright page in our historical annals; while I infer from the last intelligence from the East that, as Mr. Ward has escaped those difficulties which attended his English & French colleagues, the arrangements so happily made with China by Mr. Reed will be unaffected by the hostilities of other Powers.

With renewed assurances of respect & esteem,

I am, Dear Sir,
Your obedient, faithful Servant,
W. B. Lawrence

W. B. Lawrence
Venice, Jan. 15, 1860.

Abstract within.
The original would occupy
3-½ columns of the "Constitution."

Venice, Jan. 15, 1860

In the postscript to his letter from Dresden, written from Vienna, mentioned his introduction by Mr. Jones to Count [Johann Bernhard] Rechberg [-Rothenlöwen]. Was subsequently invited by him to an interview at the Foreign office. Conversation was directed by him to the question of maritime rights, induced by [Secretary of State] Gen. Cass's despatch. He said he knew of no objection to the adoption of our proposition except from England. Alluded however to the obligation of joint action, arising from the "declaration" of the Congress of Paris, of 1856. Told him that as a private individual I could not say if privateering would be abondoned but that Americans would never consent to the "declaration." Told him the interests of Austria were the same, & that much of their trade came through Bremen and Hamburg in American ships. The Count assented to these views. The conversation was before the prorogation of the Congress.

The project of restoring the Italian princes, or of founding a kingdom of Etruria, has been abandoned. Does not doubt now that all Central Italy will be annexed to Sardinia. The project of a confederation is no longer discussed. The good faith of Napoleon is being seriously questioned in Austria. He had more reasons than are supposed for concluding Armistice of Villafranca, & its stipulations were illusory. Austria & the Grand Dukes then had confidence, as he learned from one of their ministers at the time. Cavour retired then, & ostensible efforts made for the recall of the Dukes but it was all for policy, & Garibaldi himself was satisfied.

Is astonished at the prostration & disaffection in Venetia. Is stopping, the only guest, in a hotel capable of accommodating 300. The great *Piazza San Marco* is entirely deserted. The theatres are closed.

In receiving the new French minister at Vienna, after his presentation to the Emperor, the news came that Napoleon had endorsed the pamplet [sic] "The Pope & the Congress." The Empress was immediately declared sick, and the ceremony has never been completed. Thinks Austria should sell Venetia.

Thinks the Harper's Ferry affair will aid the Democracy, & congratulates you on the reaction in this country.[4]

Venice, January 15, 1860

Private

To the President of the United States

Dear Sir,

In the postscript from Vienna to a note, written at Dresden, in reference to the discussions, with other States of Germany, of the propositions of Bremen & Hamburgh, with regard to the insecurity of private property at sea, I took occasion to allude to my introduction, by Mr. Jones, to Count de Rechberg. I was subsequently invited, by the Austrian Premier, to an interview at the Foreign Office, during which he directed the conversation to the pending questions of maritime rights, induced by General Cass's despatch. He was not aware, he said, of any difficulty being interposed to the adoption of our propositions, unless it came from England. He alluded, however, to the obligations of joint actions, arising from the "declaration" of the Congress of Paris, of 1856. I told him that being only a private individual, I was, of course, without any authority to say, whether privateering was to be abandoned by us, even if accompanied by the immunity of private property, but that no American could have any hesitation in asserting, that the "declaration" referred to could never be acceded to by his

[4] Notation and summary made by the President's secretary.

government—placing, as it did, our commerce, now greater than that of any other nation, at the mercy of the British or French navy, while, from the smallness of our military marine, we should be wholly without the means of retaliation. In this respect, I remarked, the interests of his country were identical with ours. Though the navigation of Austria is comparatively limited, yet her trade, as well in the receipt of our cotton, as in the export of her produce & manufactures, made it important to her that no undue advantage should be given to states having great navies. I reminded him that the extent of the intercourse between our countries was most imperfectly represented by the returns of Trieste, as all articles, unless of great bulk in proportion to their value, were shipped through Bremen & Hamburg. Count de Rechberg, assenting to these views, entered into an explanation of the *patent*, which had then just been issued, and which by opening all branches of industry, except those specially enumerated, to general competition, it was supposed would give a great development to Austria manufactures. This, he observed, could not fail to be felt in our reciprocal trade.

The preceeding conversation, which took place before the prorogation of the Congress, and when it was supposed that Count de Rechberg's remarks might soon have a practical application, I deem of sufficient importance to communicate, especially as I am thereby enabled again to allude to the satisfactory relations of Mr. Jones with the government, to which he is accredited.

The inference, at the close of my last letter, deduced from unofficial manifestations in the pamphlet, entitled "le Congrès et le Pape," has since been confirmed by the retirement of Count Walewski, (a proceeding, which, however proper under the circumstances elsewhere, would seem hardly necessary where the Emperor is his own Minister of Foreign Affairs,) and by the scarcely equivocal language of Napoleon to the Pope.

The question of the Ecclesiastical States was always the most difficult matter connected with the affairs of Italy; inasmuch as the Pontiff's supremacy over the Catholic Church made his influence felt everywhere without regard to the comparative insignificance of his mere territorial possessions. That even the Emperor of France was not insensible to that influence has been apparent in all his negotations with the Holy See, during the several years that he has had the military occupation of his States. At any moment, it was certain, and such last winter was the feeling of every foreigner there, that the withdrawal of the French army from Rome would be the immediate signal of a revolution; yet the fear of giving umbrage to a large portion of the people of France prevented a resort to any extreme measure.

Now that the Romagna is free, there can be no longer any question as to the restoration of the fugitive Princes. And whatever idea, at the beginning of the war, may have been entertained of the erection of a kingdom of Etruria, the difficulties, deemed insuperable, of making acceptable, either to the population or to the great Powers of Europe, a new French Dynasty, in the person of Prince Napoleon, put an end to any such project. None could now doubt a consummation, which was certainly the object of Cavour, when he projected the Sardo-French alliance, as worthy of the patriots, who originated the later movements throughout Italy. I mean the annexation of all Central Italy to Sardinia & the creation of a great State.

In corroboration of this view, it may be noticed that, not only, is it now proposed to restrict the Pope to the city of Rome, —the future condition of whose inhabitants, confined to a mere municipal government, and enjoying the patronage accorded to the spiritual capital of Christendom, may be assimilated to that of the citizens of the District of Columbia but the idea of a Confederation, suggested in a pamphlet before the war, having the same semi-official character with the last publication, & prominently brought forward at Villafranca & at Zurich, is no longer discussed.

The course, which events have recently taken, have [sic] caused the good faith of Napoleon in his personal interview with Francis Joseph to be seriously questioned. The Austrian papers, as well in the provinces, as at Vienna, do not hesitate to charge duplicity in the strongest language. Nor, however happy the result for the cause of humanity, is the impeachment without plausible grounds.

When in Germany, I became satisfied that Napoleon had more reason to conclude an armistice than was generally supposed. Besides the opposition, which Austria could interpose with an army still equal to his own, & with the advantage of the quadrilateral line of defence [Verona, Peschiera, Mantua, and Legnano] intended to be impregnable, there was a growing disposition to war, not only among those which, concurring with Savoy, from the beginning were disposed to involve the Confederation in hostilities, but the States, which looked to an independent Germany or to an amalgamation with Prussia, had no French sympathies, and had Austria been attacked in her German possessions, & which military considerations might have rendered indispensable, it is not improbable that Prussia would have found the pressure in the [Federal German] Diet irresistible. There are those who, believing that this would have been the case, regard the stipulations of Napoleon to have been illusory from the beginning, & to have been entered into with the hope of terminating, by diplomacy or superior sagacity, that which armies could not effect. The return of the Italian Princes, without any armed intervention, to States, whose inhabitants had unamimously repudiated them,—reforms to be made voluntarily by the Pope, which a French army had, for years, in vain endeavoured to extort; a confederation of Princes, whose fundamental principles were diametrically opposed, were nominal concessions, which, from the first, might have been deemed impracticable.

Nor is it to be forgotten that, while Austria reposed in the full confidence of the restoration of the Princes, the populations of Central Italy were equally satisfied as to the favorable intentions of France. There was no manifestation with which Austria took exception, before the ratification of the treaty of Zurich. It was intervening the signing & the ratification of that treaty that I saw the Minister, at Vienna, & the new Grand Duke, in whose favour his father had abdicated. He came to Dresden to present his letters to the King of Saxony, to whom he was likewise accredited. He was on most intimate terms with the French Minister, & I had repeated conversations with him, during which he told me that the Grand Duke had many assurances from Napoleon that Tuscany should be restored to him, & he gave me, in detail, the grounds on which his convictions reposed.

It will be remembered that, on the conclusion of the preliminaries of Villafranca, Cavour retired from the Sardinian Ministry, that Buoncompagni, who had governed Tuscany, as a representative of Victor Emanuel during the war, was recalled, as well as the Sardinian Chiefs, who had gone to the Romagna & to Parma & Modena. But, although informal Missions were ostentatiously announced to the States of Central Italy to promote the return of the Dukes, there seems nowhere to have been any serious efforts made to influence the provisional rulers, in their behalf. While delegations from the Dutchies went away from interviews with Napoleon well contented, he also took care, through a relative of the Bonaparte family, understood to enjoy his confidence, to encourage the people of the Legations, whose representatives his position with the Pope prevented him from openly receiving, to maintain their attitude of independence. Garibaldi himself was satisfied with what was communicated to him, and he, like Cavour, made a temporary sacrifice of position to conceal the Emperor's ultimate policy. In the negotiations at Zurich, care was likewise taken to prevent the commitment of Sardinia to the obnoxious provisions of Villafranca, and to which as an armistice she had acceded. Notwithstanding the protracted discussions in reference to the debt of Lombardy, nothing in regard to the restoration of the Dukes, or which could affect the anomalous position of Victor Emanuel, is to be found in the treaty between Austria & Sardinia.

Notwithstanding all that I had heard, I was not prepared for the total prostration nor the extent of the disaffection, which I have witnessed. On going to the principal Hotel, which had been the palace of a family, that gave three Doges to the Republic, I found only a party of American ladies & two officers of our army. And as our compatriots left the next day, we are the sole occupants of an establishment, calculated to accomodate, in a sumptuous manner, three hundred guests. So far as regards the nobles & higher classes, they either remain on their estates in the country or have gone, with very many of every description, into voluntary exile. The great public square, the *Piazza di San Marco*, which I remember, (though my former visit was made, shortly after the suppression of a revolutionary movement of the Carbonari,) crowded at all times with the *élite* of the population, was yesterday, though a fête day, completely deserted. And today, it being Sunday, when the Austrian band, the music of which is inferior to none in the world, began to play, according to the established programme, the Italians, who had apparently come to the Square, for the mere purpose of this demonstration, at once left it. No Venetian will be found in a coffee house frequented by Austrians, & what is most emphatic, looking to the habits of the people, all the theatres are closed in consequence of a total want of support; the inhabitants not being willing to go where they would be exposed to meet the military. My bankers assure me that there is a total stagnation of all trade, & looking to how much this city depends on the monuments of past glory for the business which so many travellers ordinarily create, the absence of visitors would alone be a sensible source of distress. When the Prince di Carignano was named Regent of Central Italy, the friends of independence were exasperated at the intervention of Napoleon to prevent his acceptance, but when the treaties were exchanged—the title deeds for Lombardy—duly delivered & Austria had been induced to unite in a call of a Congress in terms acceptable to France, Buoncompagni, who had been the virtual ruler of Tuscany during the war, was allowed to return to the Dutchies under circumstances better calculated to maintain the concession of Sardinia, than if the original project had been carried out. Had Carignano been Regent, it might have been attempted to renew, in his case, what was supposed to have been contemplated from Prince Napoleon, & thereby to keep Italy dismembered.

France, as in the events, which precipitated the last war, has been fortunate in finding in the conduct of Austria a pretext for placing her in the wrong. To the simple invitation agreed on between the two however, the Cabinet of Vienna appended a protest against the appointment of Buoncompagni. This might have afforded an apology for the indefinite postponment of a Congress, no longer desired by the policy of France.

Moreover, those political reforms in Venetia, to obtain which for their brethren who remained subject to Austria, the people of Central Italy were at one time invited to place themselves, anew, under their former masters, have not been inaugurated. As the battle of Solferino had not been fought, when we were in Italy last summer, I had then no opportunity of taking my family East of Milan & to complete our tour, we came here from Vienna, a few days since.

As to the future position of *liberated* Italy, nothing would seem to be wanting, but the practical extension of Sardinia of her administrative system over the Dutchies & Romagna, as already applied to Lombardy. The recognition of the *fait accompli*, if not already effected by the signature of a diplomatic protocol, as has been asserted, with France, England & Russia, would undoubtedly receive their sanction, as well as that of Prussia. A more serious matter to arrange might be the annexation of Savoy to France, which, if the feelings of the people were consulted, judging from the personal investigations made during my residence there last summer & looking to nationality & geographical position, would be as readily conceded, as the liberation of Italy from Austrian Germany.

In Austria, great irritation prevails on account of the policy now announced by France, & it is not the less intense because, as has been already suggested, the Emperor considers himself the victim of Napoleon's subtilty. This feeling is being manifested in every form. There had been a desire to give to the resumption of diplomatic intercourse between the two Empires as much effect as possible, & the old forms of the reception of Ambassadors were strictly followed in Paris, in the case of Prince Metternich. At Vienna, I witnessed the departure from the same hotel, in which I lodged, of the Marquis de Neustrie for whose audience with the Emperor three state carriages were sent. This, according to the etiquette of the Imperial Court, was to have been followed by a reception by the Empress, and by the Arch Dukes & Arch Dutchesses, and until these ceremonies are gone through, the Ambassador is not in a position to be recognised by the Diplomatic corps. Intervening the reception by the Emperor and the period fixed for that of the Empress, intelligence of the arrival of the obnoxious pamphlet, with the dismission of Walewski, was received. The Empress was declared to be too much indisposed to admit the French Ambassador & thus matters remained at my departure & with no prospect of a change, which depended on political rather than physical causes. This affair of Court etiquette & its bearing on important political relations was specially brought to my notice, as Mr. Jones had kindly invited me as an ex-diplomat, together with Prince Esterhazy, who had recognised me as an old colleague in London, to a diplomatic dinner, which he proposed to give in return for the civilities received from his colleagues; but, as he wished to include the French Ambassador, it was necessarily postponed to await his official reception.

Not only is the Austrian press, including the official papers, both in German & Italian, here & elsewhere, very hostile to France, & in this country they, of course, reflect the sentiment of the government, but in every mode, as well through the Church as even the public spectacles, are efforts made to create those prejudices, that would prepare the general sentiment for renewed hositilities. The Clergy, who look on the Pope's cause as their own, are, of course, very efficient. In Gratz, the capital of Styria, there was brought to me the theatrical notice announcing, as the play for the evening, "Napoleon Ist his fortune & his end." The three acts were laid in Paris, in Russia & in St. Helena. The moral could not be doubtful, nor the motive for the performance at this time.

Were Austria to be governed by her resentments, a war would not be doubtful, but there are a great many reasons to deter her. There is a sincere desire to adopt economical reforms, of which the opening of the trades heretofore referred to is an illustration; and the future publication of the financial statements, the concealment of which had enabled the government secretly to augment to a great extent the debt, thereby proportionately diminishing the security of the public creditors, has been announced. Already, in consequence of the peace, & with a view to the savings arising from a diminished expenditure, not only had orders been given to forego the recruitment for the present year, but several regiments had been disbanded. For the restoration of the currency &, as connected therewith, the improvement of the industrial resources of the country peace is most important. At the commencement of last year, the resumption of specie payments by the National Bank was seriously contemplated, yet during the war, owing to the great issues required by government, the paper fell to 50% of its nominal value. It had, arising from the payments, on account of Lombardy & other causes, risen to within 20% of par, but the prospect of new French difficulties has again brought it down to a depreciation of nearly 30%. There was, at the beginning of this year a report to the stockholders, from which it appears that the bank notes & bank tokens, then in circulation, amounted to 466,758,923 florins against 383,480,789 in 1858, while the specie, then was 98,043-021 florins & the present reserve only 80,187,756 florins.

Besides the difficulties incident to a homogeneous Empire, Austria is always exposed to the revolution of nationalities, and, at this time, in addition to the general dissatisfaction of Hungary, much excitement prevails among the Protestants, who embrace about half of the population, owing to some new regulations affecting their ecclesiastical assemblies or synods. Moreover, the condition of Austria in her German relations, as I have heretofore had occasion to observe, is one of great delicacy.

There can be no doubt that the wisest course for Austria would be to withdraw wholly from Italy & confine herself to the consolidation of her other dominions, which, if wisely administered, with a population only inferior to that of Russia & infinitely better suited for industrial development, could not fail to maintain for her a position second to that of no European power. When at Vienna, I conversed with intelligent Austrians, who regarded the possession of Venetia of little importance since the loss of Lombardy, all of whose trade must now pass by Genoa. That Austria does not contemplate the occupation of Venice as permanent may be inferred from the secret removal to Vienna, from the Vice Regal palace here, of many valuable works of art, including *chefs d'oeuvre* of the ancient masters. That palace is closed to the public &, under pretence of renovating the ancient pictures, it is said that they are privately carried off. The Venetians cannot believe that, while the rest of Italy is liberated, their bondage is to be perpetuated, but as there are from 15,000 to 20,000 men quartered not only in the forts & in the neighborhood, but in convents, which in every part of the city, are converted into barracks, it is evident that, without an entire demoralization of the troops, nothing can be done by an *émeute* of the population.

A possible arrangement might be most advantageously made, I am assured, for the sale of Venetia, and which, by giving to Austria double what she received for the debt of Lombardy, would efficiently contribute to her financial relief. This the people of Venetia, all whose property would be immensely increased by a transfer to Sardinia, might themselves well afford to furnish, but it is hardly to be expected that Austria will act more wisely in regard to her last Italian possession than Spain does with respect to Cuba. But, though the extension of Victor Emanuel's sway over the whole Peninsula may be deferred, Sardinia is already a great Power, more assimilated to us by her constitutional system & the common interest of an extended mercantile navigation, than any other European state; while the development of her civilized industry holds out advantages, scarcely now appreciated, for our commerce. Of the importance of relations with regenerated Italy, England, though she neither contributed by men or money to the result, is now showing herself duly sensible; and I cannot refrain from soliciting to the subject the special attention of my own government, controlling, as it does, the destinies of a country having a commercial marine superior to that of any other people.

I have not yet seen the Annual Message, though from the telegraphic despatch in the papers, I understand that it has been delivered. It has, however, afforded me much gratification to learn that the demoniac movement at Harper's Ferry has produced a reaction among the intelligent portion of our political opponents. Reduced as the issue has been, by the proceedings of the fanatical men among the Republicans, to the question of interference with slavery in the States, there can be no doubt as to the adjudication of the people. Though my own State has, of late, shown no favorable record, I have never supposed, were the issue fairly presented, that a majority of her citizens were abolitionists. What has already occurred reminds me of your prediction, when I saw you, on the eve of my departure from America. Speaking in reference to the elections, which had just taken place, you expressed the opinion that the reaction, in favor of the Democratic party, would be found, within two years, to be more than commensurate with the momentary depression. I congratulate you on a result, already indicated, and which demonstrates the wisdom of your administration, as well as the conservative character of the Democratic creed.

I have the honor to be,
Dear Sir,
Your obedient, faithful Servant,
W. B. Lawrence

APPENDIX III

SPECIMENS OF FRANCIS LIEBER'S EXAMINATIONS

The numbers at the right of the questions in Sections A and B represent the point values of the questions.

A. SOUTH CAROLINA COLLEGE. JUNIOR CLASS IN POLITICAL PHILOSOPHY, 1855 [1]

The Juniors stand on Paley's Elements of Political Knowledge, to Chap. VII, and five lectures.

1. What is absolutism or an absolute Government: What is 35
an absolute Monarchy, and what is absolute Democracy? Why
is an absolute Democracy one of the worst governments? Com-
pare the reality of power and the responsibility of the power-
holder in the absolute Monarchy with those in the absolute
Democracy.

2. Define Obedience and state whether obeying is passive 20
submission or an attribute of rational beings and free agents.
Show how man is familiarized with the idea of authority be-
fore he becomes an active citizen, and show, moreover, how
it is that we ought to obey laws which were made generations
before us, and, in the making of which, consequently, we have
no direct or indirect share.

3. What is meant by the theory of the civil compact, im- 25
plied or positive? Give the most serious objection to this
theory.

4. Give the first and the last division of the general classi- 20
fication of all governments and politics, written in such a way
as to show the subordination of the different parts.

[1] Printed copy in Lieber papers, Columbia University Libraries. A hand-written note at the bottom reads: "N. B. These refer to a course which commenced Oct. 1, and ended Nov. 10. F. L."

B. SOUTH CAROLINA COLLEGE. SENIOR CLASS IN POLITICAL ECONOMY, 1855[2]

The Seniors stand on the entire annual course of Political Economy, including a course of lectures and the whole of Say's Political Economy, except the Book on Distribution.

Subjects.

1. Louis the Fourteenth was in the habit of saying that royal profusion is the charity of kings, or, that lavish governments are a blessing to the people. Show what is meant by this assertion and its grave error. 25

2. Define the term "Itinerant Merchant" or Pedlar. Does the Itinerant form an essential link in the long chain of commerce? 10

3. Enumerate the characteristics of a sound acceptable tax, according to Mr. Say, and also the characteristics as your teacher has given them—adding to each characteristic an explanatory note or two, in order to show what is meant by it. 30

4. Is machinery objectionable on the ground that it saves labor? If this were so, would the objection apply to machinery alone? 15

5. A hotel or bridge is built for a capital, say, of $100,000. The undertakings prove failures in spite of the prudent management of the concern either, because the buildings were erected on an extravagant plan, or because the number of people making use of them, falls short of that calculated upon. The hotel, or the bridge, is sold for $25,000 and now the number of boarders in the hotel, or of the passengers over the 30

[2] A printed copy is in the Columbia University Libraries.

Lieber elaborated the answer to the main part of the fifth question in *Some Truths Worth Remembering, Given as a Recapitulation, in a Farewell Lecture to the Class of Political Economy of 1849 Published by the Class.*

"No enterprise, failing by its own unprofitable nature, can be, at the same time, ruinous to the adventurers, yet advantageous to the community. If a railway cost $500,000, and shares fall to $25 in the hundred, because travelling and freight pay a fair interest of $100,000 only, in that case the community has for ever lost the value of $400,000, and the passengers and freight are carried at the regular and fair price *plus* the interest of $400,000 proportionately divided in the course of the year. Nothing is more common than to hear that a hotel or a canal has been ruinous to the adventuring individuals, but that the people have reaped the advantage of it. This cannot be. The case applies to government undertakings. They cannot be advantageous to the whole (as far as productive effects are concerned), although they would be ruinous to individuals."

bridge, is sufficient to pay for the interest of the latter sum, as well as for all other outlays, and yields a fair profit. Hereupon the general remark is made: "Well, the capitalist who first undertook the thing is ruined, it is true, but the people," or "the community at large have gained by it; for, here, they are living in this fine hotel," or "here is the bridge still standing." Similar remarks are made on large, yet unprofitable, undertakings, of governments, with this difference that, generally, it is added, "There is no harm in the original outlay, although it proves unprofitable, inasmuch as the capital laid out has returned to the people." For instance, one hundred millions of dollars laid out by government for a railway to the Pacific, would be no loss, although the railway should yield no profit, nor even pay for the interest of the capital, because the whole amount of the capital, would have returned to the people, by the laying of the road itself.

You meet with this argument every day in the debates in Congress, as well as in common life. Show its utter fallacy, or which amounts to the same thing, answer the question: Can the capitalist who pays for a work, be ruined by it, yet the community, or people at the same time be benefitted? And is there any difference in point of political economy, whether government, or a private individual be the capitalist? And also, whether there be any difference if the iron, in the case of the railway, be American iron, or purchased abroad?

C. COLUMBIA COLLEGE. SENIOR CLASS IN POLITICAL ECONOMY, 1863 [3]

I. Definition of Money.
II. Immigration Into the U. States considered in an economical point of view.
III. Error of Montesquieu concerning Money.
IV. Define direct and indirect taxation.
V. How does a Bill of Exchange become a commodity?
VI. Communism and Socialism.
VII. Enumerate the characteristics of an acceptable tax.
VIII. The N[ew] York Clearing House.

[3] In Lieber papers, Columbia University Libraries.

INDEX

Bei Fragen zur Produktsicherheit wenden Sie sich bitte an:
If you have any questions regarding product safety,
please contact:

Walter de Gruyter GmbH
Genthiner Straße 13
10785 Berlin
productsafety@degruyterbrill.com